For Richard L. Neuberger —

whose words and deeds
give great vitality
to the democratic ideal —

with admiration & esteem

april 9, 1941   Leon O'Loughlin

Photo by Underwood & Underwood

DEMOCRACY
AND FINANCE

THE

ADDRESSES AND PUBLIC STATEMENTS OF

WILLIAM O. DOUGLAS

AS MEMBER AND CHAIRMAN OF THE
SECURITIES AND EXCHANGE COMMISSION

EDITED, WITH AN INTRODUCTION AND NOTES, BY
JAMES ALLEN

NEW HAVEN

YALE UNIVERSITY PRESS

LONDON · HUMPHREY MILFORD · OXFORD UNIVERSITY PRESS

1940

CONTENTS

INTRODUCTION v

OUR CHANGING WORLD. 1

PART I. DEMOCRACY IN FINANCE

I. THE FORCES OF DISORDER 5
 The Centralization of Industrial Control . . 6
 Destructive Forces in Finance 7
 Lax Corporation Laws 13
 The "Curse of Bigness" 14

II. REGIONAL FINANCE 18

III. INVESTMENT BANKING 32

IV. CORPORATION DIRECTORS. 46

V. CORPORATION MANAGEMENTS 56

PART II. STOCK EXCHANGES

VI. THE DEMAND FOR REORGANIZATION 63

VII. REORGANIZATION BEGINS 74

VIII. REORGANIZATION OF THE NEW YORK STOCK EX-
 CHANGE 79

IX. MARGINS AND MARKETS 92

X. CUSTOMERS' MEN 107

XI. ON AMENDING THE LAW. 120

PART III. PUBLIC UTILITIES

XII. A CALL FOR LEADERSHIP. 127

XIII. DIVIDENDS IN ARREARS 134

XIV. THE CASE FOR INTEGRATION. 143

XV. CONSERVATIVE FINANCE AND THE HOLDING COM-
 PANY ACT. 163

PART IV. REFORM OF CORPORATE REORGANIZATIONS

XVI. THE NEED FOR REFORM IN CORPORATE REORGANIZATIONS 173

    The Stake of Business in Sound Reorganization 175
    A Thorough Appraisal of Management . . 175
    The Independent Trustee 180
    The Opportunity to Appraise a Proposed Reorganization Plan 188
    The Right to Be Heard 190
    The Place of the Securities and Exchange Commission 191
    "Shopping Around" for Jurisdictions . . . 192
    Speculation in Certificates of Deposit . . . 193
    A New Emphasis 194

XVII. PROTECTIVE COMMITTEES 197

    Participation in Reorganization Proceedings by the Securities and Exchange Commission 214

XVIII. MUNICIPAL DEBT READJUSTMENT 221

XIX. LAWYERS AND CONFLICTS OF INTEREST 230

PART V. ADMINISTRATIVE GOVERNMENT

XX. VIRTUES OF THE ADMINISTRATIVE PROCESS . . . 243

XXI. PROBLEMS OF ADMINISTRATION 248

XXII. ADMINISTRATIVE GOVERNMENT IN ACTION . . . 256

PART VI. EDUCATION IN GOVERNMENT AND LAW

XXIII. CHALLENGE TO YOUTH 271

XXIV. EDUCATION FOR THE LAW 278

XXV. THE DEMOCRATIC IDEAL 290

INDEX 297

The footnotes by Mr. Justice Douglas are indicated by reference marks; the numbered notes are the editor's.

INTRODUCTION

THE last public address which William O. Douglas made before he was appointed to the Supreme Court of the United States begins with a quotation from Mr. Dooley. "Historyans," said Mr. Dooley, "is like doctors. They are always lookin' f'r symptoms. Those iv them that writes about their own times examines th' tongue an' feels th' pulse an' makes a wrong dygnosis. Th' other kind of histhry is a post-mortem examination. It tells ye what a country died iv. But I'd like to know what it lived iv."

Mr. Dooley would have liked these addresses of William O. Douglas'. They belong to that part of the history of our times which tells what the country "lived of." They are a record of one phase, at least, of the country's effort to free its financial institutions of abuse. Moreover, they provide a vivid account of Mr. Douglas' superb administration of the Federal laws regulating finance and in doing so they illuminate many of the problems involved in the regulation of delicate economic mechanisms. It is on such problems that Mr. Douglas is qualified to speak. Mr. Douglas brings to the Supreme Court his intensive experience in the administration of regulatory laws and he has come to the Court at a time when these problems are in the forefront. For this reason alone these addresses, which are in effect a synthesis of his work on the Securities and Exchange Commission, are important.

The Securities and Exchange Commission has often been described as the product of a national protest against financial misbehavior. But abuse had been a factor in finance for years and the protest was not against that alone but against the growing acceptance of malpractice as the normal thing in finance. The S.E.C. was but part of a broader sentiment against the development of what Mr. Douglas called "a specious brand of morality for corporations." The average citizen is educated in the virtues of simple honesty and old-fashioned conservatism, and the S.E.C. voices his objection to the continued use of the corporation as "a convenient and impersonal device" whereby men in big business and finance might avoid the moral standards of conduct normally demanded of them as individuals.

The origins of the S.E.C. go back at least to 1913 when Louis D. Brandeis wrote *Other People's Money,* and many of those ideas found realization in the S.E.C. laws. Before that time there were few specific legal restraints on the sellers of stocks and bonds. In 1911 Kansas had enacted the first state "blue sky" law. Other states had followed with statutes to protect the public against stock fraud. In 1928, the Federal Trade Commission, at the direction of Congress, began an investigation of the public utility industry, and all through the 'twenties various individuals and groups, both in government and out of it, were pressing for some reform—reform for stock exchanges, corporations, public utilities, investment trusts, bankruptcies and reorganizations.

But it required the violence of the 1929 stock market crash to dramatize the immediate need for financial reform. In 1932 the Senate Banking and Currency Committee began an investigation of short-selling on the New York Stock Exchange. This inquiry proceeded at a desultory pace for a time, but in 1933 the committee intensified its investigations and retained Ferdinand Pecora as its counsel. The revelations that followed provided ample evidentiary basis for the Securities Exchange Act of 1934, wherein Congress established the S.E.C.

The financial reforms enacted by Congress between 1933 and 1940 made it the chief function of the S.E.C. to insure correct statements in the sale of securities, fair dealing in the security markets, and honesty and soundness in the financing of public utilities. Its purpose is to protect the investment and to strengthen the confidence of America's great middle class in our corporate system of liquid wealth. These are conservative ends, and as Mr. Jerome Frank, the present chairman, has repeatedly pointed out, the S.E.C. is fundamentally an institution of conservatism.

By the summer of 1940 the S.E.C. had six statutes in its armory of reform. In addition to the regulation of stock exchanges there was the Securities Act of 1933, drafted with the experience of the states with "blue sky" laws in mind, and calling for full truth and disclosure in the sale of securities. In 1935 came the Public Utility Holding Company Act, based on the Federal Trade Commission's eight-year investigation of public utilities. Investigations and studies made by the S.E.C. brought new standards for corporate trustees, S.E.C. scrutiny of corporate reorganizations in the Federal courts, and regulation of investment trusts.

It was something of a sensation in 1934 when President Roosevelt appointed Joseph P. Kennedy, now American Ambassador to Great Britain, to be the first chairman of the S.E.C. Mr. Kennedy was a banker who had had considerable dealings in Wall Street, and many people were shocked. Yet the appointment proved wise; Mr. Kennedy served the very useful function of introducing the new S.E.C. to the bankers and brokers who would have to work under it. While internally he organized, externally he won the confidence of the financial community and in a little over a year, feeling that his contribution had been made, he resigned.

At Mr. Kennedy's right hand had been James M. Landis, who succeeded him at the helm. One of the foremost scientists of the law, Mr. Landis, despite an overwhelming administrative and organizational burden, devoted himself to the building of a sound body of administrative regulations. To him, too, as much as to anyone, the S.E.C. owes its admittedly high standards of technical performance, and when he left to become Dean of the Harvard Law School the S.E.C. was well established as one of the most effective agencies of the Federal Government.

Meanwhile, William O. Douglas had been quietly gaining distinction first for his investigations in the field of bankruptcy and reorganization and later as a member of the Commission.

Each of these three men was outstanding in his own way and each left his indelible imprint both on the S.E.C. and on the financial community it regulates. But if the chairmen of the S.E.C. have been the focus of public attention, it is only fair to point out that on the Commission the chairman votes as but one of five members, and that all these men have played significant roles.

Under Mr. Kennedy, then, the S.E.C. was organized and under Mr. Landis its structure was built. And if the administration of William O. Douglas were to be characterized in a single word, the word would be action. The addresses contained in this book are essentially the story of his chairmanship.

William O. Douglas was admirably suited both by background and temperament for his role at the S.E.C. His biography is one of those remarkable stories, so often to be found in America, which outstrip fiction. The following account, which appeared in *Time* [1] just after he was elected to the chairmanship, is worth reprinting:

. . . Bill Douglas is the son of a missionary—a threadbare Scotsman from Nova Scotia who was a Presbyterian "home missionary," a sort of religious circuit rider. The second of three children, Bill was born in Maine, Minn., on Oct. 16, 1898. Six years later his father died, leaving barely enough money to build a house in Yakima, where Mrs. Douglas had relatives. At 111 North Fifth Ave., Yakima, the Doug-

---

[1] Issue of October 11, 1937.

lases lived until 1922 on a small income eked out by odd jobs done by all.

Young Bill did poorly on the high-school basketball team, so well on the debating team that he was class valedictorian. This won him a scholarship paying his tuition for one year at Whitman College in Walla Walla. With $5 and an old bicycle, he arrived in Walla Walla in 1916, landed a job washing windows and doing chores at Falkenburg's jewelry store for 10¢ an hour. He earned his meals by waiting on table at a hashhouse for day laborers. Freshman year he lived in a barn-like one-time dormitory which had no running water. The next three he lived in a tent. In summertime he worked at cherry picking, making fruit boxes, often slept in fields for weeks on end.

On finishing college president of the student body, Beta Theta Pi, Phi Beta Kappa, he gave up graduate work to become an instructor at Yakima High School and support his family. After two years of saving he had $600. He resolved on an insurance selling venture, bungled it and lost all but $75. So he registered at Columbia Law School in Manhattan, expressed his trunk ahead, set out himself as "herder" for a shipment of sheep going to Chicago for slaughter.

He eventually arrived in Chicago riding the rods of a freight. Having learned from hoboes that this was too risky a procedure from Chicago to New York, he bought a ticket, got to Manhattan with 6¢ left. By extraordinary luck he encountered a Whitman classmate, borrowed $75. Tutoring and writing a textbook on the side, he had $1,000 when summer came round again. Back he went to Yakima to marry pretty Mildred Riddle, a fellow teacher in Yakima whom he had often taken picnicking in an antique automobile. When they reached Manhattan they had precisely 35¢. This time, however, he knew the ropes and all was clear sailing. Working on the side, he finished Columbia second in his class and editor of its *Law Review* in 1925, easily landed a job with the crack Wall Street law firm of Cravath, de Gersdorff, Swaine & Wood. Planning to return to Yakima in two years, he set to work learning the fascinating intricacies of Wall Street finance and law, meanwhile teaching at Columbia on the side.

By 1928 his teaching-legal duties had worn him to a frazzle and he turned to Yakima to practice. After ten days he changed his mind, hustled back to Manhattan to teach full time at Columbia. A year later he idealistically resigned because President Nicholas Murray Butler appointed a new dean of the Law School without first consulting the faculty. Shortly afterwards at a party in Pelham he met famed Dean Robert Maynard Hutchins of Yale Law School. Next day

Hutchins telephoned from New Haven, hired Bill Douglas to teach law at Yale. There he was director of bankruptcy studies, collaborated with the Department of Commerce in the same field, did so well that he achieved the topnotch berth of Sterling Professor of Law. . . .

When Bob Hutchins became president of University of Chicago, he dubbed Douglas "the outstanding professor of law of the nation," offered him $20,000 to go to Chicago. Douglas refused because he wanted to complete his long studies in corporate reorganization and bankruptcy. A report he wrote on this subject in the *Yale Law Review* took the eye of Kennedy and Landis. Kennedy had never met Douglas and Landis knew him only slightly, but both were well aware of his record. In 1934, soon after the SEC got under way, Landis telephoned Douglas to come to Washington.

Having come up the hard way, William O. Douglas has the fiber, the sympathy, and the confidence of those who build with their own hands. Yet it is more than mere confidence that Mr. Douglas possesses, for he is one of those rare persons in our complex society who has a fundamentally well-integrated personality. Perfectly poised at all times, few of his intimates have ever seen him ruffled. Rebuff, disappointment, defeat are simply facts to be dealt with coolly and appropriately. His coolness under pressure is so striking that those who have worked with him will vouch for the statement that on occasions when most men would "turn on the heat," Mr. Douglas "turns on the cold."

Constantly, at the S.E.C., he was called upon to deal with veteran financiers and their able lawyers. For these he was always a match and frequently a master. His acute perception and shrewd understanding made him quick to sense their stratagems and to diagnose their motives. These are valuable assets for dealing with Wall Street.

Another trait which was perhaps even more important was his calm and reasoned objectivity toward finance and financiers. Most reformers who carry a big stick for Wall Street are motivated by fear, or by hatred, or by envy. Mr. Douglas is not handicapped by any such narrowing passions. Perhaps it was that his formative years had been spent well beyond the sound and reach of the market place. The remote sheep country of the Northwest and little Whitman College at Walla Walla, Washington, were scarcely the environment to develop either an ambitious reverence for wealth on the one hand or a covetous hatred of it on the other. Whatever the explanation, the regulation of stock exchanges was not an emotional experience for him; it remained a technical, if highly important, problem in law and finance.

This explains, in part, how he was able to get along so well with an ordinarily hostile financial community despite the fact that he was constantly pressing for action on the S.E.C. program. His standard for the conduct of administrative agencies is enlightening. "It [successful administration] demands a strict devotion to the law both in spirit and letter," he wrote. "It demands a fearless respect for facts, regardless of pressures or consequences. It requires a mastery of technicalities. It demands complete independence of—yet intelligent, official sympathy for—the group being regulated. It demands dispensation and fairness to all alike."

Equally significant is his concept of the proper relation between business and regulatory government:

We hear a great deal about the government-business relationship. We hear that it is good or bad, better or worse. One day there is a "split," the next day a "rapprochement." These are symptoms of transition. They do not describe the permanent level of the business-government relationship. As a matter of practical functioning, business and government cannot remain on a good-or-bad relationship, except as respects violations of law. I think there has been a growing recognition of the supremacy of the law, a growing recognition of the fact that once the broad national policies have been embodied in statutory law, the business-government relationship moves out of the realm of controversy and debate. It ceases to be an issue; it moves into the province of the technicians. The problems must be worked out under the law, but in business terms. They are to be worked out not on the political but on the technical level.

This insistence that administrative agencies must operate "on the technical level" may well be a guiding principle for all regulatory effort.

At the head of a government bureau, Mr. Douglas was no bureaucrat. It was scarcely his aim merely to maintain or augment the power of the S.E.C. Where new laws were needed he sought them, and vigorously, but in the administration of regulatory law he saw that the job could be done most effectively if business could be persuaded to take a hand itself. Business, he said, should take the leadership "with government playing a residual role. Government would keep the shotgun, so to speak, behind the door, loaded, well-oiled, cleaned, ready for use, but with the hope it would never have to be used."

This was a realistic approach. Mr. Douglas saw clearly that government could not easily assume the full burden of detailed, pervasive regulation. He was realistic enough, too, to recognize the limitations inherent in any program of reform. "Greed and fraud," he told members of the New York Stock Exchange, "beset all walks of life. They are immortal. You and we are not going to harness them. But you and we can deal with them effectively when we meet them."

As a critic of finance Mr. Douglas follows closely in the path of Mr. Justice Brandeis. In attacking dishonesty he has the same genius for cutting through corporate fictions to reveal the simple fraud. He has the same love for the free, untrammeled, democratic way, the same conviction that finance must be treated as an economic means and not as an end in itself. The investment banker, both Mr. Brandeis and Mr. Douglas would agree, exists principally to help corporations obtain capital, and corporations must not be used simply as vehicles for providing bankers with business. "Finance," wrote Mr. Douglas, "moves into the zone of exploitation when it becomes the *master* rather than the loyal and faithful *servant* of investors and business." Mr. Douglas also shares his distinguished predecessor's fears as to the consequences of bigness and the concentration of economic control, although it does not necessarily follow that they would see eye to eye on the methods of dealing with the problem.

Bigness concentrates tremendous economic power in the hands of a few, says Mr. Douglas, and in this he sees several important dangers. The first is that as structures increase in size they tend to demand managerial ability beyond human capacity and beyond available techniques. The second is a fear for capitalism and democracy. If economic units continue "at the rate of the last few decades, capitalism will be eclipsed. For the inherent characteristic of capitalism is competition, individual initiative, freedom of opportunity. If present tendencies continue, the only hope of economic order within the architecture of the present system will be government by cartels. That raises no hope in the breasts of those who love democracy."

Bigness has its impact on the spirit as well. Mr. Douglas sees a significant loss of human values as the individual is submerged in the impersonal corporation. "When a nation of shopkeepers is transformed into a nation of clerks," he writes, "enormous spiritual sacrifices are made."

Many Americans have long felt a sense of security in the political and economic views of Mr. Justice Brandeis. It is distinctly heartening to know that the Brandeis tradition is likely to be followed by his successor on the Supreme Court. The extent to which Mr. Douglas' thinking on democracy and finance follows that tradition and the manner in which he is likely to modify it may be gleaned from the pages that follow.

Nearly all Mr. Douglas' addresses are directly related to the work of the S.E.C. For the most part, each speech deals with some phase of a specific problem and is written with a well-defined purpose in view. Originally most of the speeches were designed to convey to a particular group—it may have been the stock exchanges, or the utilities, or the reorganization bar —the attitude of the S.E.C. on the problems faced by the group. This might lead the casual observer to believe that the speeches constitute merely a collection of unrelated essays. Such is not the case. With but slight rearrangement from their chronological order the speeches fall into an integrated pattern, developing each subject in an orderly manner and moving easily from subject to subject. This rearrangement the editor has not hesitated to make. Indeed, the editor has felt justified, where speeches have covered more than a single subject, in taking extracts from one or more speeches and grouping them with similar material, and in placing speeches on the same subject together. Some deletions have been made, too, but only to eliminate unnecessary duplication or to avoid purely local references. The bulk of the original material is here, and what is here has been edited only negligibly. The language throughout is as Mr. Douglas originally wrote it— or spoke it. Certainly nothing has been done to lose, or to alter, any of the original thought.

JAMES ALLEN

DEMOCRACY AND FINANCE

OUR CHANGING WORLD

These prefatory remarks are extracts from a talk given at the University of Chicago on October 27, 1936.

AS we move forward in our national development, we find ourselves in a new world. In some foreign countries the old order is gone, in the sense that these countries are under a new political regime—a despotism of one kind or another under which few, if any, old democratic institutions have survived. Such of those larger countries as have not succumbed to one or another type of despotism have maintained their democratic liberties only by reform and some attempt at control over the forces of exploitation which breed insecurity and in turn despotism. Irresponsible, laissez faire democracy is dead everywhere.

If the current phenomena abroad teach anything, they should convince us that we must attack relentlessly and continuously the various forces which breed insecurity. It should need no argument to persuade that, in order to avoid such tragedies, our course should continue in the direction of strengthening liberty by building it on security. From this there is no escape, no alternative; either we run the risks of sacrificing liberty, or we set ourselves earnestly and steadfastly to build a structure of democracy based on security and stability. We should know by now that an economic democracy in action is the only kind of democracy that can provide that degree of security and stability necessary for survival. Only by such a course can we really preserve our liberties, for they are not virile unless they are bottomed on security. The jungle psychology of everybody for himself will not work in an organized, delicately interdependent society.

There has always been change in our economic and social

order. That change is constantly proceeding. It is not change alone which is the challenge. It is the rate of change. That rate of change has been vastly accelerated by numerous factors. Peril lies not in change but in that tremendous rate of change. Democratic government to compete successfully with its virulent competitors must be mobile, bold, and intelligent. Its strength lies in its ability to keep pace with this rate of change. If we can intelligently reform our democracy to make it an effective instrument which can act swiftly and decisively, powerfully and constructively, without sacrificing any of the substance of democracy, then we can not only rekindle our confidence in democracy but make it our true faith.

PART I

DEMOCRACY IN FINANCE

CHAPTER I

THE FORCES OF DISORDER

This chapter consists almost entirely of an address delivered at the
University of Chicago on October 27, 1936. A few paragraphs have
been added from talks before the Economic Club of Chicago on
February 1, 1938, and before the Bond Club of New York on
March 24, 1937.

INVESTMENT in this country in the past twenty years
has undergone a shift from a few but very rich private
families and individuals to the masses. There have also
been substantial changes in the complexion of institutional investments. The banks are considerably larger investors in corporate securities, particularly bonds, than they were, say, at
the turn of the century. Life insurance companies are still the
largest single factor in the bond market and have become more
so in the last few years. The advent of the investment trust and
investment company and the spread of stock ownership among
life insurance companies have made the institutional buyer of
stock a greater factor than it was twenty years ago. The most
pronounced change, however, has been in the spread of ownership of corporate securities among people of small income.
A list of some thirty large companies on the New York Stock
Exchange shows that the total number of stockholders from
1900 to the present time has increased tenfold. It was not so
long ago when dividend and interest income was an unknown
quantity to the great majority of American families. The spread
of ownership of bonds and stocks among the masses has had
the result that more than one third of the dividend and interest
income of the country is now being received by individuals or
families making tax returns of $5,000 or less, while 50 per cent
of the total dividend and interest income is being received by

our large middle class, people whose total income is $10,000 or less.

This development has been accompanied by another shift—an increasing flow to New York of the local investment funds from many communities throughout the United States. Frequently, perhaps too often, these local savings have been attracted to the great national corporations at the expense of small local enterprises back home. It is true that, as New York became the national clearing house for investment funds, Wall Street supplied capital to the larger local enterprises all over the country. Still there were many instances where worthy local enterprises suffered from lack of financing. There was good reason for this. The small local investor, following the trends of the moment, poured his money into the industries and the companies which at the time were the most favored.

When airplane, motor, oil, or radio stocks are in the ascendancy on the New York exchanges, the less spectacular home industry has little chance to compete for the local investor's funds. A New York banking house, for obvious reasons, could scarcely be expected to service all of the needs of local enterprises. Wall Street, as a general rule, is not geared to small local issues. The local job cannot be done there. Yet the backbone of this country's progress has been the small companies, for the giants of today started under humble auspices and with small beginnings only a generation or so ago.

The Centralization of Industrial Control

Looking back over the past five years it is obvious that a reaction has set in against acute centralization of industrial control. The demand has been more and more insistent for greater democracy in industry and in finance. The voices of the investor and the worker (not to mention the consumer) have been heard with increasing persistence. The legislation of the past few years (the Securities Act of 1933, the Securities Exchange

Act of 1934, and the Public Utility Holding Company Act of 1935) has been a partial response to that demand. I feel that the solution of current industrial and financial problems is to be found in large measure through democratization of industry and finance. This question is one of the greater economic problems of today and tomorrow with which we in government have a deep concern and those in finance have a vital and abiding interest.

Destructive Forces in Finance

Of the many forces which breed insecurity, perhaps the most dangerous are the exploitation and dissipation of capital at the hands of what is known as "high finance." The reality of such waste and leakage comes forcibly home when one sees the tottering ruins of industry in bankruptcy or receivership. During two years in Washington we had occasion to examine into those ruins with some care. Under a mandate of Congress we made a study and investigation of dozens of protective and reorganization committees. Our examination of the files of companies, trustees, committees, and lawyers ranged from Los Angeles to Boston.

Through the window of reorganization most of the many varieties of capital exploitation and dissipation can be seen—certainly if a reorganization is studied, as it should be, in its financial and economic setting. Reorganization is frequently but the aftermath of such practices, for the result of the operations of high finance is to weaken the vitality of companies and to cause or to contribute to their failure.

In a competitive, capitalistic system business failures are inevitable. In any system of free enterprise investors will always be forced to pay the price of progress and competition. This is unavoidable. In a sense, capital is a thing to be lost, not saved, anomalous as that may seem. The silent and rotted water wheels of New England bear mute evidence to this. The onward rush of technology, the displacement of old devices by the new and more efficient, makes certain that this phenomenon will be constantly repeated. But dissipation and exploitation of capital are other matters. They relate not to progress but to tribute at the hands of those who may be accurately termed financial "termites."

The financial and industrial world has been afflicted with termites as insidious and destructive as the insect termites. Instead of feeding on wood they feed and thrive on other people's money. Enterprises ostensibly secure collapse as a consequence of their subtle operations. Their mysterious and destructive work has ruined many fine businesses. And at times the first warning which security holders have had that these termites were at work was the disastrous collapse of the company.

These financial termites are those who practice the art of predatory or high finance. They destroy the legitimate function of finance and become a common enemy of investors and business. While they are not seen in the antecedents of every business failure, they have been present with such frequency that the importance of dealing with them directly and forthrightly cannot be denied.

The wealth of many of our institutions—commercial banks, savings banks, insurance companies, public foundations and churches, and universities—is in the form of securities. In back of those securities are railroads, factories, public utilities, foreign credits, and the like. When the financial termites feed on the enterprises which underlie these securities, they breed insecurity and instability in values. When their operations are on a large scale, the whole national life becomes involved. It is estimated that there are twenty-five million persons who are direct owners of securities in this country. These persons are or should be definitely concerned with the destructive nature of high finance. Furthermore, every man who has a deposit in a bank, or has an insurance policy, or owns a home or a farm which is mortgaged, is affected and should be concerned. All of us are interested, whether we know it or not, in healthy conditions in our security markets, in the new issues that are floated, and in the outstanding issues that are dealt in in our public markets.

In the eyes of high finance, business becomes pieces of paper —mere conglomerations of stocks, bonds, notes, debentures. Transportation, manufacture, distribution, investment become not vital processes in economic society but channels of money which can be diverted and appropriated by those in control. The farmer with his raw materials, the laborer whose blood and sweat have gone into the steel and the cement, the investor and the consumer who are dependent on the enterprise, become either secondary or inconsequential rather than primary or paramount. Business becomes not service at a profit but a preserve for exploitation. The basic social and economic values in free enterprise disappear. For such reasons one of the chief characteristics of such finance has been its inhumanity, its disregard of social and human values.

High finance is interested solely in the immediate profit. Its organizations are not interested in whether our natural resources are wasted, whether we are overbuilding in one direction and underbuilding in another, whether our economic machinery is getting out of balance. Such groups are not concerned with whether our credit resources are being used up too rapidly. A larger demand for credit means high returns on money and these men are dealers in money and capital. They are in business only for immediate gain; a long-term view is of no profit and of no interest to them.

As one probes into the background of particular business failures, he finds reflected in them practices and policies which have preceded the collapse of many enterprises. He finds practices designed to siphon the money both from investors and from business. He sees that high finance has piled holding companies on top of holding companies until investors whose money has been taken have no more than a piece of blue sky for their security. He sees market manipulations. Companies have been merged and consolidated for no sound business reason but only to create profits for high finance. The overhead and costs of finance have been placed on business merely to keep high finance prosperous. High finance has levied its toll by taking watered stock and by unloading that watered stock on the public. The promoters pocket the proceeds. The company gets nothing for the stock it has issued. The public holds the bag.

It would be an error to denounce all of finance in these terms. Finance occupies an important place in our society, whether its functions are performed by government or by private bankers. But finance moves into the zone of exploitation whenever it becomes the *master* rather than the faithful and loyal *servant* of investors and business. To make finance such a *servant* rather than a *master* becomes a central plank in any platform for reform.

When I speak of reform, I mean reform by business as well as by means of legislation. Government can and should help, by pointing the way. An economic democracy in action would be recalcitrant in its obligations if it did not do so. It has done so in the Securities Act of 1933, the Securities Exchange Act of 1934, and the Public Utility Holding Company Act of 1935. But the fact that there is at last a Securities and Exchange Commission in Washington should not lull investors and business into forgetfulness of the fact that the problem of what happens to their capital is still their concern. Nor should they forget that many ultimate victories over predatory finance must be won by investors and by business. The program by which investors and business can keep the national riches from exploitation cannot be realized overnight. Yet it is clear that the necessity to eliminate the elements of instability occasioned by predatory finance will not brook delay.

The struggle between investors and business on the one hand and high finance on the other is a strenuous one, for these predatory interests, working in compact groups with friendly alliances, wield an economic and financial power second to none. The danger of that concentration of *power* is that it is not accompanied by the assumption of social responsibility. These groups, collectively divorced from social responsibility, are the chief agents through which our economic and financial blunders accumulate until the next blood-letting process. This is called a crisis. But it is nothing more than the rhythmic breaking out of the pent-up forces of abuse, mismanagement, and maldistribution of economic effort and income. Academic economists have tried to endow cycles and crises thus created with natural attributes. In this way they have cleverly washed the hands of high finance and excused it from social responsibility. But the cycles and crises thus created are not inescapable. We may in years to come look at them as monuments to the folly of the human race.

Such a program of reform involves both the organization and the management of business and a resetting of the laws under which it operates. In such a program there is one central principle. These predatory interests must be prohibited from being on both sides of the transactions out of which their profits flow. This is a simple and obvious proposition. Yet as Mr. Justice Holmes, I believe, used to say, the most difficult task is to teach the obvious. If an investment banker did not have control over a company, he would not be able to load that company with the "cats and dogs" which he as an investment banker had acquired. If a banker-management group were not in control of the protective committees in a reorganization, they would not be able to improvise a plan of reorganization which restored them to power, giving them another feudal tenure in the company. If a market operator were not in control of a company, he would not be able to use the funds of that company so that he could acquire another company and sell it to the first company at a profit. If the current moral and legal standards governing transactions of these men who are on both sides of the bargain more nearly conformed to the notions of decency and ethics embodied in the ancient standards for fiduciaries, their operations would be substantially curtailed.

The transactions themselves are often involved, intricate, and mysterious. Their legal garb is often baffling. Frequently, only the analyst or the lawyer is able to fathom them. Actually, however, the fundamental problem is neither intricate nor involved. It is not one reserved for analysts, financiers, or lawyers. It is so simple that he who runs may read and understand. It is basically nothing more nor less than a man attempting to serve at least two masters—security holders on the one hand, himself on the other. I say it is nothing more nor less than a man serving *at least* two masters, because more often than not high finance has a plurality rather than a mere duality of interest. When a man has a plurality or duality of interest, history has it that one of his several self-interests will be served first.

It is not simply a question of policing and curtailing the activities of dishonest men. If the system is provided so that honest men may have their two or more masters, the dishonest will rush to take advantage of the opportunities afforded. Furthermore, it is not solely and simply a question of honesty on the one hand and dishonesty on the other. No man's judgment can be trusted to act in a sound and disinterested way in those situations where the issue is whether he shall make a turn in the market, or some other profit, if he can use only other people's money to finance it.

This duality or plurality of interest permeates the whole fabric of our financial system. One sees it wherever one turns. The whole mechanism has become so complicated and intricate that frequently it is hidden and concealed even from the deep probings of investigation. But it exists in a multitude of subtle and indirect ways. It has been accepted in practice. It has gone so far that frequently the very cornerstones of certain institutions seem bottomed on it. In fact, it is commonly said that one who seeks to tinker with that part of our financial mechanism is retarding prosperity, interfering with the American way, and stifling freedom and initiative. As one banker recently put it, if steps are made in that direction "you are going to crab the initiative of lots of financial concerns." Hence, when protest is made against practices which violate ancient standards for trustees and there is insistence that they be discontinued, wails and objections go up, even from responsible and socially minded individuals, who protest that business cannot be conducted without these practices. More often than not these are but the protestations of spokesmen for the predatory elements in finance, though they appear in the guise of the profound judgment of practical men of affairs.

Lax Corporation Laws

Restraints both on the complexities and on the size of business must be designed. Complexities are made possible by notoriously lax corporation laws—laws designed to suit the ingenuity of high finance and its lawyers, laws drafted in Wall Street for Wall Street's purposes. Holding companies can be piled on top of other companies without end until even an astute analyst cannot divine what real values lie underneath. Corporations can be affiliated in such devious ways that huge corporate structures become as intricate as the works of a Swiss watch. These complexities make it possible to hide assets and to move them about from company to company covertly. These complexities make it possible to conceal basic business facts from investors. They create the ideal stage setting for high finance. In these circumstances high financiers can with practical immunity maneuver and manipulate other people's money to their own preferment. In a simple conservative corporation setup such maneuvers would be as obvious as taking cash from the till. Amid corporate complexities these raids become disguised and concealed in intracompany transactions. Provisions in charters purport to give officers and directors immunity against liability for acts which shock the conscience. Protective provisions of stocks, bonds, and other securities, permitted by corporation laws, become loopholes for insiders. Drastic over-hauling of lax corporation laws of the states becomes a primary requisite to any basic reform.

The "Curse of Bigness"

Complexity in corporate structures is usually an incidence of bigness. But bigness has other consequences which justify the expression, "the curse of bigness," uttered by Mr. Justice Brandeis years ago.

In the first place, bigness taxes the ability to manage intelligently. The energies and abilities of man are limited. No single man or group of men can intelligently conceive, promulgate, supervise, and execute from day to day intimate business details necessary for intelligent operation of big business. They cannot give management policies that painstaking and careful personal consideration necessary for responsible management. Those details must be assigned to others. So-called responsible management officials become removed from the active arena of their business affairs; they cannot give their businesses the personal care which they demand. They build themselves an elaborate bureaucracy to run the business. At the top they become so-called formulators of policy. But they are so removed from the actualities of their business—the laborers in their mills, their production problems, their intimate financial affairs—that they lose perspective and judgment. Opportunity for intelligent management decreases with the growth of business. The needs of a small Middle Western community are apt to be better served by a banker at the head of a small local bank than by the same banker at the head of the nation's biggest bank. It is not a question of ability but of capacity.

In the second place, bigness concentrates tremendous economic and financial power in the hands of a few. This may be used dishonestly; but an even greater risk is its unwise use from the national viewpoint. Enterprises or institutions which command tremendous resources, which hold the fate of whole communities of workers in their hands, which have a virtual or actual monopoly, which dominate markets and control vast resources tip the scales on the side of prosperity or on the side of depression, depending on the decisions of the men at the top. This is tremendous power, tremendous responsibility. Such men become virtual governments in the power at their disposal. In fact, if not in law, they become affected with a public interest. The impact between their stockholders' interest and the public interest at times becomes acute. Incompatibility is often in evidence. This does not necessarily mean that they are enemies of the democratic system. But it does increase the duties of government to police them, at times to break them up, to deter their further growth. And it also means that if their growth continues at the rate of the last few decades capitalism will be eclipsed. For the inherent characteristic of capitalism is competition, individual initiative, freedom of opportunity. If present tendencies continue, the only hope of economic order within the architecture of the present system will be government by cartels. That raises no hope in the breasts of those who love democracy.

In the third place, the growth of bigness has resulted in ruthless sacrifices of human values. The disappearance of free enterprise has submerged the individual in the impersonal corporation. And when a nation of shopkeepers is transformed into a nation of clerks enormous spiritual sacrifices are made. Communities everywhere lose men of stature and independence. Man loses opportunities to develop his personality and his capacities. He is denied a chance to stand on his own before man and God. He is subservient to others and his thinking is done for him from afar. His opportunities to become a leader, to grow in stature, to be independent in mind and spirit, are greatly reduced. Widespread submergence of the individual in a corporation has as insidious an effect on democracy as has his submergence in the state in other lands.

But the curse of bigness has other manifestations. In big business management tends to become impersonal. The huge aggregations of capital of big business mean that the number of public security holders is large. These investors are also widely scattered. Management acquires a sort of feudal tenure as a result of the utter dependence of the public security holders on them. That tends to give management a sense of a proprietary interest, though they may have absolutely no investment whatsoever in the enterprise. With their relationship to investors so remote and impersonal, they frequently take advantage of their own superior practical position to use the perquisites of management for their own preferment. There can be no question that the laxity in business morals has a direct relationship to the size of business. Empires so vast as to defy the intimate understanding of any one man tend to become the playthings for manipulation. The fact that railroads, or banks, or operating utilities lie somewhere deep underneath the corporate maze becomes incidental. Values become translated. Service to human beings becomes subordinate to profits to manipulators. The stage is set for moral decadence.

All of these facts challenge the *status quo* and demand concerted efforts to restore American business economy to a simpler stature.

So far as high finance is concerned, if its past practices were allowed to continue, their cancerous growth in our financial and industrial body would eventually consume it. It would be consumed because, when high finance thrives and flourishes, there are two consequences. First, there are dislocations in income and purchasing power which eventually upset the economic balance. Second, our faith in fair play and in equality, and hence our trust in democracy, is undermined. These two work for social disintegration.

America, including American finance, needs reëducation on these simple and obvious principles. Whatever the world of high finance may think, he who has not much meditated upon ethics, the human mind, and the *summum bonum* may possibly make a thriving termite, but he will most indubitably make a sorry fiduciary and a sorry economic statesman.

CHAPTER II

REGIONAL FINANCE

The proposal for regional finance was first made before the Economic Club of Chicago on February 1, 1938. Later it was elaborated in an address at San Francisco in June and at Cleveland in July of 1938. It is from these three addresses that this chapter has been put together.

REGIONS and regionalism have presented one of the perennial problems with which this country has had to struggle. In these days, however, it is more and more an economic rather than a political problem. We know that there is no one-sided solution to the economic side of regionalism any more than to its other aspects. We need a reasonable amount of centralization. But we also must make the economic structure of our major regions complete and strong. Entire political philosophies and economic theories have been developed around the problem of regionalism, mainly under the title of centralization versus decentralization. I propose to keep away as far as possible from both and shall restrict myself to the one field with which I have been in daily contact but on which only very meager information on a regional basis has ever been collected—the capital market.

A historian would be needed to trace or even to summarize the development of the centripetal tendencies in our capital-market organization. In the early days, of course, whatever need there existed for borrowing and lending was met locally or, at best, regionally. As the nineteenth century progressed, however, long-term borrowing and lending, and the origination [1] and distribution of marketable securities became rapidly concentrated in three or four leading Eastern cities. Later,

---

1. "Origination" is the function performed by investment bankers in planning and bringing on the market new issues of securities.

from about the 'seventies, the business gravitated more and more to New York. Many factors combined in this development. One of these was the stream of European capital which reached the United States through the intermediary of a few New York banking houses with European connections. For several decades, enterprises requiring large amounts of capital, such as railroads, were dependent on the coöperation of European capital. It was but natural that the small number of investment bankers who more or less controlled the distribution within the United States of capital imported from Europe (or who controlled huge sums under fiscal-agency contracts with foreign powers during the war) acquired a tremendous head start in building up an organization for the origination of securities and in cementing their current contacts with security distributors outside of New York into informal but very effective groups. More important still, American corporations came to look to these banking houses as their natural advisers and agents when they had to offer new securities.

The more important institutional investors [2] now control the great majority of new funds available for investment in securities, particularly in those of a fixed interest-bearing type. Some investment institutions raise and invest most of their funds locally; building and loan associations are good examples. Funds handled by these institutions frequently do not touch the central market at all. The same is true, of course, of the reinvested earnings of farmers and of small and medium-sized business enterprises. The largest institutional investors, however, collect their funds in many communities on a nationwide scale but invest them mainly in the New York market. Insurance companies, investment companies, the investment departments of commercial and savings banks, and the trust departments of commercial banks and trust companies now operate,

2. "Institutional investors" are institutions engaged in the investment of funds on a large scale—insurance companies, banks, investment companies, etc.

to a large extent, in this fashion. Probably only a small part of the large holdings of securities under the administration of these institutions is invested through the intermediary of local or regional capital markets.

The problem of financing small- or intermediate-size companies is primarily the problem of local companies which do not as yet enjoy national credit (or which may never enjoy such a credit because of size), no matter how good the risk and no matter how good the prospects. The problem is intimately tied up with the development of regional capital and securities markets. It is a problem of how to develop, with the help of local financial machinery, regional capital centers so as to keep local capital for local needs.

Granted the desirability and the necessity of having a great national market for capital funds upon which the whole country can draw, yet the dangers of leaving the small local enterprise without an adequate mechanism for obtaining adequate capital cannot be overlooked. It is a major national problem which presses for local solution in almost every community.

Strangely enough many people fail to understand how extremely important small industry is to our whole economy. It takes no statistical analysis to indicate the enormous importance to our nation of the company employing from 100 to 200 men and women. Out of a total of 411,000 corporations reporting balance sheets and filing income-tax returns in 1934, 386,000 had total assets of less than $1,000,000. Thus, the corporations with less than $1,000,000 of assets were almost 95 per cent of all the corporations. Large industry itself is to a great extent dependent upon the small company for its raw materials and for its markets. The small industry in most small cities and towns in the country is basic to our economic life.

Small business in this country has almost invariably been financed by plowing earnings back into the business, by commercial bank credit, and occasionally by private financing. The very high percentage of risk which is involved in many of the security offerings of small and unseasoned companies poses the question as to whether the public, and especially the small investor, should be urged to invest savings in this type of security. Commercial banks, whatever their attitude may be toward established companies, are chary about extending credit to a new and unseasoned business. But though the small company is seasoned it may still experience great difficulty in reaching the capital markets. There is thus a gap in the machinery of our capital markets.

There are throughout the country old, well-established companies which have given work to the citizens of their communities for years. Some have found that they can no longer compete with the larger ones unless they undertake extensive modernization. Such companies, and I have talked with the executives of many, must either restrict their activities to their most profitable lines on the present basis of operations—which of course means laying off men—or they must install up-to-date production methods. Others need capital to take advantage of new markets which lie at their doors. Looking at it broadly, this means that, while our national economic welfare rests on the welfare of small business, our national financial machinery is geared almost exclusively to big business. This is not a new problem. It is an old one. It is pressing at the present time especially because of the condition of our capital markets.

Why do we have a central capital market at all? Economists tell us that some parts of the country have more savings than they can put to profitable use, while others (in the developmental stage) do not have the resources to finance all needed investment. It is the economic function of the central capital market to match the surplus savings of some regions with the excess demand for new capital from other regions, in addition to tapping the national market for those issues which by size or nature have a national rather than a regional appeal. This function is necessary under existing conditions. If we had no central capital market, interest rates would differ much more between different parts of the country than they do now and large parts of the country would be much poorer in capital equipment than they are. That is the theory. In fact, however, the central capital market does much more than match regional surpluses and shortages of long-term capital. It is not only the final clearing house for surpluses and shortages which are left over after regional capital markets have attempted to match the supply of savings and demand for investment originating in their territory. Instead, the majority of the total supply of savings investable in new securities and of total new issues of securities go through the central market. That market combines to a large extent the function of a national clearing house with that of a dozen or so of undeveloped or underdeveloped regional clearing houses.

The real problem, then, is one of degree: To what extent could the matching of supply of, and demand for, long-term capital, which now flows to the central market, be done regionally without impairing the efficiency of our national capital market? This is a problem which obviously cannot be settled dogmatically. And it may be that it cannot be solved in the same manner in every region. Wherever a region has a very heavy excess of savings or a very large excess of demand for new capital, conditions for the development of a balanced regional capital market are not propitious. It would seem, however, that there are a number of regions in this country where both the supply of savings and the demand for capital are sufficiently large and sufficiently well balanced to permit the development of a sound regional capital market.

A wise man long ago said that figures might not govern the world, but that they did indicate how the world was governed. And figures certainly indicate to what extent the American capital market is highly centralized.

Of the nearly 7,000 brokers and dealers registered with the S.E.C., approximately 30 per cent have their headquarters in

New York. More significant is the fact that, of all underwritten issues of $1,000,000 or over registered under the Securities Act of 1933 between July 1, 1936, and June 30, 1938, 84 per cent were managed by investment banking firms with principal offices in New York City, and that the underwriting participations of New York firms in the same issues aggregated 72 per cent of the total, leaving but 28 per cent for bankers or dealers in the provinces.[3] Most of our larger insurance companies, with policyholders in every state in the Union, are domiciled in New York and environs, and even those which are not conduct most of their investment business through the New York market. About 70 per cent of the total assets of our investment companies are held by companies domiciled in or around New York City, although their stockholders are spread over the entire country. Most of the larger investment counsel firms, which have been administering a rapidly increasing amount of funds of clients residing from Maine to California, have their headquarters in New York City. Even of the total security investments of all banks in the country, about one quarter is held by New York City banks. Similarly, of total trust funds under the administration of commercial banks and trust companies, it is estimated between one fourth and one third are in the hands of about a dozen large New York institutions. And finally, a striking though well-known figure—of all stock trading on exchanges, about 95 per cent takes place on the New York Stock and New York Curb Exchanges alone, leaving only 5 per cent for the other twenty-seven (registered and exempt) exchanges. If I were to lump together all of the available indicators, I should say that, at

3. "Underwritten issues" are security issues in which investment bankers are employed to "underwrite" the success of the offering. On a large issue an investment banker will commonly invite other banking firms to participate in underwriting the securities, or offering them, or both. A syndicate is formed and the original investment banker acts as "syndicate manager." The amounts of the issue taken by the various members of the syndicate are known as the "participations."

the present time, well over one half of our capital market, so far as it is represented by the current investment in marketable securities, is concentrated in lower Manhattan.

These developments all point the way to more adequate regional recognition, to greater regional development, to a larger degree of regional independence. Much work and study remains to be done. Some light is thrown on limited aspects of the regional problem by the following statistics.

The S.E.C. analyzed all the underwritten security issues of $1,000,000 and over which had been registered under the Securities Act of 1933 and offered for sale between July 1, 1936, and March 31, 1938. In dollar amount these totaled $3,418,-820,000. There were $2,608,279,000 of bonds; $533,648,000 of preferred stock; and $276,893,000 of common stock. Then we examined the underwriting participations in these issues. Firms with principal offices in New York City had 74.05% participation in the bonds; 69.54% in the preferred stock; 64.72% in the common; 72.59% in all issues. Firms with principal offices in San Francisco had 1.18% participation in the bonds; 2.21% participation in the preferred stock; 1.42% in the common and 1.36% in all issues. Firms with principal offices in all of the Pacific Coast and Rocky Mountain States had only 1.48% participation in the bonds; 3.27% in the preferred stock; 2.59% in the common; and only 1.85% in all issues.

Another illustration may be found in the Fourth Federal Reserve District, located principally in Ohio. Although it covers only about 2% of the area of the United States, it represents, economically speaking, about 10% of the country. There is in the Fourth District about 9% of our population. It bought in 1935 9½% of all the goods sold at retail in the country. It accounts in good years for about 12% of our industrial production, and it pays about 9% of all Federal income taxes. The share of the Fourth District is, of course, much higher in a few large industries. Of rubber products, for instance, considerably over 50% is produced in the Fourth District, of steel and steel products about one third, and of stone, glass, and clay products, about one fourth. If statistics were available, comparable high percentages would be shown for a number of important but more specialized industries.

We may expect that a region of this importance and structure will also be an important source of savings funds and, at the same time, originate a large demand for new capital. Indeed, savings deposits in commercial and savings banks in the district aggregate, we estimate, nearly $2,000,000,000. Building and loan associations in the district have assets of over $1,000,000,000. The savings of residents of the district in the form of premium reserves with life insurance companies should amount to over $2,000,000,000, if population is an indicator. Interest in regional problems has in the past, unfortunately, been too small—and statistical difficulties too forbidding—to permit the citation of more exact and more comprehensive figures on the volume of saving and investment in the Fourth District. We know, however, that a considerable part of total new securities issued during the last few years was floated by companies whose plants are wholly or in part within the Fourth District. A rough calculation which I had made indicates that of total underwritten industrial and utility issues of over $1,000,000 registered under the Securities Act between July 1, 1936, and June 30, 1938, approximately 12 per cent were of enterprises which may be regarded as domiciled in the Fourth District.

Is the investment-banking and capital-market machinery of the Fourth District commensurate with its economic importance or its position as a source of savings and an originator of securities? I doubt it. Of course, there are a number of important investment banking firms domiciled in the district, some of which have more than regional importance. Statistics, however, indicate that of the more than 9,000 offices of registered brokers and dealers, less than 5 per cent were located in the Fourth District. Similar relationships appear on investigation of the underwriting participations of firms domiciled in the Fourth District. Of underwritten issues of $1,000,000 and over registered under the Securities Act between July 1, 1936, and June 30, 1938, they took but 5.2 per cent of the purchase group participations and they managed only 2.7 per cent of such issues, measured by the total dollar amount of offerings. This is to be compared with a ratio of about 12 per cent of issues of Fourth District enterprises. There are only a few sizable insurance companies with head offices in the Fourth District. Commercial banks, of course, made considerable investments for their own and for trust accounts, but mostly, again, in securities issued or traded in New York. Finally, there are three of our twenty-seven securities exchanges in this district. But during the years 1936 and 1937 they accounted for not much over $\frac{1}{400}$ of the total dollar value of the sales on all registered exchanges.

Undoubtedly, then, there is a considerable supply of funds available for long-term investment and a large demand for long-term funds originating in the Fourth District. Much of this that might be matched regionally now goes to New York to be matched there. Suppose a part of these amounts were handled locally to form the basis of a regional capital market. What would that mean to the Fourth Federal Reserve District?

I hardly need to point out that it would mean more business for the investment bankers of the Fourth District, for the trust and registrar departments of its commercial banks, for lawyers and auditors of the district, and for printers of prospectuses. It would, indirectly, mean more business for the banks of the Fourth District in the form of loans on new securities and wider opportunities for investment.

In these matters I do not wish to belittle the East. From the broad national point of view, as well as from a regional point of view, we need strong capital and securities markets in the East. There are national, as distinguished from regional, needs to serve. But the tangible and intangible values to the nation at large, and even to Wall Street, of regional development are as great as they are to the regions in question. In many instances in the past, the New York market, because of its greater financial and technical resources, has been able to render this service on terms with which the financial machinery of other communities could not compete. But this is not necessarily a permanent condition. Business and finance can will it otherwise. If the larger local enterprises were to patronize their local financial centers more extensively, those local financial centers could develop into healthy resorts for both small and large companies in need of financial assistance.

You know the industries in your community which need capital, and you know whether their need is deserving. Furthermore, you know to what extent the welfare of the entire community rests upon the welfare of the local industry. It may be that what is needed is a reappraisal of the standards upon which investment is made and loans are granted. It may be that the risks which lie in the backyards of cities throughout the country are just as good as the ones which have become glamorous because they have caught the fancy of the larger markets. In any case, we do know that our national economic welfare rests on the welfare of small or local business. Only regional facilities can care for that, for our national financial machinery is almost exclusively big-business machinery.

I believe there is a growing regional consciousness on all sides. It does not, and should not, take the form of economic barriers or trade walls. It merely recognizes that each region should stand more and more on its own feet, beholden to no outside economic power, dependent on itself for guidance and strength, and yet coördinated in its efforts with other parts of our national economy.

Small business must not be suffocated. In a capitalistic system dependent on individual initiative and freedom it must be served first. Can the ideal solution be found in the machinery of our capital markets? Can there be found or developed locally reservoirs of capital for the legitimate needs of small business? Or, as a measure of last resort, should the Federal Government do the job? We need business statesmanship on this pressing problem. We know that the glib answer that the Securities Act of 1933 has caused this closure of the capital markets is not the correct one. For we know that these problems of the small business antedated that Act. In a sense they have always been with us. But their acuteness has been increased over the years with the growth of bigness.

Moreover, financing of small business is only one phase of the problem of development of local or regional capital and securities markets. There are seasoned local industries of a larger size which are constantly in need of adequate and healthy securities and capital markets, and which frequently can be well served locally. But there is the tendency of the larger local industries to go into the New York market when they are in need of financing. I realize the predicament of those industries when they have to obtain their capital through the available investment media. At times the local or regional capital machinery is inadequate. At other times it is wholly adequate. In any event the call is clear for recognition of a regional service which will keep control and capital at home. In recent days a prominent business executive took a strong position in favor of such decentralization. He is quoted as saying:

I think New York would be better off with decentralization of management. We wouldn't have the load to carry here of justification of why there should be so much of the business of the country centered here. The advantages of moving back are obvious. The advantages to New York, I think, are equally obvious. . . . If your business is moved back you will be getting in with the local people. These local towns would have a stake in that industry. They would feel they had a greater stake than they have today.[4]

I heartily concur in that view.

Threads of this regional philosophy run throughout the

4. From an address by Mr. W. Averill Harriman before the Bond Club of New York, as reported in the *New York Times* for January 29, 1938.

statutes which are administered by the Securities and Exchange
Commission. All national securities exchanges are its concern
under the Securities Exchange Act of 1934. They are equal in
the eyes of that law. It is the Commission's duty not to prefer
one over the other. It is its task to aid and assist each better to
serve its local or regional or national needs. From the viewpoint of some of the smaller exchanges it is important to enable
them to broaden their activities and to increase their resources.
A strong local or regional exchange is symptomatic of local or
regional financial strength and vitality.

Congress also expressed a local or regional philosophy re-
specting the utility industry when it enacted the Public Utility
Holding Company Act of 1935. Under the much-abused and
misnamed death sentence in Section 11 of that Act, it is visual-
ized that geographically integrated utility systems will be the
pattern. Instead of far-flung properties held together by remote control, there will be local or regional groupings of
operating properties. This should result, more and more, in the
disappearance of absentee management; in the return of the
industry to its home region. So, when those at the S.E.C. concern themselves with these matters, they are not reading into
the statutes their own economic and social predilections; they
are expressing the implied or stated Congressional intent.

There are other indications that regional development is the
modern trend. As I have traveled in New England, the Middle
West, and the Far West, I have heard more and more of that
philosophy. I once made the charge that certain legal devices
were being employed merely for the purpose of corporate kidnaping.[5] But the term "corporate kidnaping" is not restricted
to the endeavors of a small group to wrest control from the
hands of the real owners of a company. It is likewise applicable
to formal and informal arrangements for taking the actual control of a company away from the seat of its operations.

Absentee management, no matter how honest and able, can-

5. Before the Bond Club of New York. See Chapter III, p. 43.

not equal local management. Remote financial control may be rationalized as sound, but it is likely to be unresponsive to local needs. And it certainly does not sit well with labor, investors, consumers, and the communities back home. It is their industry and they should be in on it. California control of New England would be as bad as New York control of California. I discern what I hope will be a decided trend to bring industry's headquarters back home.

The same philosophy is evident in a myriad of ways. An isolated example is taxation on dividends of companies in holding-company portfolios. This works for logical consolidations when that is possible and divestment where that is the more constructive way. Another is found in corporate reorganizations. I have been in touch during the last four years with many reorganization situations. A very large number of them involved companies and properties on the Pacific Coast or in the Rocky Mountain area. Most of them involved bonds issued under corporate trust indentures. In large numbers of cases the corporate trustee was located east of the Mississippi. In a smaller number of cases the trustee was located on the Coast. Close observers of the matter on the Pacific Coast have told me over and again what my own observation bore out, that the investors by and large fared better with a local trustee than with an absentee trustee. The difference lay in mobility of action and in the cost of operating from a distant point.

This is no disparagement of the trust institutions of the Eastern cities. It merely emphasizes the desirability of using local or regional trustees for the needs of local or regional business. This would result in the gravitation of other related business, such as paying agencies, registrarships, transfer agencies, depositaryships, and the like to the respective regions. By such use local facilities would be strengthened and improved. Regional financial facilities would grow. This would help regional independence to evolve. Such independence cannot be achieved if regional facilities are not given an opportunity. It can be achieved if regional facilities are allowed to fatten on regional business.

In sum, the development of regional financing should bring with it these conditions. First and foremost, it should bring simpler and more conservative finance, where finance is brought closer to the locus of business and where investors are brought closer to finance and investment.

Second, regional financing should produce better-planned financing, since under that system there might be greater freedom from the scramble in the central capital market for the issues of temporarily popular industries.

Third, regional finance might be able to develop an adequate organization for the supply of long-term capital, particularly in equity form, to enterprises of moderate size.

Fourth, a reduction in absentee financing would result in a reduction of absentee ownership and management, with all the advantages which flow from keeping business at home for the home folks.

Finally, the development of regional capital markets would bring new capital and new brains into the investment banking industry and the financial management of local business. Regional capital markets of sufficient stature should help retain and employ the best of their own sons at home.

The development of regional capital markets seems to be eminently desirable but it will not come just by talking and writing. Regional capital markets, even under the best of conditions, can grow up only if local bankers and local businessmen want them. With local patronage, development of regional capital markets is possible. Without it, it is impossible. The problem therefore at this stage is largely in their hands.

CHAPTER III

INVESTMENT BANKING

This is the famous [1] "Bond Club speech" delivered at a luncheon of the Bond Club of New York, March 24, 1937, when Mr. Douglas was a commissioner, but before he became chairman of the Securities and Exchange Commission.

IN large segments of the business of investment banking a noncompetitive condition prevails. This is due in large measure to the control—direct or indirect—of business by the investment bankers.[2] Others have pointed out the implications for business of the practice of having investment bankers represented on the boards of directors of corporations. Yet all of the hazards and dangers to investors arising by reason of the fact that bankers are represented on the boards of issuers

1. The audience, which included nearly every investment banker of importance in New York, was "shocked into a state of profound grumpiness," according to *Time Magazine*. "When the speaker was introduced," said the *New York Times*, "the members rose and gave a spontaneous round of applause. When he concluded his remarks the spattering of handclapping was far from cordial. . . ."

2. Mr. Justice Brandeis, in an earlier critique of investment banking, described "the proper sphere of the investment banker":

"The original function of the investment banker was that of dealer in bonds, stocks and notes; buying mainly at wholesale from corporations, municipalities, states and governments which need money, and selling to those seeking investments. The banker performs, in this respect, the function of a merchant; and the function is a very useful one. Large business enterprises are conducted generally by corporations. The permanent capital of corporations is represented by bonds and stocks. The bonds and stocks of the more important corporations are owned, in large part, by small investors, who do not participate in the management of the company. Corporations require the aid of a banker-middleman, for they lack generally the reputation and clientele essential to selling their own bonds and stocks direct to the investor. Investors in corporate securities, also, require the services of a banker-middleman. The number of securities upon the market is very large. . . . For a small investor to make an intelligent selection from these many corporate securities—indeed, to pass an intelli-

might continue even though such relationships were to be abolished. Such hazards and dangers are inherent in control. That control may result not only from having a representative on the board but also from having a voting trusteeship or a strategic investment position—usually though not necessarily in stock; or it may result from subtle ties of friendship, from long periods of association, from favors rendered, from zones of influence in financial circles, or from an inertia which has never been challenged.[3]

When I speak of control I do not speak legalistically. I do not mean possession of the necessary implements with which to emerge successfully from a contest over election of a majority of directors. Rather I mean not only working control but also domination and controlling influence over policies however obtained or preserved. Any banker knows how subtle that control is. He also knows how valuable it is or can be. Certainly when that control is in the form of directorships, voting trustee-ships, or a strategic investment position, the bankers who have it can commonly claim that company as their own. It amounts to a "no trespassing" sign on a financial empire. With control, underwritings as well as other patronage are commonly assured. These emoluments cover a wide range—depositaryships, paying agencies, indenture trusteeships, registrarships, stock transfer agencies, brokerage accounts, protective committees, and some-times even the minutiae such as printing and stationery. Those who are in a position to control cannot and do not always absorb all of these themselves; they frequently dispense them

gent judgment upon a single one—is ordinarily impossible. He lacks the ability, the facilities, the training and the time essential to a proper in-vestigation. Unless his purchase is to be little better than a gamble, he needs the advice of an expert, who, combining special knowledge with judgment, has the facilities and incentive to make a thorough investigation. This dependence, both of corporations and of investors, upon the banker has grown in recent years. . . ." *Other People's Money,* pp. 5–6.

3. For a fuller discussion, see *Report of the Securities and Exchange Commission on the Activities of Protective and Reorganization Committees,* Part II, "Committees and Conflicts of Interest."

to others in return for favors received or for favors expected. Nor can many of these emoluments be classified as illegitimate; nor are they always exploited. But the weakness in the situation lies in the fact that he who is in such a dominant position is not on competitive ground; he is dispensing the patronage of a monopoly. He is in a position to take unto himself all that he wants or needs or all that he can conveniently absorb and to dispense to others whatever he deems wise or expedient. Furthermore, he may frequently levy toll on the company with little or no economic justification. As a result of his entrenched position he may exact fees for underwriting when there is no real need for it. Thus it may not be necessary for strong issuers [4] to go through the steps of underwriting, syndication, and dealer distribution when it is known that most of the issue will be taken by institutions or that the price at which rights [5] are offered is such that the stockholders will take practically all the offering. Yet instead of advising the use of some form of agency distribution, or instead of recommending no underwriting at all, the self-interest of the banker has often dictated the use of more expensive machinery.

This raises the whole question of the relation of present compensation of bankers to risks undertaken. This question is particularly significant as it relates to offerings to stockholders by means of rights. When such offerings are made at substantial discounts from the market price of the outstanding shares, as they generally are, there are often grounds for questioning the need of any "banking insurance." Some issuers have found that they have been able to dispense with underwriters entirely. The actual experience in connection with seven offerings of rights of over $1,000,000 on listed issues made between June, 1935, and June, 1936, illustrates the absence of substantial risk.

4. A "strong issuer" is a corporation whose reputation and credit are widely known and unquestioned.

5. That is, a corporation offers directly to its existing stockholders the "right" to subscribe to additional stock at a specified price, usually somewhat below the current market price.

In six of the seven cases, underwriters took less than 5 per cent of the issue, in one case 11.7 per cent. Nevertheless, underwriters received overriding commissions at the rate of about 3½ per cent of the value of the whole issue, which would be equal to about 70 per cent on the amount actually taken up. In addition, in four cases, there was also an underwriting commission payable on the shares actually taken by the underwriters. It is clear that we cannot measure the reasonableness of the compensation by saying that the underwriter is receiving only fifty cents per share. Even fifty cents per share may be too much when it is clear that 90 per cent or more of the stock will be taken by right-holders. The trend toward democratization may well result in the elimination of the double load, so that there may be either reasonable payment for insurance or for selling the balance not taken by stockholders, but not both.

The use of options [6] as compensation to underwriters would certainly also come into question. This does not necessarily mean that the underwriters might not distribute as agents or under an option agreement. But the interests of investors and the issuers might be better served if the securities were distributed at a fixed return to the company and a stated maximum price to the public. It is not necessarily valid to say that the option route is a cheaper way for a corporation to raise money, for in the long run it is likely to be more expensive for the stockholders. If a corporation is raising capital, it should obtain enough to cover the expenses of raising the money. In the past, options frequently have been gratuities to the underwriters, who have received, in cash, the fair value of their services and then taken options on top of that. And the existence of options stimulates endeavors to "jack up" prices to make the option

6. In making a public offering of securities on behalf of a corporation, investment bankers do not always make a wholesale purchase of the securities. Sometimes they merely take an option on a block of securities, later buying the securities if they find they can be resold. Or a corporation may compensate its investment bankers in whole or in part by giving them an option to buy an additional block of securities at a favorable price.

valuable, and thus tends to work to the disadvantage of the public stockholder. Here too is a situation which more competitive conditions might rectify.

These are but a few of many like conditions which are nurtured by monopoly in finance. Under our present form of corporate organization there is no effective restraint on the banker in such a dominant position. His conscience and integrity supply the only safeguard to investors. The history of finance reveals the dangers which result from allowing such business patronage to be monopolized in that manner. The result frequently has been that under those circumstances legitimate business has become a preserve for exploitation. By reason of that monopoly tribute was exacted from investors. That monopoly made it possible for finance to become the master rather than the servant of business. The end result was a perversion of the banker's true function. The history of banker domination of industries such as public utilities and other types of holding companies shows how destructive such influences have been and may be.

This aspect of the business of underwriting deserves stress. A banker controlling a corporation whose securities he is underwriting is the arbiter of the reasonableness of his fees and commissions. Again, regardless of the strictly legal aspects, he is on both sides of the bargain. The situation is often not apparent since issuers and bankers can with facility dress the particular transactions in the garb of fairness and equity so as to give an appearance of arm's-length negotiation. Furthermore, in fairness to investors it should be said that what may appear to be modest fees may in fact conceal additional compensation, past or prospective, in other forms. Realistically the sum total of all such business patronage must be accounted for in measuring the reasonableness or propriety of any one single item. Restraint in one case may provide only the occasion for liberality, overreaching, or greed in another. Thus investors, under the impression that their company has succeeded in obtaining an underwriting on provident and modest terms, may in fact pay many fold for the ostensible sacrifices which the bankers are making.

The problem, however, is a manageable one. In my judgment the least which should transpire is that where the bankers are dispensing to themselves the patronage of a monopoly—whether by reason of directorships, voting trusteeships, strategic investment positions, or otherwise—a private sale of securities by the issuer to those bankers should not be made. Bona fide competitive bidding [7] should be had in such cases in absence of affirmative proof that it would be impracticable. As a matter of broad policy I am convinced that the interests of investors can be served only by that practice. Those who are in a dominant position then could no longer dictate. Such a system would remove the premium presently resting on domination or control and place a premium on disinterestedness: a step consistent with the broad objectives of a vitalized democracy, a necessary step if our financial processes are to be made healthy and above reproach. Such competitive bidding would effectively curb abuses. It would mitigate the practice of having the banker on both sides of the bargain. In this connection it should be observed that the economic utility of continuity of banking relationships [8] is of unestablished value to anyone except the banker. It is the more difficult to prove where that continuity

7. "Competitive bidding for corporate issues drew immediate fire," said the *New York Times*. Since then it has been a subject of lively controversy. Investment bankers generally have shown strong opposition to the suggestion that they should compete through sealed bids for the business of underwriting security issues. Nevertheless, during 1938 and 1939 certain investment bankers seeking to compete for underwriting business raised a demand for competitive bidding in connection with a number of large bond issues, among them the issues of the Chesapeake & Ohio Railroad Co., Cincinnati Union Terminal Co., St. Louis Union Terminal Co., Southern Bell Telephone Co., Consumers Power Co., Louisville & Nashville Railroad Co., and Cleveland Union Terminal Co.

8. On the continuity of banking relationships, Mr. Justice Brandeis wrote in 1913: "Long ago monarchs invented, as a preservative of absolutism, the fiction of 'The divine right of kings.' Bankers, imitating royalty, invented

is based on control or on ownership of securities whose substantial value may lie in business patronage made available by reason of the fact of domination. Certainly revitalization of the profession is not to be found in monopoly. Democratization under such safeguards points the way to development of the *service* rather than the *profit* standards of the profession. When that phase comes into the ascendancy, health and vitality in financial relationships are assured.

It may be that competitive bidding alone will not give sufficient protection to the public interest, in its broadest sense. As against its many obvious advantages may be put the disadvantage that lively competition for stylish and readily salable securities may induce overissuance. One phase of this is well illustrated by the large number of investment-company issues that came out in 1928–29. Their popularity made it possible for brokers and bankers to make themselves sponsors, incorporate an investment company, and go on producing stylish and popular merchandise until the crash came.

In its broadest phases, the investment-banking problem reaches out beyond the mere question of pricing and of striking a fair bargaining balance between the interests of the issuer and those of the investing public. It is concerned with the basis of economic balance and stability, the accumulation of capital funds, and their proper distribution among industries. The bigger problem is not one of price, but one of overissuance and oversalesmanship. It is one of making sure that the industries which are most in need of capital, and not necessarily those whose securities are most salable, will have ready access to the capital market. That is to say, the problem is to direct the capital flow to those industries which can make the best use, both economically and socially, of the available capital supply,

recently that precious rule of so-called 'ethics,' by which it is declared unprofessional to come to the financial relief of any corporation which is already the prey of another 'reputable' banker." *Other People's Money,* p. 31.

and to prevent an exhaustion of this reservoir, with available funds being siphoned to the type of security which can arouse the greatest consumer appetite. Therein lies the banker's most important function, to which all others become secondary. And the problem is, finally, one of building a system of adequate checks and balances in the issuing process.

Unfortunately, the investment-banking process often has been controlled by the salesmen. Then the investment banker tends to manufacture what the salesmen can readily sell; and he, himself, is often nothing more than the general in command of an army of salesmen. In other words, a type of dynamic salesmanship has taken root within the securities business in which it has no proper place. On the other hand, if conditions are created under which the banker who acts as underwriter is compelled to take graver risks, he will not be as promiscuous in the production of securities which do not answer a deep-rooted need, but which are merely a passing fad. To the extent that the production of such so-called salable merchandise is reduced, the opportunity for merchandising economically sound securities will be increased.

The question then hinges, to a large extent, upon requiring that the underwriter be true to his real function; that is, to carry economic risks and hence act as a selective agent, as well as a profound student of economic and industrial conditions. He has not been required to act in this capacity, and often has not, except for such studies as may cover the short period of the marketing process, which is practically nonexistent in the case of highly popular securities. Such steps will, in the long run, work to the self-interest of the bankers themselves, since what is good for our industries and our economy is good for everybody who participates in that economy. That this is so is exemplified again by investment trust history. In many cases there are definite indications that, while the underwriting profits of the bankers were large, these profits, and more, disappeared in the subsequent debacle, caused indirectly by the overissuance of securities and ease of issuing securities which permitted unsound capital structures, unreasonable management contracts, and a paucity of sound investment policies. It may be well to recall, at this point, that a number of large banking houses which resisted the trend up to 1929, realizing very well that these investment-trust securities would eventually bring no good either to the investor or to the banker, finally succumbed and, in one form or another, capitalized upon the popularity of these securities by bringing out issues of investment and semi-holding companies.

The problem is to make the issuer on the one hand and the distributor and the retailer on the other independent of the underwriter. If that were done, the underwriter would fulfill the true function of an insurer, with all the constructive features that go with a risk-taking function. It should come closer to providing an independent middleman who would stand between the buyer and the seller and represent the public generally. What is needed is someone to prevent economically wasteful issuance and sale of securities. Only theoreticians can leave this task to the forces of the "market," for the market too often likes the wrong thing at the wrong time. And there are always a number of people willing to oblige by cultivating such wrong predilections.

To be sure, this course might tend to slow up the process— certainly make it much more discriminating and, possibly, somewhat more immediately expensive. But that it will pay in the long run seems reasonable. It doubtless will require a number of important changes in the banking machinery, foremost among which is the increase of capital resources available for underwriting. This might entail the assumption of such functions by other agencies, either by themselves or in conjunction with the banking houses. But given supervised competitive conditions, these new sources should be readily found.

All current indicia make clear that the position of the banker will in years ahead be more and more restricted to the performance of one of the two functions I have mentioned; namely, either underwriting or selling. Insofar as management, formulation of industrial policies, domination or control over reorganizations are concerned, it is my belief that the banker will be superseded. The financial power which he has exercised in the past over such processes will pass into other hands. It is not merely a question of finding some other agency or single group which will perform its functions. It is a question of finding proper and adequate devices for passing that power back to the owners of industry where it properly belongs. The key to the solution of current industrial problems is to be found in large measure in a process of democratization of industry.

New tools to express and serve the investors' interests have to be found. One current development of foremost importance is vitalization of indenture trustees.[9] Enlightened indenture trustees will be found exercising wholesome influences in the cause of the security holders. This step, however, cannot be taken without necessary precautions against the ever-tempting opportunities for aggrandizement and power which are within reach of those who are in a dominant position in our financial empires. Measures designed to purge these trustees of conflicting interests cannot be thwarted or defeated by the pressure

---

9. When a corporation sells an issue of bonds it is the common practice to appoint a "trustee," usually a trust company, to act for the bondholders in enforcing their rights to the mortgaged property, should the corporation fail to meet its interest payments or default in some other way. Because the rights of the bondholders and the duties of the trustee are generally set forth in a legal document known as an "indenture," the trustee is often known as an "indenture trustee."

The study of Protective and Reorganization Committees conducted by Mr. Douglas at the S.E.C. revealed instances in which the rights of bondholders were endangered by faulty and loosely drawn indentures and by trustees who were lax or indifferent to their duties. As a result of these disclosures, Congress passed the Barkley Trust Indenture Act of 1939, setting minimum standards for trust indentures and minimum qualifications for trustees. See *Report of the Securities and Exchange Commission on the Activities of Protective and Reorganization Committees,* Part VI, "Trustees under Indentures."

of the sheer self-interest of the trustees. Should they at any time lack the foresight or vision to undertake the exacting tasks of their new stewardship, other competent and reliable agencies will be found. The fact is that the job must and can be done.

The vitalization of the indenture trustee is only one of the necessary steps in the program of democratization in industrial control. Today, as you well know, we have a practical usurpation of the rights of the great body of investors which can only be described as financial royalism. Our present situation is a carry over from a previous age when there were only a small number of security holders. It should not apply when we are today a nation of investors. The problem is how to achieve some form of real representation for those security holders who are not associated with the management. One phase of this is an implementation of the position of preferred stockholders. If preferred stockholders are entitled to elect a majority of the board of directors after a stated number of dividend defaults, then they should have real representation from such directors. When the old management stays in control of the proxy machine,[10] the preferred stock is not given real protection. If the preferred stock is sold on the theory that it will assume control of the corporation if the dividends are not paid, then some method must be devised to make this control a real thing.

Another phase of this problem relates to obtaining directors who will represent the public interest. This involves a reconsideration of the basis of directors' compensation and of the practice of directors acting on many boards. Possible solutions may exist in the principle of rotation of directors and the creation of so-called public directors. Advances in the same direction can be made through a series of related proposals. The elimination of nonvoting stock is one. The elimination of vot-

10. For a fuller description of methods used by corporations to marshal the proxies of security holders, see the *Report of the Securities and Exchange Commission on the Activities of Protective and Reorganization Committees*, Part VII, "Management Plans without Aid of Committees."

ing trusts as they are currently known is another. The latter are merely the apotheosis of the process of divesting the stockholders who own the company from control of, or any voice in, the affairs of the company. They afford promoters convenient devices for eating the cake and having it too. They merely make the stockholder an easier prey to whatever pressures are brought upon him by management or other dominant groups, whose power the stockholder is rarely in a position to challenge. If the corporation really needs continuity of personnel and policies, there are other ways by which to attain them. In sum the voting trust as currently observed is little more than a vehicle for corporate kidnaping.

Another or complementary method of reaching the same objective may be the development of some permanent national organization to which grievances could be carried and which could effectively intervene. Through such an agency views of the real owners of these vast enterprises could be articulated. They could be influential in assuring that management policies were dictated in the public interest and in the interest of investors and not in terms of the immediate and selfish interest of the management. The investors who today are by and large orphans of our financial economy must be provided with adequate representation by some such methods. Perhaps industry rather than government can provide it.

Investment bankers well know the basic needs for such representation. They have seen it in oppressive plans for mergers and consolidations, in bold but selfish endeavors to deprive preferred stock of its accumulated dividends, in inequitable plans for recapitalization, in management contracts and bonus arrangements which put a premium on inventory and other speculation, and in vicious and unsound labor policies. Many of these matters reach national proportions; all of them affect, directly or indirectly, national savings. They have an obvious and intimate relationship to our economic and social stability and cannot safely be left to the whim or caprice of a few.

The labor problem which I mentioned is one of the pressing contemporary conditions which cannot be imperiously treated. Management has a place in our economic sun, but so does labor, so does the investor, and so does the consumer. The real owners of these industrial empires have a growing feeling of distrust and lack of confidence in a management which treats imperiously, unfairly, or selfishly the contemporary demands of labor; they have an increasing recognition of the fact that mid-Victorian attitudes are neither wise or expedient on the one hand nor fair and equitable on the other; they have a growing resistance to any course which will sacrifice and not protect the human values at stake. Ways must be found to make management responsive to the desires and demands of the real owners of the business. To allow management to continue to place itself above or to pay no heed to the interests of labor, investors, and consumers is to invite disaster. Remote control by an inside few of these fundamental economic and human matters is fatal. There can be in our form of corporate and industrial organization no royalism which can long dictate or control these basic matters.

In this trend toward democratization in industrial management, bankers can play an important role, even though they lose their position of dominance over industry. In final analysis they are the ones who control the lifeblood of the enterprise— its supply of capital. From this position they can provide a large measure of protection. They can exercise a wholesome influence on protective clauses and provisions in charters, trust indentures, and the like. They can, if they desire, assert an influence second to none to prevent complicated and unsound capital structures. An insistent demand on their part for respectable and healthy corporation laws could have a profound effect in legislative halls. They could make certain before the underwriting is consummated that adequate and proper provision is made for giving security holders an opportunity to participate directly, or indirectly through competent and honest representatives, in the formulation of management policies. The investment bankers stand in a peculiarly strategic position to make constructive advances along the lines indicated. This progress cannot be delayed so as to await future developments. It is a course of action made insistent by the increasing rapidity of the rate of change in our social and economic order.

CHAPTER IV

CORPORATION DIRECTORS

This address was delivered at Fort Worth, Texas, on January 8, 1939.

MANY of the deficiencies of the directorates of our modern corporations result from the presence of so many inactive directors on so many of our larger boards. In many of our directorates there are business colonels of the honorary type—honorary colonels who are ornamental in parade but fairly useless in battle; men whose fathers and uncles perhaps were generals but who themselves are qualified to command only by the virtue of the uniform they wear.

That directorates, as they are now made up, have their serious shortcomings will not, I think, be disputed. We can all remember, back in the boom days, numerous examples of directors who did not direct. And only a short time ago a major scandal in a famous and highly respected New England concern showed that for years there was a real skeleton in its corporate closet of whose existence even the board of directors apparently was not aware. To be sure, no system is proof against individual dishonesty. But it is possible to make the way of the transgressor or the careless man a little harder and his career considerably more brief. Honest and capable directors and managements constitute an overwhelming majority. But it is often impossible for directors to exercise the functions of counsel, of guidance, and of restraint. And the consequences of error, however honest, are often more serious than the consequences of deceit.

Another aspect of the problem was vividly described to me the other day by a prominent investment banker. He was recounting on the basis of personal experiences recurrent episodes in modern corporate management where the director was nothing more nor less than a "yes man" for the person who was responsible for his being on the board. If that person was the president of the corporation, the director was always ready for a resounding vote of confidence in the president. If that person was a banker, the director had his eye perpetually cocked for such morsels at the corporate table which might interest the banker. The director was largely oblivious of any real responsibility to the owners of the enterprise. The investment banker who recounted these episodes to me called such activity of directors abdication. I agree.

I have spoken of inactive directors, and I have used the term in rather a critical way. It may be only fair to the inactive director, however, to point out that perhaps the corporation should not expect to get more than it pays for, and that it pays its directors a very small "honorarium" indeed. Yet that is small comfort to the stockholder. But in final analysis, if directors are to perform their duties honestly, efficiently, and constructively, they should get paid for their work in proportion to the actual contributions made by them. When the corporations so often attempt to get something for nothing, it is no wonder that the directors are sometimes tempted to collect invisible rewards, to make use of their inside information, their market tips, their banking connections, and otherwise to serve themselves rather than their stockholders. Such a tendency is destructive of the spirit in which a position on a directorate should be accepted, for it puts the opportunities of the office far ahead of the responsibilities. Yet it is difficult for some directors to maintain a professional attitude toward a job which is not set up on a professional plane.

Furthermore, even the most ethical, the most capable director cannot do justice to the position unless he can devote an adequate amount of time to the affairs of the corporation. He may not spend more than twelve or fifteen hours a year at board meetings, and between meetings he may never give his directorial duties a thought. Napoleon was a great general, but he did not try to practice his trade on a schedule of one day a month.

So much for the handicaps under which the director labors; now let us look at some of their unfortunate results. In speaking of directors, I have thus far been speaking of directors who are not officers of the companies on whose boards they serve. They are "outside" directors, in the sense of not being members of the executive group which constitutes the management of the concern. But of course the officers of the corporation also are represented on its board. The president is always a director, and so may be any number of his major executives. One large corporation, for instance, has fifteen vice-presidents, all of whom are directors as well and who together make up a majority of the directorate. Thus boards of directors are made up of two kinds of directors: the "outside" directors, who theoretically guide and control the management, and the "inside" directors who are the management itself. Because the "outside" directors spend so little time with the company and because their knowledge of affairs is so superficial, they tend to take the management's word for everything that comes up, if the management is strong.

In addition, there is frequently on the board a "strong man" or a not-so-strong man representing a great bank, an important company, or a single security holder (perhaps an insurance company). He may or may not be an officer of the company. But because of the powerful interest for which he speaks he can and does dominate his fellow directors, who, for the most part, have little or no stake in the enterprise and may derive little benefit from their positions. He speaks with the authority which is a product of vast accumulations of wealth and influence.

As against the informed management directors or the powerful representatives of important interest, the remaining directors are powerless. They have not the knowledge or information necessary to appraise, check, and evaluate proposals made concerning the conduct of the company's affairs; and they have not the specific knowledge and information, nor the economic interest necessary to resist the policies and program of powerful interests. Indeed, so long as a man is a director of a company merely as an avocation—devoting no substantial part of his time to its affairs and deriving no income from it—we can hardly expect that he will be very wise or aggressive in opposing the program of those who seem to speak with knowledge; or that he will jeopardize his own economic interests by opposing the wishes of influential groups.

This tendency to follow the leader violates the traditional idea of what a board of directors should be. When the ordinary citizen, or the ordinary stockholder, thinks of a director, he thinks of the independent director. He thinks of the board of directors as distinct from and superior to the management. He thinks of the directors as men whose advice the management will seek and who will exercise independent judgment on corporate problems. But this kind of director is too often nothing more than a myth.

What we frequently have today is a large majority of directors who are dominated by a few management men or men representing special interests. These directors have abdicated. It is not enough to describe them as directors who do not direct. Too often they do not even influence. They have become little more than ratifiers. They ratify decisions which they have not reached, based on arguments and evidence which they cannot appraise. What was designed as a position of great responsibility is in danger of degenerating into a position of mere routine. The average modern director does not direct the course of the corporation to a much greater extent than a conductor directs the course of his trolley car. Both of them go along with the vehicle; and one of them is often present only for the sake of the ride.

The decline of the power of these directors has seriously menaced the position of the stockholder—particularly of the small stockholder who is found in such great numbers on the books of the larger corporations of today. The position of the director has in it a large element of trusteeship. It is to him that the stockholder looks for the protection of his interests, for the safety of his investment. And when he abdicates his position, the stockholder has no one to whom he may turn. Since the beginning of corporate history—and particularly since corporations began to turn to the public for their funds—it has been recognized that the interests of stockholders could not be adequately served by managements alone. Managements, occupied with day-to-day problems and subjected to day-to-day pressures, cannot provide the necessary dispassionate, long-term guidance. The check of a board of vigilant, well-informed directors is needed to assure that management is always loyal, honest, and prudent.

Neither has the stockholder—except the occasional very large stockholder—the slightest possibility of representing himself. There are corporations with thousands, tens of thousands, even hundreds of thousands of stockholders, each with a very small interest in the concern. We all know that a man with ten shares is not an influence in a big company. We all should know that ten thousand men with ten shares each are not an influence either. For no matter how many shares the small stockholders may hold as a group, their voice in the company is as small as their microscopic holdings as individuals. They have no way of acting together, and so their votes are counted apart. This situation is a commonplace of corporate history, but it is a dangerous commonplace nonetheless.

So we have a situation in which a very large numerical majority of stockholders in American corporations has a dangerously inadequate representation on their corporate boards. We have ownership without authority and we have authority without ownership and, what is worse, without responsibility.

The attitude of the "insider" toward the "outsider" is well

illustrated by the remark of a prominent investment banker who was on several directorates during the worst years of the depression. Conditions were so bad that even the stockholders were making themselves heard, although they were rarely successful in making themselves felt.

"I went to the perfect stockholders' meeting the other day," said the banker.

"How was that?" asked a colleague.

"Well," said the banker, "it was this way. None of the stockholders came."

The failure of so many directorates to live up to the responsibilities of their position and the consequent peril to the small stockholders who constitute the great bulk of investors in American business demonstrate the need for a change in the directing personnel.

In Great Britain, progress has already been made along the lines that we are now discussing. In a conversation I had the other day with Ambassador Joseph P. Kennedy, he told me:

In England directors are sometimes chosen for their prestige, but more often they are elected for their special knowledge of the business. Directors are expected to take and actually do take an active part in supervising corporate affairs. The result is on the whole that the British enjoy a higher standard of directorate responsibility than obtains in this country. Moreover, usually the membership on a board is small with the result that it is seldom found that directors serve on more than a few boards. The English, with a sense of reality, compensate their directors for the time and effort they are required to devote, and do actually devote, to an enterprise. In line with the duties they assume, their compensation is fairly substantial. We (in this country) must find a way to restore in practice what has always been our theory—the principle that a director is a fiduciary owing obligations to the stockholders to protect them in supervising the management.

According to Mr. Kennedy's statement the British have taken steps to change their directorates so as to make them less ornamental and more useful.[1] It should not be difficult to take similar steps in this country. Corporations can and should take steps to place upon their boards working directors who are adequately compensated; and the responsibilities of these directors should be made commensurate with their trust.

Furthermore, we should have smaller directorates. It is in the unwieldy boards of the larger companies that inactive directors are most numerous. Corporations under their own motive power can reform their system of multiple directorships so that no man can sit on fifteen, forty, or even fifty boards. A man who belongs on fifty boards obviously can work on none.

Particularly significant are Mr. Kennedy's references to the time and effort that English directors "actually do devote" to their enterprises and to the fact that they are compensated "in line with their duties." For here the English have apparently gone far toward realization of the idea that I wish to present to you today; that is, the idea of the paid director—the professional director to take the place of the inactive director who does so little in the way of actually directing or supervising corporate managements. The paid director, familiar with the affairs of his company, could not live in peaceful and happy ignorance, oblivious to the fact that warehouses and inventories which his company owns are figments of a criminal imagination.

The term "paid director" may come as a novelty, but there is really nothing startling about the idea. Perhaps we might put it better by saying that we need more efficient directors and we can get them only by putting the position on a salaried basis. The paid director would have no business interest other than serving on the boards of a few corporations. He would acquire a thorough knowledge of these corporations, and he would sit as a representative of the public interest—particularly of the investing public which owns such a large part of our corporations and has so little influence in them. He would, of course,

1. Samuels' *Shareholders' Money* is an earlier commentary on English directors.

be elected by the stockholders. And his influence would, I believe, be immeasurable. Salaried, professional experts would
bring a new responsibility and authority to directorates and a
new safety to stockholders. The interests of the general public
would also be more carefully considered than they frequently
are today.

With no conflicting interests whatsoever, the paid director
could give his full attention to his company's affairs. He could
visit the factories and the warehouses. He could know if the
plant was being carried at too high a value; he could look not
merely at statements of inventory but at the inventory itself.
He would be able to penetrate the mysteries of the balance
sheet and see the realities that lie behind it. He would not be
merely a director at board meetings; he would be a director
between board meetings as well. He could give the directing
job more time in a week than many a director gives it in a year.

Furthermore, the paid director would revive and strengthen
the tradition of trusteeship. His job would not be to represent
the management or to represent himself. It would be primarily
to represent the stockholder—to return to the stockholder the
protection which today's stockholder has too frequently lost.
In a larger sense, he would not be so much a paid director or a
professional director as a *public* director, representing not only
the present but the potential stockholder, and representing the
general public as well.

Today it is generally recognized that all corporations possess
an element of public interest. A corporation director must
think not only of the stockholder but also of the laborer, the
supplier, the purchaser, and the ultimate consumer. Our economy is but a chain which can be no stronger than any one of
its links. We all stand together or fall together in our highly
industrialized society of today. One function of the paid director would be to harmonize those various elements so far as
possible. For, although those elements may superficially appear to conflict, the fundamental interests of all social groups

are identical over the long term. The corporate officer frequently recognizes these principles; but he is so close to his work that it is hard for him to look beyond its immediate necessities. But the paid director need not be afflicted with such nearsightedness. It would indeed be one of the defects which he would be paid *not* to have.

The problem of working out the paid-director plan would of course present many details. But I feel the principle is sound. There would be no lack of capable, mature, experienced men to enter the new profession of full-time director. There are any number of men whose successful business or banking experience has qualified them to act in an advisory capacity. It is one of the major deficiencies of our business system that we throw away so many matured intellects, so much wise counsel. In the paid directorship we would open up a new profession, a profession which would tap a tremendous reservoir of experience and wisdom, much of which finds no adequate outlet today.

The most serious body blows to capitalism do not, as some would have us think, come in the form of legislation. They come in scandalous mismanagement and reckless disregard of the ancient principles of trusteeship. Episodes of the type which have been currently in the public eye dissipate the confidence of the investors and thus weaken capitalism. Confidence is the bulwark of capitalism as it is of democracy. We should take such steps as are reasonable and practicable to perfect the corporate mechanism so that investors will be safeguarded—actually as well as ostensibly—against at least the more flagrant type of management abuses. And I feel strongly that this should be preëminently a job for business and industry. Continuous alertness by an agency like the S.E.C. can go far toward prevention. But our powers quite properly fall far short of supervision of management and within its limited powers any agency like the S.E.C. can seldom be more than a policeman. An effective job requires a leadership by business and an alertness of industry to its own responsibilities. Industry has in its power to take the lead by putting its whole corporate house in order. Every such chore should not be left to government.

I believe that we are on the eve of a real resurgence in our economic life, a resurgence in which changes in our corporate directorates will be an important and an inspiring factor. Some such changes I consider inevitable, because it will be very difficult in the future to find men of responsibility who, without adequate compensation, will assume the real duties and the real responsibilities which should go with the directorships of today.

CHAPTER V

CORPORATION MANAGEMENTS

This address was given in Washington, D.C., before the meeting of the International Management Congress on September 27, 1938.

RESPONSIBLE management has always recognized its position as the servant of the stockholders. Yet the blight of capitalism has been a specious brand of morality for corporations, a morality which drew a distinction between the allegiance which the management demanded of its staff and the allegiance which management owed to its stockholders. There can be no such distinction. Once capitalism forsakes the standards of trusteeship, it bids fair to destroy itself. It is the job of such agencies as the Securities and Exchange Commission to eradicate that specious brand of morality and to restore old-fashioned standards which place business above suspicion or reproach for questionable financial practices.

The efforts of the S.E.C. to buttress our corporate standards of trusteeship obviously serve the interest of all responsible management. For misrepresentation is unfair competition, whether it is used to attract capital or to solicit new business. But misrepresentation in bidding for capital, or in any dealings with security holders, is more than unfair competition. It is a direct undermining of that free economic system which is necessary for the preservation and perpetuation of capitalism under a democratic form of government. That is why, when a company enters the capital market for funds with which to carry on or expand its business, it is important that it has told the truth about its affairs. And when a company solicits proxies for its annual meeting of stockholders, or for some special project, it is important that investors feel that they have a solid basis of facts for an informed judgment. When your securities are listed on stock exchanges, it is important that no one make a football out of them. The country has learned that a manipulated security is a poor rather than a good advertisement for a company seeking additional capital, as well as a curse to investors. Business at last knows that it does not pay to become a stooge for market traders, since it knows that no conscientious management can divide its loyalty between its bankers and its stockholders. When finance becomes the master rather than the servant of business, a process of disintegration sets in.

There are those who would have it appear that the cost of living up to the requirements of our new securities regulation constitutes a restrictive burden on financing. That charge I feel perfectly confident in denying. The S.E.C. itself has been careful to guard against costs which might be burdensome or restrictive. Whatever costs there are, they represent only the pains which conscientious management has always taken in all of its activities.[1] Obviously, they are a restrictive influence on irresponsible managment. For that, we may all well be grateful.

In its aims and ideals the Securities and Exchange Commission has much in common with responsible and conservative business management. Both seek, above all else, a careful conservative stewardship of the interests of investors. The responsibility of corporate management is to its own stockholders and bondholders. The duty of the S.E.C., as a public servant, is to American investors as a group.

The contact which the S.E.C. has with management comes from the financial aspects of business. The managers of companies which have brought out securities issues in recent years have come into contact with the S.E.C. through the Securities

1. The Research and Statistics Section of the S.E.C. studied the registration costs, as supplied by the issuers, of all security issues registered under the Securities Act between 1936 and 1938. The study showed that the cost reasonably attributable to the S.E.C. (i.e., registration fee plus that share of legal, accounting, printing, and other expenses fairly allocable to registration) in no case exceeded 1 per cent of the proceeds of the issue. Statistical Release No. 418, May 4, 1940, Securities and Exchange Commission.

Act of 1933. This statute, probably the simplest administered
by the Commission, requires that those who seek to sell their
securities to the public must make a full and fair disclosure
of their business history, their financial condition, the purposes
for which the funds are to be used, and the rights of the various
classes of security holders. The theory of the Act is not to control the raising of capital through the sale of securities but
simply that capital cannot be raised without full disclosure of
all the facts when you are asking for other people's money. The
S.E.C. does not pass on the merits of securities to be offered;
that is left to the investor. All it asks for the investor is the
facts. Managements of companies which have securities listed
on stock exchanges have come to know the S.E.C. through the
Securities Exchange Act of 1934. That law calls for a similar
statement as to the company, its business, and its financial condition for all so-called listed companies; it also calls for annual
reports keeping that information up to date. In addition, the
Securities Exchange Act operates to prevent pools and manipulations in the securities of your companies. It sets up standards
for providing certain minimum information in the solicitation
of proxies. Equally important, it recognizes that officers, directors, and dominant stockholders are fiduciaries and should not
trade on inside information; and accordingly it penalizes certain purchases and sales. Public utility managers, if their companies are members of holding-company systems, may have
done business with the S.E.C. through the Public Utility Holding Company Act of 1935 in the issuance of securities, in the
purchase or sale of securities or properties, in the solicitation
of proxies, or in making adjustments in accounting methods
or financial structure. Under this law, the S.E.C. is required
to give approval or disapproval to many holding-company activities. Here there is an element of supervision over the acts
of management which does not characterize the other laws. For
example, there is a limitation by the Act of the geographical
area embraced by any one holding-company system; there is

protection of investors against payment of dividends out of capital; there are limitations on the presence of bankers on the boards of directors, and the like. Finally, under Chapter X of the new Federal Bankruptcy Act, the managements of companies which have the misfortune to go into bankruptcy for the purpose of being reorganized will find the S.E.C. serving in an advisory capacity to the courts and rendering them technical assistance in the analysis of plans of reorganization.

These tasks are varied. But whatever they are—whether they be insistence on disclosure of the truth, prosecution of manipulators, simplification of holding-company structures—they constitute various types of patrol of finance for the purpose of preventing malpractices. They are in tune with the standards of conservative management, for they reflect the simple fundamentals which should govern the relationship of a manager to an owner.

Service to stockholders cannot be a passive thing. It is not something to be rendered with the lips. It calls for constant diligence and tireless devotion to the standards of fiduciary responsibility upon which our capitalistic system is based. It is not enough to make an honest and revealing annual report. Management must, in every act, inspire the confidence of investors whose funds are its lifeblood. For, if the American public has a large stake in the country's corporate business, so American corporations have their stake in the public confidence. It is in that respect that this part of the President's program has its greatest significance to those who believe in capitalism and democracy.

PART II
STOCK EXCHANGES

CHAPTER VI

THE DEMAND FOR REORGANIZATION

The Securities Exchange Act of 1934 provided only the framework for Federal regulation of the stock exchanges. The building of the machinery of regulation had been left to the S.E.C., and its first requirements were simple and temporary. This allowed time for the perfection of permanent procedures. There was extensive consultation with the technical experts of the exchanges and the various provisions of the law became fully operative only as rapidly as experience warranted.

Wherever possible the exchanges were encouraged to anticipate detailed Federal regulation by meeting the requirements of the Act with their own rules. In fact, in 1937, the Commission had not imposed upon the exchanges any rules of its own governing trading. While the exchanges had, at the request of the Commission, adopted certain rules from time to time, the feeling was growing within the Commission that the exchanges were not making a genuine effort to bring their disciplinary machinery up to the new standards of the Act. Many of the exchanges were still under the domination of the Old Guard which had been at the helm through the "roaring 'twenties" and that point of view continued to dominate exchange managements.

In October of 1937, Mr. Douglas had but recently been elected to the chairmanship of the S.E.C. and was preparing to speed up the exchange regulation program when the stock market collapsed. The break, one of the most severe in market history, touched off a series of attacks by Wall Street spokesmen upon Federal securities regulation.

Sharpest of these was the statement made by Winthrop W. Aldrich, chairman of the board of the Chase National Bank. In an address, Mr. Aldrich insisted that the crash in security prices "was not initiated by a change in the business facts," charging that "excessive regulation" had impaired the efficiency of the market. Meanwhile, Mr. Douglas, acting for the Commission, had been trying to secure from the New York Stock Exchange an agreement to sponsor a thoroughgoing reorganization. Negotiations were carried on for several weeks but finally broke down. The Commission decided to make its demand for reorganization publicly. The atmosphere was tense when, on November 23, Mr. Douglas delivered to newspaper correspondents the following statement of the Commission. The statement had been carefully prepared in advance and had been gone over by all the Commissioners. It was the most important statement of attitude on stock-exchange matters yet issued by the Commission.

THIS Commission has reached a point in its administrative development where it has become imperative that an early decision upon the future course of our relations with national securities exchanges be reached. That decision, of course, rests between either a continuation (perhaps even an extension) of the past policy of leaving to the exchanges much of the regulation of their own business, or an immediate and more pervasive administration directly by the Commission of all phases of exchange business coming within the purview of the Securities Exchange Act of 1934.

Ideally, of course, it would be desirable to have all national securities exchanges so organized and so imbued with the public interest that it would be possible and even desirable to entrust to them a great deal of the actual regulation and enforcement within their own field, leaving the government free to perform a supervisory or residual role. It is my belief that local self-government in the light of local conditions should be possible and could be highly efficacious within the meaning of the letter and the spirit of the Act.

At the present time, however, I have doubts as to the desirability, from the standpoint of the public interest, of assigning to exchanges such a vital role in the nation's economic affairs, before they adopt programs of action designed to justify their existence solely upon their value as public market places. I have always regarded the exchanges as the scales upon which that great national resource, invested capital, is weighed and evalued. Scales of such importance must be tamper-proof, with no concealed springs—and there must be no laying on of hands. Such scales must not be utilized by the inside few to the detriment of the outside many. The importance of keeping them free from those elements which have in the past tended to distort their balance seems obvious. Furthermore, they frequently become generators of storms on the one hand or of intoxicating overconfidence on the other which cause grave dislocations in unrelated parts of our economy. Such an important instrument in our economic welfare, affected as it is with so vital a public interest, must be surrounded by adequate safeguards. Yet it is also obvious that such restrictions must be consistent with the profit motive, which in final analysis is and must remain the driving force in our economy.

For these reasons it seems imperative at this time to reappraise the traditional methods of exchange administration. The evolution of exchanges has been from small groups of traders and brokers, to small private membership associations, to great public market places. Their public aspects have come more and more into the ascendancy. It is essential that their organization keep pace with that evolution. This is especially true of the New York Stock Exchange.

Operating as private-membership associations, exchanges have always administered their affairs in much the same manner as private clubs. For a business so vested with the public interest, this traditional method has become archaic. The task of conducting the affairs of large exchanges, especially the New York Stock Exchange, has become too engrossing for those who must also run their own businesses. And it may also be that there would be greater public confidence in exchanges (and the prices made thereon) which recognized that their management should not be in the hands of professional traders but in fact, as well as nominally, in charge of those who have a clearer public responsibility.

As is well known, the Commission has in the past made a practice of permitting the exchanges to adopt as their own the rules governing the trading practices of their members. This method appeared to have two distinct advantages. First, it would permit the necessary elasticity required because of varying conditions on the various exchanges. And second, it was thought that it would add the weight of the exchange itself as an enforcement agency having jurisdiction over its own members. It was thought that government might avail itself of this already established enforcement machinery. We were encouraged in this belief by the exchanges, and consequently not only invited exchange representatives to the drafting table, in these particular matters, but forewent entirely the adoption of any rules of our own in governing such practices. The net result is that of all the rules now in force governing the trading activities and practices of members of the New York Stock Exchange, in accordance with the requirements of the law, not one was formally adopted by this Commission. True, their adoption by the Exchange was at the suggestion of the Commission but only after full consultation with the Exchange. And in no case where the Exchange refused to act did the Commission promulgate its own rule. In short, all of them are the Exchange's rules, enforceable primarily by it.

That raises the question, which I have previously indicated, as to whether the exchanges have equipped themselves to continue in this important role and to be entrusted with even greater responsibilities in this direction. A vigilant, vigorous, and full-time enforcement of existing regulatory obligations is essential; but even more important is a progressive assault upon the roots of practices which make many of these rules necessary. That assault can be a joint venture of the Commission and the exchanges—and it is my hope that it will be exactly that.

Any realistic approach to the problems confronting exchanges must soon meet the question as to whether the exchanges should attempt to provide a livelihood for their present huge memberships. In short, are the exchanges attempting to feed too many mouths? The prolonged periods of great activity in the late 'twenties provided an income sufficient perhaps to justify a

25 per cent increase in the membership of the New York Stock Exchange. But the vast changes which have occurred are well known. Not only was there a normal shrinkage in volume as the national speculative fever died down, but a very substantial portion of trading activity (the kind that bred more activity) was wiped away forever, we hope, when manipulation was outlawed. But the principal overhead of the exchanges, their membership, has never been reduced. It may be that, until such a deflation occurs, there will always be a substantial obstacle in the way of any attempt to reconstitute the exchanges as public market places. Certainly, that kind of economic pressure is a great deterrent to the growth of realism in facing squarely the advent of governmental regulation.

The problem of the permissible field of operation of the professional trading member on the floor of the exchange for his own account is one which has long pressed for solution. The exact point at which the interests of the floor trader become inimical to that of the general public is the subject of widely divergent points of view, but there is substantial agreement that over a long period of exchange history these interests have not been coextensive. Any study of our markets over the past twenty-five years will reveal that there has always been a tendency upon the part of the professional trader to accentuate a declining market by selling short for speculative profit at a time when public distress adds a factor of demoralization.

That such activity has not died out with the advent of the Act is evident from a consideration of the figures lately assembled by the New York Stock Exchange concerning trading in five leading stocks during a recent period of abnormal activity. Those statistics show us that during the period under study members effected for their own accounts about 30 per cent of all transactions in these stocks on the Exchange. This figure, when compared with that of 21 per cent for similar trading by members in all stocks during the period, indicates a further problem—the apparent excess of professional attention to the active stocks with a corresponding neglect of the inactive issues. Furthermore, in spite of the recent adoption by the two leading exchanges of rules covering member trading, the proportionate position of the professional in the market has remained more or less constant for more than a year and a half.

The proper readjustment of exchange trading practices in the interest of the public cannot overlook the problem of the specialist. To point to only two or three significant instances in our market studies which are by no means exceptional—on September 7 and September 10 of this year, two days of spectacular price losses, members of the New York Stock Exchange in general, and more particularly the specialists, were heavy sellers on the decline. On September 7, when the industrial average declined 8.14, and the total volume of trading was 1,870,000 shares, the record of the members was as follows:

	Specialists	Other members on the floor	Members off the floor
Bought	176,300	95,600	67,105
Sold	219,500	129,300	107,775
Balance	− 43,200	− 33,700	− 40,670

On September 10, when the same average declined 8.32 points and the turnover was 2,320,000 shares, the record was:

	Specialists	Other members on the floor	Members off the floor
Bought	205,420	129,700	83,170
Sold	272,630	170,620	92,000
Balance	− 67,210	− 40,920	− 8,830

In the same period, in contrast to those two days, on September 11, when prices recovered slightly, each of these member groups, particularly the specialists, bought heavily on balance.

Another period of widely fluctuating markets tells the same story. On October 18, when the largest decline of the year occurred in a 3,230,000 share market, we see the floor groups, particularly the specialist, playing a vital role:

	Specialist	Other members on the floor
Bought	250,600	168,500
Sold	320,400	230,000
Balance	— 69,800	— 61,500

And with the volume at 7,290,000 shares on October 19, when the pronounced weakness continued until about 11 A.M., followed by a very sharp rally wiping out a great part of the previous day's losses, we see the following:

	Specialist	Other members on the floor
Bought	935,900	329,200
Sold	749,100	267,300
Balance	+ 186,800	+ 61,900

These figures serve only to fortify further the conclusion indicated repeatedly in our studies that members of the Exchange trading for their own account—particularly the specialists— either create the daily price fluctuations or else contribute materially to their severity.

The force of this trading by members of the New York Stock Exchange for their own accounts is even more clearly indicated in another study now in process by the Commission. In thirty-five trading days between August 16 and September 25 this year, twenty members alone accounted for 16 per cent of the total trading in the U. S. Steel common and twelve members accounted for 13 per cent in General Motors common. Here we see how extensively the members tend to concentrate their activities in the stocks which are so-called market leaders— stocks the price movements in which undoubtedly have a tremendous effect upon the general trend of prices.

The most arresting data compiled in the recent New York Stock Exchange study, however, concern short selling. It is revealed that short selling represented as much as 31 per cent of the total trading in one of these market leaders and constituted almost a quarter of the trading in the above-mentioned five leading stocks. Of this amount 46 per cent, or almost half of the entire volume of short sales, was that done by members for their own account.[1] This striking fact constitutes an excellent example of the nature of some of the particular problems with which the New York Stock Exchange is presently faced. In fact, these figures as a group are a challenge to the validity of the common assertion that the existence of the specialist and the floor trader is justified on the basis of their stabilizing influence on the market, and their resultant benefits to the members of the public who enter the market. In a market in which there is such an enormous public interest—in which not only 300,000 small traders but 10,000,000 investors have a stake, it is essential that no element of the casino be allowed to intrude and that all such elements be obliterated.

One of the most important public considerations at the present time grows out of the great increase, in recent years, in odd-lot buying and selling. This type of trading, generally considered to represent the activity of the little investor, has reached a point where it now averages up to 21 per cent of the total reported volume of transactions on the New York Stock Exchange. The problem is how to transmit accurately the net effects of this activity to a market in which the unit of trading —the only thing that appears on the ticker—is one hundred shares, or round lots.

For the past year or so, the actual purchases and sales by odd-lot customers have averaged from 16 to 21 per cent of the total volume on the New York Stock Exchange. The record of these transactions shows that odd-lot customers were selling during almost the whole of 1935 and have been buying heavily on the balance in the recent decline. Yet it rests almost entirely with

1. The S.E.C., on January 24, 1938, published a report on short selling on the New York Stock Exchange during two weeks of market declines and adopted rules which operate to restrict short selling in market declines. See Securities Exchange Act Releases Nos. 1548 and 2039.

the odd-lot dealer as to whether or not these important balances of purchases or sales are passed on the market. The odd-lot dealer may, if he wishes, fill the order from his own inventories. He does not always have to go into the market to buy or sell, and there are times when he does not and when, if he had, there might have been a beneficial effect on the market.

There were crucial points in the movement of prices recently where odd-lot dealers failed to pass on to the round-lot market a substantial part of the support which their customers' purchases might have afforded. For example, on September 13, 14, and 15, when odd-lot customers' purchases exceeded their sales by 316,000 shares, odd-lot dealers in turn bought only 216,000 shares in the round-lot market, and supplied some 100,000 shares from their own positions. Again, on October 20, when odd-lot customers bought 570,000 shares more than they sold, odd-lot dealers in their turn bought only 328,000 shares on balance in the round-lot market, supplying 242,000 shares from their own positions. While some part of this balance undoubtedly was necessarily supplied from dealers' positions because positions in individual issues failed to total a full lot, nevertheless, the extent to which offsetting purchases were withheld from the round-lot market seems clearly to indicate that dealers in part were taking advantage of their odd-lot customers' buying to reduce their own long positions or increase their short positions in some stocks.

It may be argued that these are exceptional cases, but the fact remains that on the three days cited in September, the odd-lot customer was disfranchised to the extent of nearly one third of the net balance of his buying over his selling—the only part which could have contributed to the trend of prices—and that on October 20 over 42 per cent of the net balance of his votes was not counted. And even under normal circumstances, day in and day out, the dealer holds hundreds and sometimes thousands of shares of public orders in individual issues wholly outside of the main current of prices.

This condition emphasizes the acuteness of the problem of how the buying and selling of this important group of small investors and small traders is to be given its proper influence in the creation of prices in a great public market place.

Of course it is the province of neither the exchanges nor the Commission to interfere with the basic trends of security prices, though it may be that we jointly have some responsibility to insulate the economic life and business morale of the nation against the severity of the shocks which have in the past been the unfailing accompaniment of violent shifts in the trends of security prices, so that the seismograph does not itself create the earthquake. Prices of securities should at all times freely reflect the ups and downs not only of the enterprise against which they are issued but of basic economic conditions. However that may be, certainly the entry of artificial forces, stimulating or accentuating a trend in one direction or the other, is of constant concern to the Commission, and it should become equally the concern of the exchanges.

These problems constitute a challenge to the exchanges and their members as well as to the Commission. It is a challenge which can only be met with progressive action, just as any public institution must meet the challenge of time and altered conditions. Such challenges must usually be met with change. In this case the changes called for should be a constitutional revision of the administrative and functional techniques of the exchanges. Perhaps this is the only way in which the exchanges may gain the public confidence necessary for them to be effective in performing important supporting roles in the administration of the Securities Exchange Act of 1934. For that reason it transcends mere matters of internal management.

From conversations I have had with many exchange leaders recently, I have gathered that certain technical administrative changes are being contemplated within the New York Stock Exchange. Such changes, involving as they well might, the introduction of a greater degree of public responsibility and independence from the many private and personal interests which are exclusively those of the membership, could indeed clear the decks for an approach to the more fundamental problems I have described. It should not be thought, however, that whatever changes may be made, either by the exchanges or by the government itself, can possibly insure against the risks of loss which are an inevitable ingredient of any kind of human dealings in any kind of public market place. The insurance which we must seek can only be against unfair dealings and inequitable opportunity between public and member. To the degree that the changes I have heard discussed are in that direction, I wish to state emphatically that any such action will have the wholehearted and active support of this Commission. And I feel certain that it will also have the heartiest support of the investing public.

CHAPTER VII

REORGANIZATION BEGINS

The Chicago Stock Exchange was the first exchange, following Mr. Douglas' statement of November 23, 1937 (Chapter I) to approve a reorganization. On January 26, 1938, it announced that its governing committee had accepted a plan simplifying the governing system of the Exchange, instituting a salaried management and creating an advisory committee to represent the public and the corporations whose stocks were listed on the Exchange.

The following discussion of the problems of the Chicago Stock Exchange was contained in a speech delivered before the Economic Club of Chicago on February 1, 1938.

SYMBOLIC of the common problems of various regional financial centers are the stock exchanges. They are an integral part of the machinery of the capital and securities markets. Their health and vitality are important to those markets. Their management in the public interest is essential. Their growth and development as adjuncts to the financial community are basic and of deep concern to us in Washington.

Hence I am heartened by recent activities right here in Chicago. I viewed with great interest the survey which the Chicago Stock Exchange has made, and the recent proposal of the governing committee to turn the findings of this survey into a program of action. This program, as I understand it, would discard an admittedly archaic system for a modern one along business lines, with a paid executive staff fully authorized and responsible for administrative action. I want to emphasize how truly significant it is that Chicago had the foresight and initiative to take the lead. It is of significance because it indicates that the Chicago financial community is thinking about—and acting upon—its own problems, without waiting to see what the East intends to do. Too often, in finance, cities outside of New York have been content to sit back and wait for

New York to assume the leadership. I am encouraged and gratified to find an important mid-Western stock exchange proceeding under its own motive power and assuming a position of
leadership in a movement of such great moment.

This effort of the Chicago Stock Exchange in the direction
of a modernized stock-exchange mechanism, and the similar
insistence on the part of the Securities and Exchange Commission, received hearty encouragement from the recent report of
the committee which studied the New York Stock Exchange.
On past occasions I have been critical of stock-exchange practices and methods, and, I am afraid, with good reason. But
I think the report of the New York Stock Exchange's committee [1] shows real wisdom and courage in an effort to solve a
perplexing problem. I feel that the members of that committee,
like your Chicago group, have displayed a sound appreciation
of the demands of the public interest as well as a far-sighted
understanding of the business of the modern stock exchange
and its members. They have recognized the public role that
the modern exchange plays and the public responsibility that
it bears in our economic system. In their report they have dealt
realistically and forthrightly with the problems and the trends
that any stock exchange must face today.

Their report recommends a stock exchange governed on
business and democratic principles; an exchange organization
in which the balance of power would be held by those whose
interest is and must be to serve the investing public. It calls for
a new type of exchange organization where the public interest
has greater opportunity to remain paramount. Of course, to a
major extent, the eventual success of this program must rest
on the quality of the men who are chosen to head the exchanges.
Given the power which these plans propose, there is no question that men of broad vision, wisdom, and courage, approaching the problem with this fresh point of view, can do a really
first-class job.

1. The Conway Committee. See the note on page 79.

In this connection I would like to lay a ghost. Persistent rumors have it that the Commission wants the power to choose the new president of the New York Stock Exchange (and even members of its new board) or at least to have a veto on such selections. There are several things wrong with those rumors. The only one I need mention is the fact that those statements are complete falsehoods. Management of such institutions is not, and I hope never will be, for government.

Yet I do say this. The advantages of going to the outside to seek men qualified to assume the new administrative duties of the exchanges have considerable weight. I recall that after the Hughes investigation of insurance companies, when the companies reorganized as a measure to regain public confidence, a great many of the major companies chose as their principal executives men who had never been associated with the business. In the case of the stock exchanges there is a further consideration. Some institutions by their very nature are excellent training ground for executive administration. But it may be doubted if, even in the largest commission houses, there is the opportunity which exists in a large industrial or other organization to develop this kind of ability.

But the choice of men for such posts is not ours. We have no candidates. It is not so much the method as the results which are of concern to us. Any exchange which demonstrates by action that it intends to assume—and actually does assume— a vigilant role in conformance with the letter and spirit of the Act will find in us its strongest ally. An exchange which does not will find in us a fair and honest but exacting taskmaster. In other words the job will be done.

This new concept of how a stock exchange should be run really has its roots in developments that began twenty years ago. It is the result of forces that have been in operation for a long time. Before the World War, stocks and bonds were, for the most part, bought and sold either by institutional investors or by individuals whose profession was finance. The savings of the individual found their way into investment only indirectly, through the investments of the banks and insurance companies with which the individual left his money. Since the war, however, while the indirect investments of the public have been growing in several directions, there has been a great increase in the direct investment of savings by individuals who put their funds directly into the securities of corporations. The elementary steps of investing relatively small sums of money in corporate enterprises have become widely disseminated. To put it bluntly, the stock market has more and more invaded the American home.

Now I do not imply that this is bad, but it has created many new problems. The individual investor is not the well-informed, highly skilled security buyer that the big institutional investor is. For the most part, the small security buyer has purchased and sold on native business judgment and hunches. Yet our whole system of converting the savings of many individuals into the invested capital of our national industries must rest, to a large extent, on the ability of this small, unskilled individual to invest successfully. It is in the light of this problem that the stock exchanges are today beginning an appraisal of their adequacy and effectiveness. The exchange members who are supporting these movements for exchange reorganization are far-sighted businessmen who are facing their business problems realistically. They have discarded those friends in disguise who prefer to cling to an outworn system, who fear change of any sort. They are foes of those who cut corners at every opportunity, and of those few whose actions bring discredit upon the community as a whole. They are displaying that quality of business leadership which is so earnestly needed in these times.

Past attempts to improve the stock-exchange mechanism or to bolster its regulatory powers have indicated, I think, that a sound reorganization of the exchange is a basic prerequisite to either effective control or management of them in the public interest. I also think it is absolutely essential for building up a confidence in those market places on the part of investors and for justifying that confidence which is created. There should be no doubt as to the desirability of such a degree of conformance of exchange practices to the law of the land as to make it possible for government to act in a purely residual role. That is my oft-stated philosophy.

An exchange organized along sound lines would, I feel, be equipped to handle adequately many of the difficult problems posed by the Securities Exchange Act of 1934. The delicate question of what constitutes fair practice on the floor of the exchange, the question of conflicting functions of broker and dealer in the same person, the task of controlling overtrading on the floor, the problems centering around the specialist and his relation to his customer, the practices of issuers and houses of issue, manipulation—these could be effectively handled by a properly organized exchange. On these problems exchange management can have profound prophylactic effect. Such questions as the proper use of discretionary accounts, the soundness of the capital position of all exchange members, standards of practice for customers' men would be taken care of in exchanges run on sound business principles. The list is a long one. They are matters relating to the standards and business methods of all persons engaged in doing an exchange business. I know they are of such a nature as to lend themselves to ready solution by any forward-looking public-minded organization. While I appreciate that they may appear to be but the minutiae of our larger exchange problems, they are nonetheless fundamental in character. Here, there is offered to exchanges the opportunity for harmonizing exchange machinery with the law of the land. Compliance with the standards of the statute can be effected and business conducted on a high plane without the irksome presence of the policeman. In the movement toward this objective, I am gratified at Chicago's leadership.

CHAPTER VIII

REORGANIZATION OF THE NEW YORK STOCK EXCHANGE

On November 23, 1937, the S.E.C. issued its demand for stock-exchange reorganization. Seventeen days later Charles R. Gay, president of the Exchange, appointed a committee, headed by Carle C. Conway, chairman of the board of the Continental Can Company, to study the problem. On January 27, 1938, the Conway Committee submitted its report, recommending a sweeping reorganization. The report called for a paid president for the Exchange, three governors to represent the public, and a wide revamping of the Exchange's committee system of government. The report was quickly adopted by the Exchange, and on May 20, 1938, the Association of Stock Exchange Firms gave a dinner to honor the Conway Committee. Mr. Douglas was the speaker of the evening. His address follows.

REPRESENTATIVES of business and government meet tonight to hail a joint achievement and to launch a joint program. We are proud of what we have done working together. We are confident of what we can accomplish by pooling our resources and combining our energies. What we can do, other groups can do. Working together we can overcome any problem which besets capitalism and democracy. Working together we can make this profit system work and at the same time sacrifice no whit or tittle of our government's objectives.

Greed and fraud beset all walks of life. They are immortal. You and we are not going to harness them. But you and we can deal with them effectively when we meet them. But they are not our chief problems because most people are honest. Our main efforts lie along the lines of making as certain as possible that honest business has opportunity to make honest and substantial profits. Freedom of opportunity is as essential to healthy capitalism as it is to healthy democracy. By our joint efforts we can preserve that freedom of opportunity. By doing so we will preserve capitalism and democracy. Let us not be diverted from that effort by indulging in the pastime of looking for motes in each other's eyes or in the calling of names. Only by a joint and united front can we keep from these shores the plagues that have descended elsewhere.

Fair play and simple honesty are a part of our inheritance. Individualism is our pole star. A united front on current problems has been one of our greatest assets. We know how to pool our energies in attacking a common enemy whether it be an army, a depression, or a burning issue. We need not offer each other olive branches. Unless we will it, our enemy is not ourselves but deep economic problems. This government needs you and you need this government in attacking those problems. Let us not be deluded into mistaking personalities for issues. The issues live on, though personalities change. The answer to those problems cannot be found by reliance upon dogma or smugness. They cannot all be found in laboratories. They can be found at conference tables and at forums. Free speech carries the answers on its wings.

The value of this approach is demonstrated by the joint achievement of your Exchange and my Commission. We were and are in the same boat together. We knew that all of the brains and character did not rest with one group. We knew that if we joined forces we could lick our common problem. In this manner can other groups work together, irrespective of creed or politics. We live in perilous times. We can ill afford anything but joint action. If there is failure here, we all fail. When the hearts of Americans are bound together in a common purpose, there can be no such thing as defeat. That time has come, for the common enemy of economic forces has invaded us.

But I want to speak tonight more particularly about this joint achievement and this joint program of ours.

You and we have come a long way together since last autumn.

The road which we chose to travel was not the easiest. Some said it was impassable. Others said it was dead end. But you and we knew that we chose wisely. We were bent on a complete reorganization of the New York Stock Exchange. We insisted that it be a truly public institution, managed and operated so that the interest of the public be served first. Our joint acceptance of that basic principle made possible our joint achievement.

Many of you have been clamoring for these changes over a period of two decades. In your ranks there have been many who have been rebels against the smugness of those who stand resolute against any change. Out of the daily contact with Exchange problems came the realization to many of you that the public's interest was not always being well served. As early as 1914, some of you went on the line for a full-time, independent, paid president of the Exchange. You felt then what subsequent events have clearly demonstrated—that the private-club form of government was not suited to the operation of the Exchange as a servant of the public. Some of you clamored, too long in vain, for the plan to have all stock-exchange houses file with the Exchange periodic statements of their financial condition so that the public would be better protected against the risk of insolvency. Recent events have shown beyond doubt the tragic error of the long delay in accepting your proposal. Still others in your membership have been champions of similar reforms. Your capacity to agitate has been productive of many constructive changes. Dare I say that, for that reason, a goodly number of you would qualify for admission into the ranks of the New Dealers? Tonight I salute those who have been endeavoring with heart and soul to preserve this ancient institution by remodeling and modernizing it.

A large part of your success has come as a result of the work of the Conway Committee whom we are now honoring. That committee gave implicit recognition to the public interest as a prime motivating factor for future administration of the Exchange. It properly recognized that "the integrity of the Stock Exchange is of first importance even with a program of governmental regulation." It also set forth as basic the proposition that a huge business enterprise such as the Exchange should be run in a modern, efficient way rather than in the manner of a private club. But it talked in no vague generalities. It laid down a concrete plan of action—a new constitution, a paid president, a trained personnel, a reduction, nearly in half, of the size of the board of governors—in short, a businesslike administration of one of the most important businesses in the country; a streamlined administrative machine geared for high-speed action in the interests not only of the members but of the general investing public.

Intervening events have proved the wisdom of the principles which the Conway Committee laid down for you. And the speed and dispatch with which you adopted these proposals for reorganization are a sign of a new spirit in the Street. For that reason I congratulate you and the Conway Committee. As a result of your acceptance of its platform, you can face the future with the hope and belief that you can reclaim the public confidence in the integrity of your business.

So tonight we turn our eyes from the past to the future. And the question on all lips is: "What next?" Last winter I told a committee of the Congress my views as to the proper relationship of an agency of the Government like the S.E.C. to a stock exchange. I said:

My philosophy was and is that the national securities exchanges should be so organized as to be able to take on the job of policing their members so that it would be unnecessary for the Government to interfere with that business, and that they should demonstrate by action that they were so organized. Now, that is something more than coöperation. That is letting the exchanges take the leadership with Government playing a residual role. Government would keep the shotgun, so to speak, behind the door, loaded, well oiled, cleaned, ready for use but with the hope it would never have to be used.

That is still my view of the matter. I do not relish governmental intrusion into your business any more than you do. And you know, as the public knows, that I am as sincere in that statement, as I am in saying that we will faithfully endeavor to do the job which is ours under the law.

We are first and last the investors' advocate. But we are also your advocate. A proprietor of a business such as yours can render a high service to his customers and to the nation. With full sincerity I can say that if we can help you render that service we will have helped you help our whole national economy. For it must be remembered that your vitality and strength are symptomatic of the health and vitality of all of our financial processes.

That is why it must not be forgotten that the way your Exchange is run is a matter of national concern and of national importance. Your Exchange is one of the greatest market places in the world—a place where buyers and sellers throughout the world meet and do business together. It is important to those buyers and sellers, whether they be big or small, that this market place be above suspicion. To satisfy the demands of investors there must be in this great market place not only efficient service but also fair play and simple honesty. For none of us can afford to forget that this great market place can survive and flourish only by grace of investors. A man who wishes to buy or sell stocks or bonds must be convinced that this is his exchange, not an insider's exchange. He cannot be convinced by mere words. But I am sure he can be convinced by action. You have made a splendid beginning. It clears the decks for action. And if I am any judge of the attitude which prevails among the men who have been chosen to your new board, we shall have convincing action.

The course which that action should take seems clear. As I have said on other occasions, those intricate matters cannot be solved in the manner of debating societies. They are hard practical problems which can be answered only by dint of hard work and study and by an exchange of ideas between you and us. No one has a corner on truth in these matters. We must expect change and flexibility as conditions change. Our standard is and can be only the welfare of investors. Your self-interest also lies in that direction, for the welfare of investors is on the long pull your welfare.

In the first place, it should be clear to all that neither you nor we can or should endeavor to fix it so markets go up or down. And, of course, neither you nor we can be held responsible for rising or falling prices so long as those movements are not artificially generated. These markets should mirror and reflect what the world of business is doing. He who tries to interfere with those natural movements is not a true advocate of the investor. Out in the Far West, we used to have annually a county fair. The side shows at those fairs used to be more popular with the younger ones than the exhibits of cattle, sheep, and apples. One of the most intriguing was the tent containing the magic mirrors which would make fat men out of thin ones and dwarfs out of tall ones. Too often have our exchange markets been magic mirrors, not reflecting real conditions but distorting true facts. You and we must by action eliminate so far as possible those magic-mirror effects. That means among other things a joint attack on manipulative trading. Hitherto, we in Washington have carried the brunt of such policing. We have had to exercise the greatest vigilance to see to it that the law was enforced. Detection of pools is one thing; legal proof of the existence of pools is another. We operate under the law. That means full opportunity for a hearing by the accused. It also means a fair trial and a careful weighing of the evidence by us. All of that takes time. Furthermore, the doing of our job in a legal way has required collection of facts from hundreds of brokerage offices and from customers. Brokerage offices and customers naturally find us somewhat of a nuisance when we are bent on such a mission. But to enforce the law we have to have facts. We cannot manufacture them out of thin air. The only way we can get them is to go to original sources. This may be called gathering of evidence or snooping, depending on your point of view. But on that issue, here is where we stand. Congress has outlawed pools and manipulation. We intend to carry out the Congressional mandate, though some may say it took a snoop to do it. But I am convinced that through united action by the exchanges and by us we can do the job much more effectively. An exchange properly policed should seldom create such onerous tasks for the S.E.C. policeman. I am confident that, through your activities, you can make manipulation and the manipulator as unpopular here as they are in the country at large. Hence, I look forward to the day when policing of the Exchange by you is so effective that there remains little for us to do on that score.

Secondly, there is the troublesome question of the insider on the Exchange as contrasted to the outsider. I would not be frank if I did not mention it. Some of you members and member partners have yourselves in the past complained as vigorously as members of the public about the undue advantage which the inside trader has had over others. You have also let it be known in no uncertain terms that this trading advantage has too often been used not alone for the insider's profit but to the detriment of the outsider. Due to this foment and discussion both within and without the Exchange, the popular impression has been clear and strong that someone on the inside has a mirror—not a magic mirror this time but a clear, sharply focused old-fashioned mirror—behind the backs of the investors who enter this market. The feeling that one member at the table has a mirror strategically located behind the other players is not conducive to confidence here, any more than it would be in case of a game of poker or bridge. It does not create an eager desire on the part of others to become participants. It is repellent to the American sense of fair play. It adds a casino element to what should be an old-fashioned, open auction. This is the most difficult problem confronting you and us. I do not come here this evening with a ready answer. The mechanism of the Exchange is as intricate as a Swiss watch. All of its parts properly synchronized are essential for effective operation. In a real sense, members on the floor—the so-called insiders—and the commission houses who do business with the public are dependent one on the other. There is no good reason why they should not pull together. What is good for one part is found in the long run to be good for the other. So this problem is a joint one for solution by all of you and by us. I face this problem with confidence that working together we can solve it in a way which will be sane and sensible and at the same time protective of the best interests of the man or woman who enters this market place to buy or sell. We must soon get on with that problem for it is a constant source of irritation. If we neglect it now, it will come back to haunt us all on less favorable occasions. But over and above all else it is not fair to the investors of this country for us to neglect that problem longer, no matter how difficult its solution may be.

In the third place, there is the problem of affording the person who buys or sells securities protection against the risk of loss of the securities or cash which he has left with or delivered to his brokers. Occasionally a broker has become insolvent. Still less frequently there have been misappropriations by him of his customers' securities. On these scores the record of Exchange members has been exceptionally good. But these occasional cases have raised in the minds of some customers fear and suspicion. We might as well be frank about that. This condition recalls the story of the Indian out in the Far West who wanted to borrow $1,000 from the local bank. The banker wanted some collateral for the loan. The Indian could not understand. The banker finally made the Indian see that he could not have the money unless he left with the banker his twenty ponies. So the Indian brought in his ponies and got the loan. Later the Indian struck it rich. He came in with his huge bank roll, peeled off a $1,000 bill, paid the loan, and retrieved his ponies. The banker, seeing the large bank roll, suggested that the Indian deposit the money in his bank.

"How many ponies *you* got?" asked the Indian.

Some of that Indian's blunt skepticism and simplicity crops up when one out of a thousand honest businessmen comes a cropper. The problem has been accentuated in periods of business recession.

In the simplest form of cash transactions, a broker often holds for his customer either cash or fully paid securities. The length of time during which cash or securities are held will vary with the details of the transaction or with the wishes of the customer. The risks inherent in this holding of cash or fully paid securities depend upon the care with which a broker's business is handled. In a situation where a broker holds cash for his customer, the customer has what is known as a "free credit balance." In effect, it is like a deposit of money in a bank. It is apparent that many customers make a practice of having cash balances with their broker, for we know that those few brokerage houses alone which reported to the New York Stock Exchange by questionnaire as of March 31, 1938, had free credit balances belonging to their customers aggregating $245,000,000.

Now a broker has his own cash funds as well as those that he holds for his customer. He may commingle his customer's funds and his own funds, or he may set the customer's funds aside in a separate account. Better-run brokerage houses have taken appropriate measures to hold apart, or segregate, assets approximating the amount of the total credit balances carried by them. Just as money balances belonging to customers may be commingled by the broker with other customers' balances or with his own, similarly securities belonging to customers which are carried on margin may be in the house of the brokerage business so commingled.

In the past there has been general regard on the part of brokers for high standards in the conduct of their business and this has given protection to customers. By and large there have not been many losses to customers resulting from causes of the brokers' own making. The record of your Exchange is exceptionally good on this score. But there have been some cases where these high standards have not been followed. Overspeculation and other forms of excessive commitments in securities by a brokerage firm or its partners have involved unjustifiable risks to the customers and in some cases actual losses. The shades of a recent example of such disregard of the customer's property still haunt financial districts. And other cases of insolvency or peculation have from time to time revealed potential weaknesses in the present system. Thus, there still remains a problem of the utmost importance to the public as a whole and we feel, as we know you do, that an attempt must be made to find the answer.

How desirable it would be to achieve a greater measure of security for the customer's property. How simple, from the broker's point of view, it would be if brokers were relieved of worry over the mechanical operations of handling securities or funds; over performing these banking functions; or over the difficulties and responsibilities of custodianship. I should like to offer a suggestion, and it is no more than that, for reaching at least a partial solution to these problems.

I may say that this suggestion is not an original one with us. It emanates from the brokerage business itself. It was suggested at least as long ago as 1932 by some of your own members. It comes down to this—the establishment of an institution in the nature of a trust company to be formed for the purpose of taking over the functions of banking, clearing of securities, and the custodial duties of all members of the exchange. As I recall, this was originally suggested by some of you as an economy measure. Changing events indicate that today it has acquired additional merit by reason of the real assurance and protection which it would appear to afford customers.

The suggestion contemplates the formation of a trust institution under state law whose functions would be confined solely to acting in a fiduciary relationship as agent for both brokers and customers. It would not operate for its own account, nor would it engage in a commercial banking business. The usual functions with respect to purchases and sales of securities would be carried on by brokers just as is the case today. But brokers who had the benefit of the services of this institution would be relieved of many of their present functions. For instance, the trust company would act as cashier for brokers; receive from and make payments to customers for securities bought or sold; transfer, receive, and deliver customers' securities upon instruction of the brokers; and as respects margin transactions, act for brokers not only in relation to their customers but in relation to the banks as well. Clearances could be readily and conveniently handled.

An institution along these lines would of course reduce the number of operations involved in the securities business, and should effect substantial economies for the brokers. But more important should be its service to investors and to the public generally in reducing or eliminating the risks at present involved in the performance by brokers of the quasi-banking and custodial functions which I have mentioned before—the holding and commingling of the funds and securities of their customers.

From another viewpoint such a measure should also answer many of the administrative problems of the Commission as well as of the Exchange. It would simplify the task of making inspections of the margin accounts of our far-flung brokerage community and also the handling of the other details which are the necessary incidents either of enforcement or self-regulation. Certainly, when considered in this connection, this suggestion has great appeal for us.

The suggestion is, of course, only tentative and the details of the functioning of such an institution have not been thoroughly explored. We hope to explore them with you to see if practicable ways cannot be found for effecting such a measure within the near future. If, as a result, you and we agree that the idea has merit, we will be happy to coöperate in the establishment of such an institution in a form which can best serve the interests of all.

These then may be regarded as cardinal problems worthy of our joint endeavors. Their solution holds out great promise of entrenching the Exchange in public confidence and of building it up as an integral and vital cog in the financial machinery of the nation. In no sense do they constitute what might be called an official agenda. And they can be called a program only by virtue of the fact that they are a part of the unfinished business which is before you and us. Tonight we face them together and I firmly believe that we can solve them together in the near future. There are other parts of that unfinished business, though there are not many. There is the persistent question of bond trading. How can the quality and quantity of bond trading on the Exchange be improved? There is the question of the amount of commissions and other service charges which members of the Exchange should receive. There is the question of whether or not the odd-lot business and procedure can be improved in the interest of the public and in the interest of the Exchange. These in main constitute our immediate unfinished business. Other problems will doubtless arise in the future. But we have in this list our chief problems. Our solution of them will switch on the green light which will open the broad highway which lies ahead. Let you and us see to it that that green light functions. We need not long delay. We need not await endless study. Much spadework has been done. Common sense and informed judgments will point the way. The conference table rather than the laboratory is the place for us to do most of our joint work.[1]

1. About ten days after this speech there began a series of conferences between the technical staffs of the S.E.C. and the New York Stock Exchange on the problems presented by the Conway Report. These conferences, which

We may make mistakes—that is human. But let us not allow fear of error or of complexity to promote inaction.

Some will always look with longing, backward glances to the gay days of 1929. But you and we know that as a nation we cannot and should not turn back. You and we know if we work together rather than apart, if we expend our energies on the problem rather than on each other, that we can make this segment of capitalism work. That will mean profits for your business. That will mean health for our national economy. That will mean a vivid demonstration that the aims of this government and the objectives of business are wholly compatible. So as the green light flashes, I bid you safe riding down this broad and open highway that lies ahead. I do more than that—I offer you a police escort.

Mr. Douglas termed "the round-table," were held periodically for almost a year.

CHAPTER IX

MARGINS AND MARKETS

The New York Stock Exchange sponsored a round table on business and finance at the 1936 session of the Institute of Public Affairs of the University of Virginia. Charles R. Gay, president of the Exchange, had spoken in strong defense of speculation and the rights of speculators. The following discussion is taken from Mr. Douglas' reply to Mr. Gay, delivered July 11, 1936.

TWO years ago there was launched a long-needed program of Federal regulation of the securities markets. That program is still in its nascent stage. Its full development will be a matter of years. By its very nature it calls for gradual approach and tentative measures tested in the light of experience. We have to date attacked only segments of the problem. It is still too early to make adequate appraisal of some of the measures which have been adopted. But there are some current aspects of the problems which are arising in connection with the administration of the Securities Exchange Act of 1934 which I would like to mention briefly.

In the first place there is the problem of margins over which the Federal Reserve Board has jurisdiction. In this connection there have been some interesting developments. Following the decline in stock prices which occupied most of the month of April of this year, some people became apprehensive concerning the restriction of margin accounts which was caused by the combination of stiffer margin requirements and the stock-price decline.

Under Regulation T of the Federal Reserve Board concerning loans by brokers and dealers, there was prescribed, effective April 1, a maximum loan value for registered securities (other than exempted securities) of 45 per cent of current market value. Regulation U, covering direct loans by banks for the purpose of purchasing or carrying registered stocks, effective May 1, also prescribes a 45 per cent maximum loan value.

It is likely that speculators have been inclined to purchase stocks to the limit of lawful credit accommodations inasmuch as even that full amount is considerably smaller than they had been accustomed to carry with equal cash or collateral in preregulation days. Obviously, when margin accounts are filled to capacity even a small dip in stock prices will have the effect of restricting further purchases. Moreover, the accounts may remain thus restricted for some time, since a subsequent market rise may not include, to any worth-while extent, the poorer-grade issues that fall sharply.

In former times it was not unusual for some classes of speculators, intent on greater profits, to attempt to carry as much stock as their funds and collateral would permit. When a dip occurred in prices, these buyers, even as today, were in no position to make further purchases. Often it was only a matter of a small further decline that brought about a number of calls by brokers for additional margin. Thus, restriction of margin-account buying is not new, but restriction today does not mean enforced selling.

Contemporary stock buyers, as well as those of any previous period, might be grouped in two classes: those who cannot resist the temptation to overtrade and those who are wise enough to "restrict" their own accounts by purchasing no more than a very reasonable risk will permit. The second group would include true investors who confine their dealings to cash transactions. Every investor and every smart speculator sees the wisdom of self-restraint in stock-market matters. A cautious investor "restricts" himself to the amount of cash at his disposal.

The two main purposes of the margin sections of the Securities Exchange Act of 1934, prevention of the excessive use of credit in security transactions and limiting speculation, are to a substantial extent accomplished by Regulations T and U. Their existence is justified by the creation of greater safety for investors on the exchange and in the capital markets.

As of May 29, 1936, there were 418 reporting member firms of the New York Stock Exchange which carried margin accounts for customers. The number of these accounts totaled 205,884. It may be liberally estimated that these 205,884 accounts involved 200,000 persons, or less than two tenths of 1 per cent of the population of the country. It may also be estimated that these accounts represent the great bulk of margin trading through brokers in this country. During this year New York Stock Exchange brokers' loans have averaged about one billion dollars. From other data which we have it may be estimated that the brokers supply about one quarter of a billion dollars more money, making a total of about one and one quarter billion dollars of customers' debit balances owed to brokers. Taking the market value of New York Stock Exchange stocks alone, it appears that the ratio of the total debit balances of customers to the market value of these stocks is 2.51 per cent.

It can fairly be said that present margin regulations do not impose an undue burden upon security buyers. With $5,500 one may purchase securities valued at $10,000, a value about 82 per cent in excess of the funds available for the speculation. It is difficult to rationalize a more liberal credit extension, to find reasons why stock buyers should take greater risks.

Our national income in 1932 was less than forty billion dollars. In that year retail sales on the installment plan were estimated at three and one half billion dollars.* Thus, assuming forty billion dollars of funds were available, the three and one half billion representing installment sales bore a ratio of only 8¾ per cent to total national income. Thus it will be

---

* Evans Clark, *Internal Debts of the United States*, p. 307.

observed that the average man's general installment obligations amounted to only 8¾ per cent of his annual increment.

The buying of a car on the installment plan is the equivalent in many cases of money saved which might otherwise have been used in various ways. There is little difference between saving ten dollars a week for the purchase of furniture for the home and buying it on ten-dollar weekly installments. The purchase of securities on borrowed money is a different story. Money placed in securities represents savings. The purchase of securities on credit is an outright oversaving which may jeopardize true saving, since a price decline forces liquidation.

The popular view, however, is that we must make some allowance for American gambling proclivities. And it is said that Congress did this in writing Section 7 of the Securities Exchange Act, which deals with margin requirements for securities registered on national securities exchanges. However that may be, a thoughtful student of the subject cannot fail to be impressed with the necessity for examination of the hypotheses upon which margin trading is based. The ramifications of that subject have never been adequately studied. Constant and attentive consideration of the incidences of margin trading becomes essential for the immediate and long-range program of control of security speculation and security manipulation.

In the second place there is the problem of the "thin" market, which in some respects is closely related to the problem of margin trading. Blame for the relatively thin stock-exchange markets of recent months has been attributed by many to the Commission and to the Federal Reserve Board. And fears have been expressed that continuing regulation of this character will tend to accentuate this condition of "thinness." [1]

1. The stock market is said to be "thin" when the ranks of potential buyers and sellers are thin; this reduces the speed with which a given amount of securities can be bought or sold at a specific price.

We have had occasion to study this problem intensively in recent months, especially in connection with our study of the segregation of the functions of brokers and dealers. Recently we have submitted a preliminary report on that subject to Congress.[2] In that report we recognized the grave risk of fundamental conflict of interest existing when one person acts both as broker and dealer; i.e., when he acts as an agent or fiduciary for others on the one hand and as a trader for his own account on the other. As we pointed out in that report, this conflict may react to the disadvantage of the brokerage customers:

A broker who trades for his own account or is financially interested in the distribution or accumulation of securities may furnish his customers with investment advice inspired less by any consideration of their needs than by the exigencies of his own position. The securities, equities and credit balances of his customers may be endangered by the risks which he incurs in making excessive commitments for his own account. A complicating factor in these situations is that the average investor too frequently is unaware of the distinction between the broker and dealer relationships and hence takes no account of the possibility that the advice and service proffered by a broker may be affected with a powerful, independent interest at variance with his fiduciary obligation.

We also pointed out that the prevalence upon exchanges of a type of dealer activity which exerts undue influence on prices and incites public speculation, leads to disorderly markets and interferes with the effective fulfillment of the brokerage function.

That study and report were "preliminary in character." Rather than adopt a comprehensive program of immediate segregation of all brokers and dealers, we chose the course of an "evolutionary but direct approach" with the view of moving forward progressively toward a thorough solution of this aggravating problem. To that end we proposed, among

2. *Report on the Feasibility and Advisability of the Complete Segregation of the Functions of Dealer and Broker* (1936).

other things, a "functional segregation of all members on the floor of the exchange with the exception of the specialist in the stocks in which he specializes." Under such a requirement, floor traders could not act as brokers and floor brokers and commission brokers could not, while on the floor, initiate orders for their own account or the account of their firms.

We also suggested further proposals for control of floor trading, for restriction of the activities of the specialist, for trading by members in stocks off the floor. These additional requirements move in the direction of an insistence upon a singleness of allegiance on the part of brokers acting in fiduciary capacities. We do not leave the problem with these admittedly partial solutions. We are committed to a continuing and increasingly intensive study of the whole problem with a view of moving progressively forward toward the objective of high standards of conduct in our security markets.

Admittedly such measures will have their effects on the quality of the securities markets. They may contribute to the "thinness" of such markets. But let us stop at this point to consider some of the aspects of this quality of thinness not from the point of view of brokers and dealers whose income may be affected but from the viewpoint of our national economy. Disregarding the proposed segregation rules which we have sponsored and looking solely at present rules and regulations, what condition do we find?

If rules and regulations under the 1934 Act have reduced the numbers of potential buyers and sellers of securities on the stock exchanges, or limited the extent of their trading, it should be remembered that they are those same rules which were devised to prevent manipulation and controlled prices, to prevent excessive use of credit in security speculation, to prevent excessive speculation itself, to remove the advantages formerly accruing to insiders, and to regulate the trading by members of the exchanges. Some contend that these rules and regulations have contributed to thinness in the markets. But it must be remembered that volume of trading usually dries up after a long upward trek in security prices is halted, even temporarily, by a swift decline. Thereafter, speculative activity is lethargic until primary causes are found for renewed upswing or further decline. In fairness, then, it cannot be contended that these natural causes be disregarded and full blame be attributed to Federal regulation. The normal lassitude of markets which follows speculative excesses cannot be overlooked.

Furthermore, what is this thing called "liquidity" and how important to our national economy is it? Liquidity means not only convertibility into money but also conversion into money within a reasonable period of time and at a price not out of line with that deemed appropriate for the particular commodity. The fact that a ready market may exist for a commodity does not necessarily mean that the commodity possesses liquidity, for the market price may be so out of line with current conceptions as not to provide a price within the limits which are deemed appropriate. Some are apt to think of the 1929 stock market as being the norm for liquidity. But what degree of liquidity was there, for example, in October, 1929, when stocks listed on the New York Stock Exchange lost over $15,000,000,000 of value? At that time it would seem that instead of liquidity we had evaporation.

Now if there were reason to sell a large block of stock in a short period of time and within a reasonable range of prices, one should not be surprised to find the problem more vexing now than in the summer of 1929. Yet compared with October, 1929, such a transaction would perhaps not be so difficult. On the other hand, it is self-evident that if in the average day's trading in regulated markets there are fewer buyers and fewer sellers, or if there are as many as in previous years but they are trading in smaller amounts of stock, the need of "thickness" of the market also has been reduced proportionately. It would also seem obvious that to the extent that these markets are freed from manipulation, the need for thickness in the market is likewise reduced proportionately.

As I have stated, the so-called "liquidity" and "continuity" of security markets during past periods of large volume of trading were, while they lasted, due in large part to excessive trading by professionals and insiders. Still worse, a substantial portion of the activity was provided by manipulative efforts of pools and by the overtrading of misguided individual speculators who bought securities, not because of merit or intrinsic worth, but because of the glamour of pool-made markets and whispered tips originating with the pool managers. Markets which are free from these influences and in which purchases are made after mature deliberation are more permanent markets, if not as liquid for the short term. When a pool advertised its wares by sudden market price movements in its stocks, the public buyer was drawn in at high prices. After a sharp decline, that buyer did not have the necessary funds to purchase similar shares at a reasonable price level. This means that, on a broad scale, more and more speculators and would-be investors were drawn into the maelstrom of a gambler's market at higher and higher prices. Obviously, many of these persons were automatically released from their holdings as prices declined sharply. The aftermath of the speculative orgy was low prices and low public participation. Thus the liquidity of the boom market paved the way for the illiquidity and lack of continuity of later markets.

Let us look into the short periods of liquidity associated with earlier bull markets. The same floor trader who was willing to buy stock at twelve o'clock on a certain day was a willing seller at two o'clock. The insider, who supported his favorite issue at attractive prices on a decline, generally let the purchased block of stock go on the first good rally. The manipulator who created fancy prices also caused sharp declines when he had completed his distribution and was taking a short position. The eighths and quarters of the floor traders and the larger profits of insiders and manipulators resulted principally from the fact that many "outsiders" paid more for their stocks or received less upon their sale than might otherwise have been the case. If we cannot countenance such abuses—and we should not—we cannot have the high degree of liquidity which was a concomitant of the extremely active markets of limited periods in the past, unless such liquidity is the result of public interest not artificially stimulated. Such liquidity and continuity were normal resultants of the manipulation and excessive speculation of those periods.

It has been stated that specialists' books in recent weeks have been very thin. That is to say, there are few buyers and sellers who have open orders to buy at prices below current prices or to sell above current prices. Perhaps specialists' books are always thin, when a long rise in the market has been followed by a sharp decline and speculative activity temporarily has been reduced because many brokers on the floor, who in busy days leave their orders with the specialists, attend themselves to their execution on quiet days. In the second place, as markets become less active, the true books of orders at or near the market, in the majority of fairly active stocks, are in the pockets of various floor brokers and in the minds of speculators and investors who will buy or sell without advance notice to the specialists. Markets are not as thin as the specialists' books would indicate.

What we ought to remember is that those who buy with sufficient capital, and not merely to take advantage of one-quarter- or one-half- or one-point movements, neither depend upon, nor are interested in, markets featured by the degree of liquidity for which our speculative and manipulative markets have been notorious. Markets of this sort, which were prevalent in the late 'twenties, ended in practically complete nonmarketability. Investors' markets necessarily are different markets, but this does not mean that the investor fares worse. The most liquid markets are those *made* by manipulation, but the investor who remembers the experiences of 1929 and 1932 should certainly be aware of the fact that they are not *made* for his benefit.

Or to state the matter in another way: *

The economic value of an exchange is popularly measured by the extent to which it possesses the quality of continuity and imparts liquidity to its securities. Respect for these attributes, particularly where stocks are involved, has become generally ingrained in the consciousness of investors and lenders. Investors and lenders are accustomed to regard current exchange quotations as accurately reflecting the realizable value of a security. . . . Our economy as presently constituted not only holds these attributes in high esteem, but has attuned many of its institutions, such as our banking system, to them.

On the other hand, the experience of the past suggests that the creation of claims that demand liquidity can be carried to such lengths that the result is an unstable economy. Over-emphasis upon liquidity promotes artificiality in the economic structure, because it is based upon the assumption that the wealth represented by securities is and will continue to be readily convertible into money and at not too great a deviation from current quotations. Inasmuch as a belief in the continued existence of liquidity makes for lending capacity on securities, independent of what may be the purpose of the loan, it induces expansion in bank credit, and, as the past readily illustrates, undue expansion of bank credit has reverberations throughout the entire economic structure.

The total volume of credit extended upon securities may at any time be wholly disproportionate to the credit that lenders would extend directly to the corporations which issued these securities, even though the latter type of loan has a legal position ultimately superior to the loan made upon the securities. Such a result largely flows from the fact that the market imparts for the time liquidity to the securities held as collateral, though the ultimate security in both instances may be the earning power of the corporate assets. Again, the prominence of the quality of liquidity increases the inclination, already too prevalent, of buyers of securities to think in terms of the appreciation in the value of the security rather than its promise of continued and substantial earnings. This inclination impairs the

* *Report on the Feasibility and Advisability of the Complete Segregation of the Functions of Dealer and Broker* (1936), pp. 98–99.

value of the market as an accurate barometer of investment opportunities and thus tends to vitiate the judgments of even those buyers who do think in terms of underlying worth.

That activity as such is desirable because it promotes liquidity, and that speculative activity is an essential to the maintenance of liquidity are by no means established economic truths. Generally speaking, lack of balance in the market between investment inflow and outflow operates to bring about changes in price trends. When the outflow exceeds the inflow, prices fall; but if they fall below a certain point, the sacrifice which would be involved in the sale of a security may induce its holders to treat it as non-liquid rather than as liquid wealth. Consequently, speculative activity, which accentuates price trends, has its bearing upon such a phenomenon. Furthermore, if liquidity involves an appropriate balance between investment inflow and outflow, and a disturbance of that balance occurs, speculative activity that accentuates price trends tends to increase the lack of equilibrium already present, and, though convertibility into cash may be maintained, that accentuation brings about the type of artificial instability making for price declines and rises totally out of line with basic economic conditions, and destructive of a fundamental element of liquidity.

From this it is clear that our problem and concern are not with thin markets as such, but with that type of speculation which brings about artificial instability. Speaking generally it may be said that the interests of investors and speculators are basically divergent. By his very nature the investor has to buy when he has a surplus of funds or has to sell when he needs to realize on his invested funds. A speculator does not have either to buy or sell. He simply does it in the hope of making a profit. It was stated by the House Committee Report on the Securities Exchange Act of 1934:

There is plenty of room for legitimate speculation in the balancing of investment demand and supply in the shrewd prognostication of future trends and economic directions; but the accentuation of temporary fluctuations and the deliberate introduction of a mob psychology into the speculative markets by the fanfare of organized manipulation, menace the true functioning of the exchanges, upon which the economic well-being of the whole country depends.

On this basis there is room for speculation which furnishes a bridge between the investor-buyer and the investor-seller. But that bridge does not have to be so wide, and the multitude of speculators so large that the number of investors will be overwhelmed. As I have stated, such excessive speculative markets, with all their liquidity, have been fertile ground for abuse and actual fraud, for distorting the real prices, by divorcing them, through an intervening speculative enthusiasm or despondency, from their economic background. At times this caused wholesale distress, because everybody relied on liquid markets, and got themselves accustomed to thinking of liquidating, even wanted to liquidate at the same time, which, of course, is impossible. It is a fundamental weakness of the liquidity concept—and a reflection on the way we have been educated to react to it—that there are times when thousands of people want to buy for speculation, while there is only a small number of investor-sellers available, and, at other times, still greater numbers all wanting to liquidate at the same time, while those who would have been investors have been tuned up to the speculative state and, instead of being buyers themselves, for no good investment reason join the already too disproportionately large ranks of the sellers.

If we have recurring waves of ups and downs; i.e., market swings, or cycles, to the extent that we have a large number of speculators that play such swings rather than take an investment position, the danger is that, if all are equally smart to catch the trend, stocks will shoot stratosphere high at one time and drop abysmally low at another.

In view of this it is obvious why we should not be as solicitous in permitting freedom of action on the part of the speculator as we are in safeguarding the interests of investors.

It is not uncommonly contended that the professional speculator should be left free and untrammeled and that, if that course were followed, the public speculator would be protected. There is, however, a fallacy in assuming that professional speculators protect the public speculators. This fallacy flows from the assumption that there is a certain definite amount of stock to be traded, say, a thousand shares. If three hundred of such shares are bought by professional speculators, there are only seven hundred shares left for the less wise public speculators, and hence they get to that extent less hurt than if all the thousand shares were bought by them. The truth of the matter is that trading has a totally different aspect. The professional speculator does not take off so much stock from the public speculator. Rather, the more he buys the more the public will buy. He sometimes generates movements in stock, and, because of the facilities of the ticker, the public joins him. It is not at all proven that increased speculation by professionals means decreased speculation by the public. It is likely that the opposite is true.

It is proven, however, that certain professional trading accentuates price trends. Thus our analysis of daily trading reports from members of the New York Stock and Curb Exchanges, gathered over a period of six months, showed that the floor trader traded against the trend only one third of the time, but traded with the trend two thirds of the time. However, when fluctuations in prices were small, floor trading was neither preponderantly with nor preponderantly against the trend. But when the market definitely moved in one direction or the other floor trading was with the trend 73.5 per cent of the time. We concluded that "floor trading on most of the days under review accentuated the trend of market prices."

To put the matter another way, if you let speculation alone and set up no controls over it, what starts as moderate speculation will feed on so-called injudicious speculation; the speculative excesses are quickened and the investment process is weakened. And finally, by depleting the ranks of investors in favor of those of speculators, speculation inevitably, sooner or later, destroys its own foundation and builds a debacle.

What is frequently forgotten is that the cost of speculation

to the public is very high. There are as many, or more, transactions in the odd-lot market, for example, as in the round-
lot nonprofessional market. The average purchases in the odd-
lot market amount to about twenty shares, or less than $1,000
per transaction. The double taxes paid, the high minimum
commissions, the differentials, are such that it may be estimated that a customer, starting with about $1,000, as a result
of sixty-six trades, has contributed to the kitty $1,000. If he
buys on a 50 per cent margin, thirty-three trades will result
in the $1,000 going to the kitty. If he uses still smaller margin,
and buys that much more stock, it means, of course, that the
kitty will take the amount in fewer transactions. This assumption is, obviously, based on the fact that in his sixty-six
trades he will buy and sell, on the average, at the same price;
that is, that he has an average chance of neither losing nor
winning. Whether he has such an average chance is still to be
proven over a term of years. That so-called injudicious speculation is not only economically harmful but harmful to the
individual has been long recognized by conservative brokerage
houses, who have insisted upon margins higher than the stock
exchange, and discouraged their customers from overtrading,
and too rapid a turnover, even though it meant a loss of
commissions.

All speculative theories agree that the fundamental basis of
all markets is legitimate trading. In the grain market, for
example, the basic idea is to distribute the crop to the proces-
sors; in the security market it is to give an opportunity to
those who have accumulated funds to buy and, when they
need cash, to sell. It is sometimes said that the speculator is
actually a "middleman" between the original seller and the
ultimate buyer. This is something simple and comprehensible;
but, whether, in order to render this service, it is necessary to
turn over the capitalization of some stocks several times in one
year is far from proven. It is true that this furnishes "great
liquidity," but, as I have stated, the greatest liquidity is al-

ways in artificial markets, made by pools and manipulators for as long as the making goes on. And, whether such markets are made by manipulators, or the liquidity results from spontaneous speculation, it usually ends in a condition where there are no markets, and neither speculators nor investors can sell. Rapid turnovers mean increased brokerage commissions. But from a broad, national point of view, there is little economic significance in whether the turnovers are high or low.

So in conclusion, let me say, first, that our primary concern is with the protection of investors. The objective is neither creation of "thin" markets nor "thick" markets, but with curbing of speculative excesses which are so dangerous to our national economy and with the injection into these market places of higher standards of fiduciary relationships. And let me say, secondly, that the appearance of thin markets is not of itself a matter to be decried. Nor is the fact that this may possibly be due in part to actions taken by the Securities and Exchange Commission and by the Board of Governors of the Federal Reserve System any proper condemnation or criticism of the propriety and necessity of the kind and degree of Federal regulation which has been imposed. Nor is the fact that insistence on higher fiduciary standards of conduct in the securities market by segregation of brokers and dealers may accentuate the quality of thinness any justified criticism of that ethical proposition. Thin markets may promote true liquidity, as well as the contrary. We need to forsake the blind faith in that kind of liquidity for which the markets of the late 'twenties were conspicuous and to examine *de novo* the validity of the hypotheses upon which that kind of liquidity is based. Until we approach the problem in that manner and from the viewpoint of our total national economy, rather than from the viewpoint of brokers and dealers bent on increasing their income, we will never reach a satisfactory solution of the problem of attuning the security exchange markets to the public interest.

CHAPTER X

CUSTOMERS' MEN

The "customers' man" is the stock exchange's point of contact with the investor. Since he is not a salesman, but a broker, his function presumably is limited to receiving and executing his customers' orders to buy or sell. Yet his value to the firm which employs him is measured largely in terms of the amount of business he obtains. This conflict gives rise to many problems.

The following talk was delivered in November, 1936, at the Stock Exchange Institute, a school maintained by the New York Stock Exchange for the employees of member firms. In the spring of 1939, a group in New York organized the Association of Customers' Brokers and adopted a code of ethics and standards of practice for customers' men employed by New York Stock Exchange firms. The new association gave customers' men the new title of "customers' broker."

SINCE this is a little university in Wall Street, I wish to speak to you in terms of education. I have no concern over the lack of any adequate opportunity which this institution will afford you to obtain necessary training and equipment for your professional work. I believe that you will be introduced to many of the mysteries of Wall Street. I believe that your studies in economics, accounting, and finance will stand you in good stead and give you a broader perspective on your vocation. I believe you will be well trained to master the complicated financial machinery of which this spot is the physical center. I believe you will receive instruction designed to draw the line for you between legitimate and illegitimate, honorable and dishonorable business. I have no worry on the quality of your instruction. My only worry is what will happen to you as you move forward in your business.

I am particularly happy to discuss with you some of these

problems, because you are and represent youth. Youth has both ambition and idealism—an ambition to conquer, an idealism to make the homely virtues living realities. Youth is anxious to preserve the best from the past and to discard the worst. Youth is eager to repair the damage of those who preceded them and to build constructively and permanently. Youth is open minded and forward looking, not oppressed by prejudices engendered by habit, routine, and convention. Youth is the generating force whereby we move forward toward a fuller and better national life.

Hence, I welcome this opportunity to lay before you some constructive ideas for your consideration—ideas which relate to the business into which you are fast being integrated. One of the most difficult jobs is to view objectively one's own activity and conduct. This is likewise true of one's vocation or business. But I feel it will be worth your attempt if you undertake to do so.

In this connection, youth faces perplexing problems. There always have been and always will be subtle and subversive influences at work to corrupt the high functions which business, finance, and the other professions perform. For this reason one of the chief problems of youth is an ethical one. Friends, associates, environment, indeed time alone, work for this corruption. When I speak of corruption I do not mean gross extravagances in the form of larceny and the like. I refer to the practice of gentlemen teaching youth gentlemanly ways of redistributing the wealth of their clients so that they may get an inordinate share of it in extravagant ways. I mean the use of the ideal of freedom of opportunity and private initiative to warrant or excuse exploitation. I mean the application of pressure from employers that these high virtues be exercised solely to the end that their earnings will increase. I include temptation to ape the activities of clever market operators so that acquisition of material wealth may be easy, effortless, and immediate. I refer to the urge to keep the customers' portfolios well churned so that by the quick inflow of commissions one may the sooner join the elite of high finance.

Some of your elders say that the thing that was wrong with 1929 was that they were too commission hungry. But human nature has not changed. I see no reason to believe that youth cannot develop as ravenous an appetite. There will be inducements to do so, for the pressure to move onward and upward, according to cash-register standards, will be almost irresistible, and the end of the rainbow will at times appear to you, either by example or by precedent, to be merely a carnation in your lapel and the comfortable club life of your city. These are not matters which should depress youth and make it jaundiced and bitter. Rather, they constitute a challenge to youth to make constructive conquests and to capitalize opportunities missed by their elders.

Your profession has no particular claim to distinction in this respect. The same elements appear as a corroding influence in other professions. Our educational system has been too virile in production of men immunized from a sense or feeling of social responsibility, trained in the art of plunder in gentlemanly ways, imbued with the false ideal that the American way means exploitation. There has been too little emphasis on the principle that the basic essential of an education is the ability to think—to think in terms of human values, to think in terms of social responsibility, to think in terms of what the cumulative effect of your daily activities is in terms of your clients' welfare and of your character. This need, while not peculiar to your profession, is especially accentuated there because in final analysis yours is a profession affected with a public interest.

I can perhaps sharpen and make more specific some of the matters which cause this worry and concern, if I restrict my comments to one vocation which at least some of you will enter and which doubtless holds out bright prospects and hopes, especially as we move forward on the road of prosperity. This is the vocation of the customers' man.

I suppose you would say that a customers' man is not a salesman but an order clerk who transmits customers' orders, who makes sure that the orders are executed, and who reports the execution of the orders to his customers. You might say that although he contacts customers and solicits business for his employer, he does not have an inventory of securities to sell. When a customer makes a purchase through his firm, the firm does not, or certainly should not, sell the security which the customer buys. But, in spite of all this, the customers' man is a salesman, though he has nothing to sell but himself, his services, and his counsel.

The function of providing a mechanism whereby buyers and sellers can be brought together is an important function to perform. Its importance is not restricted to the securities field. If you have mice and I have a mousetrap, the one who supplies the ready machinery whereby we may come together is performing an important function, at least judged from the viewpoint both of those who do not like mice and of those who desire to sell mousetraps.

Securities exchanges similarly serve high functions in providing the mechanism whereby buyers and sellers can readily come together. One of the problems raised by the institution of customers' men is the basic question of how far these markets should go toward providing salesmanship as distinguished from a market where purchases and sales can be effected. Salesmanship like its brother, advertising, may be an indispensable ingredient of our system of business organization. Salesmanship in the field of securities, however, has given rise to such a host of abuses that the most conservative safeguards are necessary. Finance has used salesmanship as a short cut to profits. Salesmen have not been able to forego those profits by telling customers not to buy this or that because it is not economically justified. Salesmen have been told and have believed that their task is to sell customers whatever they want, and, if necessary, make them want what the salesmen have, at any price which the traffic will bear. Those who have selling organizations on their hands would not take the larger view, since that is against their financial interests. These selling organizations clamor for salable securities. They like merchandise which is stylish and which has a popular demand, even though such merchandise usually reflects an exploited situation. Hunger for commissions thus becomes at times the sole arbiter of the process of capital distribution and preservation. When that happens, the securities business becomes not a legitimate enterprise conducted for a profit but a business engaged in exploitation.

This type of salesmanship which I have described has no necessary relationship to the business of securities exchanges. These could be conducted without it and it could be conducted without them. And I do not wish to attribute to the exchanges, as such, the evils and abuses which such salesmanship has engendered. But it is important to consider the impetus to excesses which is provided when salesmanship of the type supplied by the customers' man is added to exchange trading. There is then added a stimulating factor. The glamorous limelight of exchange trading is sufficient in and of itself to attract the moths of speculation and investment. Customers' men may make that light seem brighter and more attractive than is warranted.

History teaches that the interest of customers' men frequently lies in encouraging customers to buy and sell not only often but promiscuously and indiscriminately; to be satisfied with small profits or to accept small losses; and to make the daily pace and direction of the stock market their measurement of value. Customers' men, being in constant contact with tickers and news, are frequently influenced by short-term considerations, rumors, inside dope, and the like, and

disseminate this influence among their customers and prospects. Furthermore, they have not only distributed other
people's rumors; they have manufactured and distributed their
own. Customers' men frequently have been primarily interested in generating trading by speculators, since their compensation is dependent, indirectly at least, upon the volume
of business transacted through them. At times their activities
reach the proportions of high-pressure salesmen whose frantic
telephoning and whose conduct are more compatible with the
boiler room than with customers' rooms of member firms.
Accordingly, they become an influence which stimulates speculation and encourages active and in-and-out trading.

Perhaps the tendency to such speculative activity has been
accentuated by the nature of customers' men since, as I have
said, they are primarily engaged in the solicitation of commission business in securities. By their constant observation of
the market, of news, and of tickers, they keep their customers
apprised of price trends of securities in which they cause
their customers to be interested and of new developments
affecting those securities. But it should be remembered that
as to counsel or advice rendered by customers' men, they are
not, for the most part, trained statisticians or economists.
Their experience with securities has been largely gained in
the Street or financial district. At times their contacts in the
financial district and elsewhere give them insight into the
merits of certain securities. Yet even though they may make, at
times, studies of corporation reports and statistical data, the
advice or counsel which they are generally prepared to offer is
neither that of the statistician nor that of the professional
investment counsel. Thus it is that there is a growing belief
that customers' men are of no use to bona fide investors, that
persons who desire to invest money have ample facilities
among the many sound and reliable institutions and member
firms of securities exchanges without the necessity of the intervention of an additional agency like the customers' man.

These facts emphasize one of the dangers of attaching such a person to our already complicated and impersonal market machinery. It tends to separate by one further degree *values* from *things*. It tends to accentuate the dominant characteristic of securities exchanges as inanimate objects—impersonalized to such a degree that human and social values disappear and economic facts become blurred and indistinct.

This separation of *values* from *things* is one of the most conspicuous danger points in our entire system. The progressive movement from barter, tokens, and coins to paper money and securities has enabled finance to treat business as mere conglomerations of stocks, bonds, notes, debentures. Finance has not neglected the opportunity thus afforded. Through complicated financial structures, holding companies, collateral trusts, tribute in the form of hidden charges, and the like, it has created a system which at times makes almost impossible any intelligent determination of the relation between *values* represented by the securities and the *things* which securities represent. Or if the determination of such relationship is possible, the tendency is to treat the facts of transportation, manufacture, wholesaling, retailing, as secondary rather than primary. The weather vane of business becomes not the profit-and-loss account and the balance sheet, but the gyrations of these pieces of paper as revealed on the ticker. Under such influences the ticker cannot become the pulse of business. Under such influences the ticker cannot follow business—the tendency is the false illusion of business following the ticker. In other words, economic facts disappear from the picture or become blurred and indistinct. The fact that people who have saved are involved, and that their future and security are at stake is also forgotten. The social and human values disappear. When that transpires, the market becomes a place for games rather than orderly investment and liquidation processes. The consequence is, as I have stated, an inanimate and impersonalized market devoid of human or social values and irresponsive for periods to economic facts. Tragedy in the form of social disintegration is the end result.

Customers' men, to the extent that they stimulate trading by their solicitation methods, accentuate this tendency. They add an artificial element to the market processes. They breed excitement and feverish interest. In their small way, they add to the churning of portfolios which in terms of basic economic functions has no significance. It is important only as measured in terms of cash-register standards. The activities of customers' men can have no other effect, so long as they parade themselves as understanding and knowing markets, market trends, and securities values, when in fact they do not have such understanding and knowledge.

These facts make abundantly clear that the whole institution of customers' men is at least of unestablished value. They stress anew the question of whether or not such a stimulating influence has any proper place in our sensitive and delicate market mechanism. They challenge you who are moving forward toward that profession to produce living evidence that the economic, human, and social values involved in the exchange process not only will not be sacrificed, but, in fact, will be enhanced by virtue of your activity. If you do not produce that evidence, society or your exchange may feel that your function performs such a distinct disservice to investors as to justify a change in the system.

But if, and so long as, this vocation continues there are certain practices which need be eschewed, lest you further corrupt it and lest it corrupt you. In this brief paper I cannot mention all of them. A few will suffice for illustration. The first relates to the fiduciary position of customers' men. He who holds himself out as rendering this investment counsel and this service to customers should be held to high fiduciary standards of conduct. If he who gives this advice and encourages and stimulates his customer's purchases and sales has a self-interest in the transaction over and above his salary or

regular compensation, his customer is apt to receive not un-
biased and disinterested advice but advice discolored by the
self-interest which such purchases and sales will serve. The
presence of this self-interest will deprive the customer of the
benefit of disinterested and impartial advice, the very thing
which presumably the customer thinks he is getting. The
courts of law have refused to admit that the average individual could stand the stress and strain of such dual interests.
When the issue is resolved in final analysis, it means that the
counsel given will be likely to follow the bias and self-interest
of the agent rather than the best interests of the customer. In
any given case the factors in motivation are too subtle and
tenuous to result in anything but guesses. But human experience teaches that a man cannot serve well two or more
masters. In terms of customers' men, this fundamental principle of fiduciary relationship should mean at least two things.

1. First and foremost, customers' men should have no interest, directly or indirectly, in any security for themselves,
except that which they have acquired for bona fide investment
purposes. To many this will appear to be not only a mistake
in business judgment but also a meticulous and unnecessary
stretching of these ethical and legal rules. To be sure, such
standard of conduct outruns the rule of law. But as a working
rule of thumb, it is essential if the market place is to be rid
of some of the subtle influences of biased and discolored advice by those who purport to be objective advisers. The question is not simply one of preventing specific transactions
wherein the customers' man or his firm has a special adverse
interest, transactions which should be beyond the pale; it is
broader than that. It entails also avoidance of a situation
whereby the customers' man, influenced consciously or otherwise by his own glowing prospects in particular speculative
transactions and impressed by his own infallible judgment,
proceeds to advise his customers to follow in his footsteps.
Meticulous regard for these standards should be had by re-

liable and competent persons purporting to render investment counsel. Needless to say, this would entail prohibition of margin accounts for customers' men, directly, or indirectly through their wives, fathers, brothers, etc. In such cases, there are further reasons: Not only will judgment be warped and biased; fair-weather customers' men will be so concerned with their own margin accounts that their clients' interests will suffer, especially in times of market reactions.

2. Customers' men should be prohibited from having any interest in an operation designed to distribute securities. Great abuses have occurred in the past by reason of the presence of such an interest. The practice of paying customers' men, directly or indirectly, for the placement of securities with their customers has not been abolished. Reputable firms will shun and avoid this practice. Eager and ambitious (and hungry) customers' men will be tempted by it. The temptation will always be present. Operators engaged in a secondary distribution will be vitally concerned with the task of putting the securities away in permanent hands. If they can work through the good offices of the customers' man and reach such purchasers, their operations will be made easier. Accordingly, they will attempt to buy the customers' man for a consideration. The end result is that for that consideration the customers' man is giving not disinterested advice but advice corrupted and biased—irreconcilable with his fuduciary status. His corruption violates legal and ethical standards of conduct of ancient origin. He then becomes not a useful or permissible cog in the financial system but a corroding influence. He may be able to survive the fair weather of the markets. But the day of accounting comes sooner or later if he departs from the standard of giving advice on any basis other than his own free belief in the merits of the security.

In the second place, the extravagances of the customers' men in connection with margin trading and discretionary accounts weaken the case and challenge the justification for their existence.

Justifiable criticism of customers' men has been directed to their tendency to encourage overtrading by their customers. Frequently they have had no regard for margin regulations and they have permitted their customers to load up their accounts beyond the point of conservatism. Some customers' men have encouraged customers who have a limited or restricted account to make new commitments which they cannot afford and which they must liquidate within the limit of the three business days allowed by Regulation T. Thus the spirit, if not the letter, of such regulations has been violated. This malpractice is not, to be sure, traceable entirely to the door of the customers' man but is one for which his employer should receive equal, if not greater, blame. The problem, as you know, has been recognized by your Exchange in its rather recent ruling that no member shall permit a customer "to make a practice" of effecting transactions requiring a margin and then either defer the furnishing of a margin beyond the time when such transactions would ordinarily be settled or cleared, or of meeting such demand for margin by the liquidation of the same or other commitments in his account. But the problem from the point of view of the customers' man is not only to see that there is no such regular practice but to prevent all other transgressions. As to the prevention of such excesses, the customers' man stands in a peculiarly strategic position and is derelict in the performance of his obligations if he neglects to insist on meticulous fulfillment of such rules.

More important, however, are the abuses which have arisen in the past as a result of the employment of discretionary powers by customers' men. After your Exchange had adopted a rule according to which customers might delegate discretionary powers only to partners, it was known that such powers were in turn delegated by partners to customers' men, so that the spirit, if not the letter, of the rule was violated. That rule has, as you know, been altered by the Exchange so that no discretionary accounts may be handled either by partners or by customers' men without the consent of the Committee on Customers' Men. But there appears to be valid consideration for a rule which would effectively prohibit customers' men from employment of any discretionary trading power. The interests of customers' men in general and those of their customers would be well served by such a prohibition.

The dangers of any other course are self-evident. Compensation of a customers' man will always be dependent indirectly, if not directly, on the commissions he brings the firm. If he has a discretionary account, the temptation will always be almost irresistible to keep that account well churned for the sake of commissions. Discretion, in other words, will tend to disappear. The daily or weekly record of the customers' man can be bolstered by a few transactions in the discretionary account. The guiding principle will tend to be the record of the customers' man in terms of commissions rather than his record in terms of sound and conservative judgment in the interests of his client. Here again motivation is a complex thing. Cause and effect will not always be easy to determine. But human experience—the record of the past—teaches us that an employee in such a position will tend to sacrifice the client's interest for his own record of achievement in terms of commissions.

In sum, if the institution of customers' men is to survive, it must have meticulous regard for the standards of conduct governing fiduciaries. It cannot survive if it ostensibly serves the customers but actually serves the employees and employers. It must redefine its functions. It must forsake the idea of salesmanship and concentrate on investment service. If the institution desires to survive, let customers' men become serious students of corporations; let them be in a position intelligently to advise clients on reorganization plans; let them qualify to render counsel to those solicited in proxy campaigns; let them be competent to advise on mergers, consolidations, recapitalizations, and the like; let them lose their consuming interest in intermediate price movements; let them desist from calling their customers unless requested or except in serious emergencies; let them become studiously concerned with the fundamentals of business and of finance. The only social vindication of that institution is to be found in such a course. Whether or not such a program of achievement can be attained will be in issue. Perhaps it is impossible of realization. Perhaps the fact that the customers' men are not paid by the clients but by the firms, from which the pressure to produce business will be strong, will provide an irreconcilable factor.

But, as I stated earlier, the institution of customers' men has at present an unestablished value. In the past it has served as a method of churning portfolios, of creating frenzy and excitement, of manufacturing and distributing rumors and tips —in short, of serving as a fair-weather device to make the market a gaming place. Whether it can be made a valuable investment-service adjunct to organized exchanges rests in the hands of your generation. It will not and should not survive if the corruption of which I earlier spoke intrudes.

CHAPTER XI

ON AMENDING THE LAW

On March 13, 1939, representatives of fifteen stock exchanges attended a conference in Washington, D.C., called by the chairman of the Stock List Committee of the New York Stock Exchange. The S.E.C., which had been holding regular round-table conferences with the New York Stock Exchange for many months, was not informed of the nature of the meeting. The newspapers hinted that its purpose was to attempt to secure amendments to the S.E.C. statutes. The committee deliberated for two days and on the evening of March 14 made public a report, a copy of which was sent to the S.E.C. The report proposed the amendment of the anti-manipulative provisions and four other sections of the Securities Exchange Act, as well as certain provisions of the Securities Act. The next day, March 15, the Commission replied to the committee's report with the following statement.[1]

THE Securities and Exchange Commission has received the report of the committee, headed by John M. Hancock of Lehman Brothers, proposing amendments to the Federal securities acts. We have considered those proposals and make the following observations as respects the chief one.

1. Mr. Douglas met the newspaper correspondents to give them the statement of the Commission. Discussing the committee's report, he pointed out at the outset that the only comment authorized by the Commission was its prepared statement and asked that his remarks be "off the record." In the course of the discussion, however, at the request of the newspapermen he granted permission to quote certain of his observations. The stenographic transcript of this portion of the press conference is here quoted:

Mr. Douglas: "So, again, not speaking in terms of motives, not attacking the Hancock Committee—because I haven't discussed this with them at all —but just looking at the end result, if you try to measure this in terms of a program for business recovery, all I can say is that it is a 'phony'."

Chorus of Questions: "Can we quote you on that?"

Mr. Douglas: "That's right, you can quote me on that. Furthermore—"

The chief proposal of this committee is a relaxation of the law against market manipulation. Stripped of its legal phraseology, this proposal would bring the pool operator back into the market. This strikes at the very heart of stock-market regulation. The Securities and Exchange Commission is unalterably opposed to any attempt to legalize manipulation in the stock market. The finding of Congress in 1934 * is the conviction of the S.E.C. today, after five years of experience with the law.

This proposal is presented on the ground that it will aid the capital markets. The S.E.C. is deeply concerned with the problem of maintaining a free flow of capital, from the savings of the investor through to the productive channels of industry. To this end the Commission is vitally interested in stimulating the confidence of investors in the securities of American industry. But this Commission cannot stand idly by while any attempt is made to bring investors back into the market on a 1929 basis. Such a proposal would redound only to the benefit of those whose primary interest is served by an increased volume of trading—the broker to whom more trading means quicker profits, the insider, and the market rigger

[At this point, at the continued request of the gentlemen of the press, the reporter began to read, as follows: "If you try to measure this in terms of a program for business recovery."]

Mr. Douglas: "Put it this way, if it is set up as a business recovery program it is a 'phony,' or, it would be a 'phony' on any standards of a business recovery program.

"Again, I am not attacking anywhere along the line the motives of these men. They have their own ideas and they are entitled to express them."

Q. "Could we quote you as saying you are not attacking the motives?"

Mr. Douglas: "Oh, sure. I never talked with them about this. They probably feel very keenly about this and they have set convictions. They have stated them. Well, we are stating ours for what they are worth. And I will tell you this, that if you got this program intelligently interpreted to the American public they would turn it down a hundred to one; there is no question about it. Because there is nothing in here for the investor. You can write that down in your hat, there is nothing in here for the investor."

* "House Report No. 1383," 73d Congress, 2d Session, p. 10.

—not American industry nor American investors. Sound recovery cannot be had through the use of injurious stimulants.

The law as it stands today has for five years been increasingly effective in protecting the stock market against manipulation. The modification suggested by the Hancock Committee would weaken the law and make its enforcement exceedingly difficult.

The recommendation would first make the prohibitions against market rigging dependent upon rules drafted by the Commission. The committee asks clarification of the law in the interests of certainty. The proposal, however, only adds uncertainty and confusion by superimposing on the present single statutory test of purpose additional tests of a far more indefinite nature; e.g., the committee's proposed standard of purchases or sales "for the purpose of unduly or improperly influencing the market price of such security." Furthermore, it would make enforcement of the rules dependent upon standards of conduct so indefinite and so subject to differences of opinion as to render the protection of the statute illusory.

The Hancock Committee's suggestion would inevitably involve the Commission in a determination of appropriate price levels for securities bought and sold in our markets, if not in the actual evaluation of such securities. Such activities on the part of the Commission would be directly contrary to one of the basic philosophies of our Federal securities legislation. The proposal would also call upon the Commission to foresee and define every conceivable variety of manipulation. Such a procedure might well result in the ceaseless invention of new techniques to evade regulation. It is in recognition of such human ingenuity that our courts have consistently declined to lay down hard and fast definitions of fraud that might in any way be relied upon as delimiting precedents in future cases involving new and different schemes.

The present prohibition was placed in the statute by Congress as a guarantee against manipulation. To alter the provisions of the statute on this point would involve a change in national policy with respect to manipulation of our public-securities markets. No longer would manipulation be outlawed as a matter of national policy, but the definition and prohibition of manipulation would be left to the discretion of the Commission. Out of almost five years of administrative experience the Commission finds no evidence to indicate and no reason to believe that market manipulation would be less of an abuse today than it was prior to the passage of the Act.

Weakening our safeguards against market rigging will not contribute to business recovery. On the contrary, it will serve to destroy whatever investor confidence has been built up through efforts to clean up the stock exchanges. It will not produce "healthy buying power."

It is interesting to note that the proposal to permit market rigging and pool operations is accompanied by another proposal which would exculpate the corporate insider who wishes to take personal and private advantage of his inside information. Let us not forget that stock-market pools were often the most successful for the manipulator when he worked hand in glove with the corporate insider.

Similarly it is interesting to note that some of the other proposals of the Hancock Committee (such as those dealing with gross sales and cost of sales) go principally to a reduction in the amount of information available to stockholders and the investing public. A stripping away of the protection against pools, a nullification of corporate insiders' responsibilities to their stockholders, and a curtailment of truth to investors— these are not harmonious with old-fashioned, conservative standards for finance.

PART III
PUBLIC UTILITIES

CHAPTER XII

A CALL FOR LEADERSHIP

The Public Utility Holding Company Act was passed on August 26, 1935, and within a few months utility companies brought over fifty lawsuits challenging its constitutionality. When the registration provisions of the Act took effect on December 1, 1935, the S.E.C. was immediately faced with a multitude of injunction suits to prevent enforcement of the law. The Government, desiring a prompt and fair test of the Act, brought a test case against the two-billion-dollar Electric Bond and Share Company, meanwhile agreeing to withhold prosecution of violators of the Act until a Supreme Court decision could be had.

On January 29, 1937, the United States District Court for the Southern District of New York decided the Electric Bond and Share case by upholding the constitutionality of the registration provisions of the Act and ordered the Electric Bond and Share Company to register. The case was appealed and on November 8, 1937, the Circuit Court of Appeals sustained the decision of the District Court.

With the constitutionality of the Act becoming increasingly clear, Mr. Douglas sought to persuade utility leaders that further delays were unnecessarily obstructing progress within the industry. He urged certain financiers that if they would take the lead, the constructive program of the Act could get under way and the country would benefit. When this effort failed, Mr. Douglas determined to ask publicly for leadership in the utility industry.[1] The following

1. The *New York Times,* on February 4, 1938, described Mr. Douglas' position: ". . . Mr. Douglas recognizes, as does nearly everyone else, that the utilities could use many millions of dollars during the next few years to increase their plant capacity. He recognizes that the spending of this money would be a tremendous force in bringing about the recovery of business. Then why are the utilities marking time? It is Mr. Douglas' thesis that the investors in public-utility securities have nothing to fear from an intelligent enforcement of the so-called 'death sentence' on holding companies, but that the managements of these companies, being essentially concerned with retaining economic power, are holding back from the expenditure of funds. The industry itself is eager to go ahead. But its real operating heads, 'under the whip hand of New York finance,' are paralyzed into inaction. . . ."

speech was given at Chicago, before the Commonwealth Club on February 2, 1938. Two months later the United States Supreme Court, in the Electric Bond and Share case, upheld the constitutionality of the basic registration provisions of the Act.

W ITH the Public Utility Holding Company Act of 1935, the Congress attempted to provide new standards for the utility industry in its relations with investors, consumers, and the public generally. The country had long demanded more conservative practices from that industry. The abuses disclosed by the Federal Trade Commission's investigations [2] were too grave to be ignored.

This legislation had to be forged in the heat which a long-felt demand and an urgent need for change always generates. That heat was generated largely by the powerful public-utility lobby which used every artifice and device to defeat the bill. Emotions on such occasions usually run high, especially where a modern system supplants an archaic one, where monopolistic activities are throttled, or where valuable franchises for individual preferment are impaired. Intense advocacy, intelligence, and courage alone can carry the day on such occasions. Every hardheaded liberal knows that. That is why life in the front-line trenches is usually intense and at times lonely. Those who over the years have been trying to put the public-utility house in order know that only too well. But that does not mean either that this measure was conceived in hatred or that its administration (if and when its provisions are found valid by the courts) will be governed by intolerance or vindictiveness.

Of course, one who insists that financial wizards be not allowed to construct or maintain holding-company structures which are oppressive to business or dangerous to investors will always run the risk of being dubbed a protagonist of

2. Utility Corporations, "Reports of the Federal Trade Commission to the Senate of the United States Pursuant to Senate Resolution No. 83," 70th Congress, 1st Session.

strife who would pit Main Street against Wall Street and business against finance.

But Congress intended to preserve the real values in the utility systems (as part of the capitalistic system) for the common good of investors, consumers, and management, and not to destroy them. Preservation means a harmonious relationship between finance and business, between management and stockholders, and between industry and Government. That is no formula of sweet sentimentality. Nor is it a formula for inaction or drifting. The country wants to reap the benefits of a constructive program for the utility industry. It is no achievement to have a Holding Company Act if nothing is to be done to clean up the conditions which made holding companies and the practices of financial wizards in that field disreputable.

The nation calls for action—direct, forceful, and intelligent action in dealing with the utility situation, not by government alone but by the industry. Such action means constructive work of the highest order, with the industry being given freedom and the opportunity to take the initiative but with Government pointing the way and taking the lead if it falters or delays. A fusillade of words will not suffice. We may change the climate of opinion but we can hardly move forward a millimeter if holding companies and Government agree upon abuses or maladjustments but make no effort to do anything about them. Nor can we view with approval attempts to rewrite these new charters of freedom for investors and consumers in order to satisfy the special interests of management.

All of us, I am sure, conceive that the best government is that which reaches the stated objectives with the least possible interference with business and finance. Then, there is greater opportunity for individual growth and development. How much governmental intervention there must be depends upon industry. The aims and objectives of the Public Utility Act of 1935 have been clearly defined by the Congress. If the industry undertakes to conform to these standards, there will be no need or excuse for prodding from Government. If the industry works with the law rather than against it, setting the pace in tune with the national will, as defined by this legislation, Government will need to act only in a residual role.

There are sufficient brains, courage, and integrity in the business to do this. Those who have created the real values in the utility industry can provide anew a leadership under this new program of reconstruction which the nation has demanded. They will find coöperation on those terms in Washington. They will find fairness, intelligence, and genuine assistance in solving their problems. They will also find sympathy and coöperation—sympathy without weakness, coöperation without capitulation. Those who seek to evade this program, those who are willing to be bound merely by those of its terms with which they agree, will find us unyielding. Such an attitude is indispensable to democratic government; it and it alone makes possible the attainment of the objectives of Congress.

A large part of the industry continues to ignore the Act, pending litigation testing its constitutionality. During this interval, which has already continued for over two years, much time and many opportunities for constructive work have been missed. A basic industry which ought by now to have been ready for much of its needed financing has largely neglected to put its own house in order to make that financing possible and practicable. I regret it; I do not resent it. But I am shocked at the far-flung cry of "wolf, wolf" from the mouths of management over the grave dangers of the misnamed "death sentence," [3] for I know the fears which that specter generates in investors. And I know how unfounded that fear

3. Section 11 of the Act, which sets standards for the geographical integration of scattered holding-company systems and for the simplification of complex corporate structures, was dubbed the "death sentence" by utility spokesmen.

is, because I know that its basic threat is not to investors but to certain types of management essentially concerned with retaining economic power.

But these are matters in retrospect only. Our job is not an autopsy but reconstruction. We live today, not yesterday. The tide of events moves us forward to the constructive work that lies ahead. The once united front against the Act no longer exists. Many realists in the field have taken a full measure of the Act and have concluded that they can and will live and prosper under it.

But the great bulk is still silently resisting. I see operating managers pressing for the opportunity to work under the Act, because they know that by complying with it they can perform a service which, quite properly, would be profitable not only to their stockholders but to themselves. Yet I see these men under the whiphand of New York finance, paralyzed into inaction. I see realists chafing under the domination of these bankers who are forestalling them from moving forward to obtain equity money which the companies sorely need. I see finance thwarting the will of those who place the vitality of the industry above emotions and collateral self-serving motives. I have spent hour upon hour with leaders of companies who extol the virtues of the Act yet are prevented by untold intangibles, such as the fear of offending New York investment bankers who hate the Administration, from participating in its health-giving benefits.

These are tragic episodes. While the nation awaits restoration of its capital markets, financial leadership slumbers. An industry which its leaders say could use millions of dollars a year in capital for the next few years does not quicken to the possibilities which have been, and are, in store for it. An industry which has the opportunity to make a major contribution toward recovery is stymied by a small group who stand squarely in its path intent on preserving their own intangible interests regardless of the costs. An industry which has a signal opportunity to put its promotional phase behind it and to enter upon an era of conservative but widespread growth neglects the constructive work which can be done immediately. In Washington we can supply, I believe, the action which is needed from government. We have long been prepared. But this is in essence a coöperative undertaking. It is an undertaking which, to be preëminently successful, must proceed under the motive power furnished by the industry. If we were in a position to compel, compulsion should be reserved for the marginal group. Voluntary action points the way to revitalization of the industry. I know that that can be successful. It took financial ingenuity and initiative to do the original job. What financial ingenuity and initiative at times did fantastically it can do conservatively.

Perplexing to me is the failure of the so-called financial leaders to appreciate the force of public opinion which brought about this law. History clearly shows over and again that the nation never surrenders such gains. It appears too obvious for question that the public will never again tolerate the conditions and practices of this industry and its financiers in the past. Progressive leadership cannot fail to recognize the imperative quality of this call for change. It is time for some leadership in the industry to assert itself before the parade of progress passes it by altogether. An ostrich with his head in the sand has no vision.

One of the outstanding men in the utility industry recently said: "In the next ten years consumption will double and at least ten billion of new capital will be needed. The cheapest way to get this new capital, half of which at least must be in stock, will be to simplify existing capital structures. The electric-power industry has only one reason for existence and that is to render dependable service as cheaply as possible. To do this the capital invested must have reasonable certainty of return. The corporate form that it takes should be simple and understandable and workable. The management should be as

close as possible to the territory served." This man obviously
is no ostrich. He is a realist. He reflects the views of many
others, not subject to the whip hand of New York finance.

As I have said, there are brains and imagination aplenty.
We need only the leadership from the industry. The need for
this surpasses the requirements of individual companies; it
goes to the very heart of one of our major national problems
—the capital markets. But aside from the point of view of our
national economy, and thinking only in terms of the self-
interest of the industry, the need for immediate action is
strong. What is in store for the industry in the long vicissitudes of time no one can predict. And under a capitalistic
system no guarantee obviously can be given to it any more
than to other basic industries. It is clear, however, that the
greatest opportunities for survival flow to those companies
which adopt conservative standards of finance of the character
supplied by the Congress under the Act.

Business, the professions, and finance all have their elders.
These elders supply leadership. Though they are not responsible for all that happens, they can and do give constructive
counsel and advice at least in emergencies. That leadership
has always been needed. It is needed now in the industry. Yet
it is almost completely lacking. That leadership can provide
a cohesive quality, imagination and courage, and a singleness
of purpose, undiluted by suspicion or temerity. That leadership with a courage and will to do the job can put the private
utility house in order. The small world of finance can supply
that leadership if it will. If it will not, it is high time for it to
step aside and let the realists do the job. Give us that leadership and private utilities will enter a new era of vitality; and
the national economy will be well served. Deny us that and
the industry, its investors, and the nation will pay the cost.

CHAPTER XIII

DIVIDENDS IN ARREARS

During the booming 'twenties many a utility holding company floated more securities than its earnings could ever justify.[1] The result has been that there are hundreds of millions of dollars of preferred stocks outstanding on which no dividends have been paid for years. The problems raised by the ever-increasing accumulation of dividend arrearages are discussed in the following chapter, a combination of two articles which appeared in June, 1938, one in *The Annalist*, the other in the annual public-utility edition of *The Wall Street Journal*.

THE purpose of this article is to outline a specific program for coöperation between business and government in the financial rehabilitation of a substantial part of the utility industry. The project is to unfreeze, by means of recapitalization, the capital structures of many units of this vast industry, substantially a half of which, measured by assets, is now bogged down in a morass of accumulated unpaid dividends amounting to some $432,000,000 on about a billion and three quarters par value of preferred stock. Substantially 46 per cent of the $3,860,000,000 of the preferred stocks of registered holding companies and their subsidiaries outstanding in the hands of the public are in arrears.

The correction of this situation will serve the threefold purpose of opening the way for resumption of dividends, of facilitating new financing for construction, and of creating sound financial structures on which to build for the future.

The implications of these figures must be faced. They do not appear to have been faced even by the industry. In effect, they virtually forbid equity financing to about half the in-

1. See the report of the Public Utilities Division of the Securities and Exchange Commission, "Dividend Status of Preferred Stocks of Registered Public Utility Holding Companies and Their Electric and Gas Utility Subsidiaries as of December 31, 1938," issued November 21, 1939.

dustry, since plainly enough investors will not invest without hope of return. They preclude the use of earnings for dividend payments, since often companies which cannot finance must keep earnings for corporate purposes. In addition, many of the companies which have any accumulated and unpaid dividends on their preferred stock cannot legally pay dividends.

The accumulations stand in the way of that full revival of public confidence and trust in the utility industry which cannot come until there is a rebuilding of unsound financial structures. Whatever other burdens rest heavy on the industry's back, the hand of this accumulation is by far the heaviest. The accomplishment of this program is pressingly necessary. The task is of a kind we have elsewhere mentioned—an "obvious thing to do first" if the industry is to make great progress toward setting its house in order. Also it supplies a concrete situation for the application of the best coöperative endeavors of which the industry and this Commission are capable.

In other days, conditions of this character were corrected by a process of private bargaining which was often palpably inequitable. The history of reorganization is replete with proof of that contention. To prevent the recurrence of such abuses in the utility industry is a responsibility of this Commission. The law now sets up certain standards, and the task of coöperators necessarily lies within the framework of those standards.

Within the statutory framework, reorganizations and refinancing should proceed in an orderly, equitable fashion. Under the new system, they should be constructive and beneficial to the industry, to investors, and to consumers. These ideas serve to illustrate concretely why the Commission calls this statute constructive. The destructive way is the old way, a way which was directed with little or no heed except to that interest which was able to dominate.

Sound recapitalization programs mean that the flow of earnings from the utility industry to investors will be resumed. We all know that the utility industry is an earning industry, as strong or stronger than any in the nation, not in the least decadent. It is a thriving industry, and still young.

Recapitalization is the most serious task currently confronting the utility industry and this Commission. It is primarily a reconstruction job which will require recognition of all the interests involved that they must exchange their weak securities for securities that will stand up in the market to the end that they may again receive that which they are not now receiving—a return on their investment. The earnings are there; the sound properties are functioning efficiently. There is more to be gained by prompt action than can be lost by delay.

The present financial problems of the industry had their origin in the fair-weather policies of finance which for many companies reached an all-time peak of irresponsibility in the late 'twenties. The Holding Company Act did not create the situation. It is a result, not a cause, of this financial headache, and it is also a prescription for cure.

In spite of the relative stability of the electric and gas industries, the depression not only completely wiped out the income of the common shareholders in many holding companies but also yielded insufficient income to pay holding-company preferred-dividend requirements. This came about not merely because of the reduction of gross earnings, but also because of the tremendous overcapitalization of electric and gas companies. Bonds and preferred stocks, carrying with them an inexorable charge upon earnings, were freely issued. When the storm broke, therefore, the companies could not continue to meet the demands upon their earnings. Some defaulted on fixed interest charges, but a great many failed to pay preferred dividends. In terms of the national situation, the latter present the most pressing problem.

Here are the detailed figures: On January 1, 1938, out of

158 holding companies having outstanding preferred stocks with a par or liquidating value of $2,413,255,930, there were 48 companies with outstanding preferred stocks of $1,330,616,-237 which were in arrears as to dividends to the extent of $336,-657,749.

The arrearages represent an average accumulation of 25.3 per cent of the par or liquidating value of the stocks, or more than four years' dividends. It will also be noted that more than half of the par value of the outstanding preferred stocks of these holding companies have accumulated arrearages.

Turning now to the operating subsidiaries of registered holding companies, there were 224 companies with preferred stocks in the hands of the public amounting to $1,447,460,196 par value. Of these, 70 companies, having $442,976,005 par value of preferred stock, were in arrears to the extent of $95,745,276. Thus over 30 per cent of the par value of the subsidiaries' preferred stocks held by the public are in arrears. The amount of arrears averages 21.61 per cent or over three years' dividends.

In most cases, it will probably be some years before earnings are sufficient to eliminate these arrearages. Until the arrearages are eliminated in some way, these companies cannot do their financing job nor can dividends be paid on the common stocks. In a great many instances, recapitalization will be necessary. Typically, the financially weak holding-company systems have an excessive amount of senior securities outstanding. In many cases the parent company has some debentures and a large issue of preferred stock with three or four years of accumulated unpaid dividends. The parent company's common stock represents a relatively small part of the total consolidated capitalization, but it enjoys all or a majority of the voting control. It is obvious that there are reasonable limits to the amount of pyramiding that may safely be allowed in utility-holding-company structures. It is equally obvious that these limits have been greatly exceeded in many instances. Thus only a small decline in the rate of return on the operating companies' properties has caused the huge accumulations of dividend arrearages which now exist. Clearly, then, our present task is to coöperate in reconstructing these unsound financial systems. The requirements of the Holding Company Act, particularly relating to the issuance of securities and the acquisition of properties, should prevent a recurrence in the future of such widespread financial difficulties.

Consider in more detail some of the effects of the weak financial condition of holding-company systems. If utility operating companies are to continue to fulfill their obligations to the public, they must be able to obtain relatively large sums of money through the sale of new securities. A considerable part of the new money should be raised through the sale of additional preferred and common stock. If operating companies are to obtain equity money, they must be able to sell their own securities directly, or perhaps indirectly, to the public. Those companies, therefore, with large arrearages on their preferred stocks must undergo a readjustment of their capital structures in order that such earnings as are available may be equitably distributed to their shareholders and the securities placed on a basis that will attract new money.

Here then is the industry's dilemma. We are reliably informed that with a revival of business the operating companies should resume their construction programs on a basis approximating the 1923–30 level of seven to eight hundred million dollars annually. While a substantial amount of the funds would come from current earnings, including accruals to depreciation and retirement reserves, it is probable that new financing would be required to the extent of three hundred and fifty to four hundred and fifty million dollars annually. Yet without recapitalization, many companies would be unable to sell such additional common stocks as would be necessary to insure a proper proportion of equity money in new construction programs.

We have no illusions as to the difficulties of effectuating voluntary reorganizations. Ordinarily such recapitalization plans are devised by the management. The management, in almost every instance, has been placed in office by the votes of the common stock and frequently is financially interested as well. Recapitalization plans, formulated under such auspices, while calling for sacrifices by the common stockholders usually in the form of a dilution of their interest in the equity of the company, have invariably called for disproportionately large sacrifices by preferred stockholders.

Preferred stockholders particularly may become apprehensive as they contemplate the inevitability of "voluntary reorganization" of their companies. Let us explore the source of this apprehension and examine its validity. From time to time, students of corporate finance have pointed out weaknesses under state corporation laws in the position of preferred stock in the usual corporate structure and the inequitable treatment which it has received in many voluntary reorganizations. Frequently the preferred is voteless. Too often, in such voluntary reorganizations, assets and earnings belonging to the preferred stock have been taken for the benefit of the common. It was not uncommon to see "voluntary" plans which gave to common stockholders new stock of substantial value for old shares which were way under water. The common stock was able to do this because of its superior power—a direct product of the common's voting rights and its control over the management of the corporation. It was not the orderly result of the common's legal right, when it is remembered that its claim upon assets and earnings is inferior to that of the preferred. This kind of plan was not defensible. Simply and baldly speaking, it amounted to a sacrifice of the preferred for the benefit of the common. In view of this history, the apprehension of preferred stockholders is understandable.

Congress, however, has provided safeguards for investors involved in reorganizations of public-utility holding companies and their subsidiaries. Under the Holding Company Act, the

Securities and Exchange Commission is charged with the responsibility of reporting on reorganization plans. No proxies or consents to a plan can be solicited unless the solicitation is accompanied or preceded by a copy of the Commission's report on the plan. In addition, the "securities" to be "issued or sold" under the reorganization plan must be approved by the Commission. In passing on these securities, the Commission is governed by the provisions of Section 7 of the Holding Company Act. Among other things, this section requires that the security must be reasonably adapted to the security structure of the company and other companies in the same holding-company system; it must be reasonably adapted to the earning power of the company; and its terms and conditions must not be detrimental to the public interest or the interest of investors or consumers. These provisions give to the Commission the duty and the power to scrutinize the plan for its fairness and equity.

Standards of fairness and equity must govern this Commission's action and clearly indicate the path we should pursue in discharging these duties. All security holders affected by a reorganization plan must receive just treatment, in accordance with their legal rights. The word "preferred" in the designation of a senior stock cannot be regarded as surplusage—as merely an advertising slogan which facilitated the sale of the stock. Preferred stockholders must receive recognition in reorganization plans for the interest in corporate assets and earnings to which they are entitled by the terms of their contract and on the basis of which they presumably made their investment.

On the negative side, this means a great deal to preferred stockholders. It means that they can rest assured that their interests will not be sacrificed for the benefit of the common stock. With respect to affirmative results, I should be less than frank if I minimized the difficulties, the primary one being the attitude of some common stockholders.

It is to the interest of preferred as well as of common stockholders that companies in need of reorganization accomplish it as speedily as possible. But speed alone is no safe criterion. We want speed; but we also want fairness. If the Securities and Exchange Commission allowed fairness to be sacrificed for the selfish interests of the common stock, it would not be carrying out the mandate of Congress. This does not mean that the rights of common stockholders may be disregarded. The Commission has the same duty to protect the rights of the common stockholders that it owes to the preferred holders. It must fairly protect those legal rights but it cannot permit either class of stockholders to impair the rights of the other.

The sensible way out is for common stockholders, encouraged by this Commission, to abandon the pattern of the past and to devise plans which give to each class of stock its lawful and rightful deserts. This may mean that some common stockholders will have to content themselves with less than they might have been able to obtain in the days when reorganizations were effected without check or restraint. Recognition by common stockholders of this basic requirement is essential to solution of the difficulties.

Needless to say, the intervention of the Commission in this situation will not produce perfect plans. There is no such thing as a perfect plan. The question in every case is whether "the bargain made is, under all the circumstances, within the permissible limits indicated by the rights and priorities of the various classes" of securities.* Virtually always there is room for legitimate disagreement in reorganization, voluntary or otherwise. But in spite of the absence of hard and fast rules, this principle is clear: The Commission will not permit any particular group to profit unfairly at the expense of other interests.

On the basis of the standards set by the Act, the Commission is ready to coöperate in the formulation of sound recapitaliza-

* *In the matter of the Application of International Paper and Power Co.* (*1937*), Holding Company Act Release No. 770, Securities and Exchange Commission.

tion plans. Our policy in this, as in all matters under the Act, is to place our staff at the industry's disposal with a view to discussing their problems informally. Thus when a plan is presented to the Commission, the applicant will have had the views of the staff concerning the equities of the situation and the requirements of the law. To be sure, the ultimate decision will rest with the Commission. Nevertheless, we feel that this is a helpful procedure. It tends to overcome the frequent complaint of businessmen that they can never get from an administrative department of the Government an indication as to whether or not a proposed course of action is in the right direction.

Many members of the industry have already expressed their realization that coöperation is an effective technique. It is needless to emphasize that this job must be done. We have urged the industry to assume leadership. And that leadership seems to be emerging. But whoever leads, this job remains as one of the most pressing ones.

CHAPTER XIV

THE CASE FOR INTEGRATION

Many public-utility executives long opposed the provisions of the Public Utility Holding Company Act which call for the geographical integration of holding-company systems.[1] In July, 1938, at the Annual Convention of the American Bar Association at Cleveland, Mr. Douglas read the following paper before the Section of Public Utility Law. He defended the soundness of the principle of geographical integration and compared the record of companies whose properties were integrated with the record of companies having scattered properties.

THE problems of corporate simplification and geographical integration are intensely practical and difficult ones. The Commission recognized that in the case of American Water Works where we announced that "the problem of consummating integrated public utility systems under the Act is of necessity, in many cases, an evolutionary rather than a revolutionary process. As a practical matter, it will often be necessary to accomplish the ultimate objectives of the Act by a series of steps rather than by one direct and final step." Adoption of this formula makes for workability and progress, in a field where words rather than action have been too long the keynote.

This inaction has in part been the product of misunder-

1. In a letter dated May 5, 1938, J. F. Fogarty, president of the North American Co., and C. E. Groesbeck, chairman of the board of the Electric Bond & Share Co., wrote to Mr. Douglas on behalf of a committee of fourteen leading utility executives, offered to work with the S.E.C. on problems of the Holding Company Act, but stated in part: "In this connection, these executives also expressed their belief that the fundamental principle of diversity of investment, which is represented here by both geographic location of operating properties and character of business served by them, is a very important factor in the raising of additional capital, and that such principle should be preserved in the public interest."

standing. Prophets of disaster have usually spread alarm where great advances have been made—whether those advances were in medicine, in engineering, in finance, in sociology, or in government. There was no exception here. And in this case alleged disaster and misunderstanding have been pronounced because a catch phrase has obscured the issues. The characterization in the heat of battle of that part of Section 11 which calls for corporate simplification and geographical integration as a "death sentence" has done inconceivable harm. Publicity-wise it was clever; practically it was very damaging. It cast the shadow of a hangman's noose on a purpose and program that are constructive and beneficial. It is my hope that I can today aid in dispelling this ominous shadow. Facts, I think, will do it. I have a deep faith in the power of facts. I have confidence that a problem well understood is half solved. Once having understood the problem, the public-utility industry and we can, and will, devote our joint resources and intelligence to a solution.

There has been substantially no opposition to the provisions of Section 11 (b)(2), which call for the simplification of complex corporate structures and the equitable distribution of voting power. Attack has centered on the requirements of Section 11(b)(1). This section provides that it is the duty of the Commission, as soon as practicable after January 1, 1938, after notice and opportunity for hearing, to require each registered holding company to limit its operations to a single integrated public-utility system and to such other businesses as are reasonably incidental or economically necessary or appropriate thereto. By definition an integrated public-utility system means a system whose utility assets are physically interconnected, or capable of physical interconnection and which under normal conditions may be economically operated as a single interconnected and coördinated system, confined in its operation to a single area or region, in one or more states, not so large as to impair (considering the state of the art and the area or region affected) advantages of localized management, efficient operation, or the effectiveness of regulation. The Commission is empowered, however, to permit a holding company to continue to control one or more additional integrated systems if they are located in one state, or in adjoining states, or in a contiguous foreign country; if each such additional system cannot be operated as an independent system without the loss of substantial economies; and if the whole aggregation is compatible with the advantages of localized management, etc.

Insofar as these provisions call for geographical integration of operating companies, they are entirely in tune with what has been a trend for many years. That trend has been evidenced not only by the extent to which operating companies have expanded but also by their mergers and consolidations in various regions. That policy of the statute is not new to the industry; its leaders have seen for some time its many virtues. Improvements in business organization and technological advances within the industry have demonstrated the economies and efficiency of unified operating territories. They have shown the value of integration based upon a sound rationalization of the industry within areas not so large as to lose local character, but not so small as to prevent the realization of engineering progress. The most casual familiarity with the utility industry as a whole will reveal that these economies frequently have been sacrificed. In large part, they were neglected in the scramble by rival holding companies to acquire local operating utilities. I need not remind lawyers of the recklessness with which this was done in those halcyon days. This business of buying properties, helter-skelter, resulted in highly undesirable operating conditions. Operating units owned by rival holding companies cut across territories in the fashion of a crazy quilt, with the result that the power requirements of many areas were not planned or served in an efficient manner.

For example, an area in a Middle Western state, ideally suited to the operation of a single system or at the most two systems, is actually served by half a dozen operating companies controlled by as many holding companies. Waste results; power costs are unnecessarily high; returns to investors are affected; and the stability and efficiency of each of the operating units are unnecessarily diminished. Let me give one simple illustration. One of these companies recently built a new generating plant to provide for a load of less than 10,000 kilowatts. It was located somewhat less than twenty-five miles from a large efficient plant of a neighboring company which had ample capacity to supply this load. In all probability, if these companies were integrated, duplication would not have been needed.

Such apparently uneconomic developments often flow from the strategy of immediate expediency, nurtured by individual system rivalries. I can understand the cause of these situations without condoning their indefinite continuance. Insofar as the Public Utility Holding Company Act calls for, or will result in, rational integration, it will substantially eliminate these forces of disharmony.

An executive in the electric light and power industry recently stated the advantages which his system had derived for both its investors and its consumers from an integration of operating companies. He summarized these as follows:

1. It makes possible the substitution of one or more large generating stations for numerous small units, and thus introduces economies in production, while at the same time increasing capacity and insuring adequacy of supply.

2. Where territories have been integrated it is often possible to dovetail steam generation with hydroelectric generation, making the most economical use of each source.

3. Integration permits planned transmission facilities in a manner which obviates frequent and costly rearrangements of lines.

4. Where operating territories are integrated, it is possible to develop greater uniformity in rates and rate structures, to introduce on a wider and more effective scale promotional activities, and to encourage wider and more diversified use of power.

5. Under integrated operation many duplicate services and overlapping departments are eliminated.

6. If the territory of a system is integrated, there is a natural tendency toward simplification of corporate structures within the system, through consolidations and mergers, with consequent economies in corporate reports, taxes, accounting supervision, and the like.

7. A sound integration of operating territories promotes sound financing of the enterprise.

But it is not geographical integration per se with which the Act is concerned. The Act is not aimed at operating companies as such. In terms of geographical integration it has no impact on isolated operating companies. The fulcrum of Section 11 is the holding company. It is through the holding company— and only through it—that the Act attempts to exert leverage on this problem of geographical integration. To put it simply: isolated and independent operating companies remain unaffected by Section 11; * a holding company must be confined, with few exceptions, to a single integrated public-utility system. Theoretically, then, only a part of the private utility problem is touched by Section 11. Actually it has a pervasive effect on most of the industry in view of the dominance of the position of holding companies.

The policy of the Act in restricting holding companies to single integrated systems is not difficult to divine. In the first place, it reflects the desire to diminish concentration of control in the electric and gas utility industries. In the second place, and as a corollary of the first, it is designed to promote the formation of strong regional or local operating systems—rid of absentee management and remote financial control. On this matter, the National Power Policy Committee has said:

---

* Isolated companies, rid of holding-company control, may be expected to respond to technological and operating considerations in development of integrated units—perhaps in some cases to state-wide integration. This is not to mention the important realm of state regulation not affected by the Act.

Numerous studies have already shown, and the report of the Federal Trade Commission further demonstrates, that the concentration of control in the electric and gas industries through the device of the holding company has assumed tremendous proportions. While the distribution of gas or electricity in any given community is tolerated as a "natural monopoly" to avoid local duplication of plants, there is no justification for an extension of that idea of local monopoly to embrace the common control by a few powerful interests, of utility plants scattered over many states and totally unconnected in operation. Such intensification of economic power beyond the point of proved economies not only is susceptible of grave abuse but is a form of private socialism inimical to the functioning of democratic institutions and the welfare of a free people.*

The fact is that the electric and gas utility industries have become essentially local monopolies by virtue of their economic characteristic; yet many of the large holding-company systems have succeeded in expanding their financial and economic control far beyond any reasonable limits. In Section 11, Congress has ruled that the financial and economic power of the utility holding company must conform, roughly speaking, to the economic area of the regional or local operating monopoly. Section 11 places a natural limitation upon concentration of control, for as different systems map out their single integrated service areas and in the process acquire the scattered properties of other systems, each system's boundaries impose a limit upon the future expansion of its neighbors. In contrast, when a holding-company system could pick up properties anywhere and such properties did not have to be geographically related, there was no effective limitation upon the size of a holding-company system or the number of units which it might control.

The philosophy is that while our technological advances have created economic principalities in many spheres of national activity, the size and power of these principalities must correspond with the economic or social facts. No man or group

* *Report of National Power Policy Committee on Public Utility Holding Companies* (1935), "H. R. Document No. 137," 74th Congress, 1st Session at 4.

of men should be permitted to expand this financial and economic control beyond limits justified by those facts. In the electric and gas industries, as in some others, a situation which logically arose because of certain inherent, operating characteristics was pushed far beyond its logic. The local units of the electric and gas industries have been referred to by some as "natural monopolies," and they have been given peculiar legal status because of the characteristics which led to this designation. This may have been wholesome and desirable; but, if so, one of the factors which made it such was the essentially local characteristic of these industries.

Now, one of the consequences of this status was some stabilization of rate of return for these industries. But this stabilized return made these industries peculiarly attractive to those who had a lust for power and profit. These persons collected more and ever more electric and gas companies and properties and combined them into huge holding-company systems. The result was not merely absentee ownership, but absentee management and remote control. An essentially local industry was managed from a far distant metropolis. It was run not merely to serve the local consumers and the people who had invested their money in that company, but as part of a huge empire. It was, so to speak, a member of a scattered family with the controlling grandparent dwelling in distant parts. The local or regional unit lived not for itself, but for all of its kin. If money were needed in any part of the holding company's system, a local company was subject to raids of one sort or another to produce that money to support the ailing members. In many instances its officers and employees were used to sell securities of its remote parent or of one of its remote brothers. Its good will was dependent not upon the local life of which it was essentially a part, but upon the fortunes of dozens of remote brothers or second cousins and the vagaries and humors of several degrees of parents.

In Section 11 of the Holding Company Act, Congress has

recognized not merely that reorganization of the electric and gas utility industries on a regional basis is necessary in order to promote their health, but also that the huge scattered empires must be broken up into regional systems in order to prevent the destruction of the utility industry itself. This is the philosophy of the statute. And I, like all others who believe in keeping business at home, think this philosophy is sound. And there is strong support for it in the industry itself. An executive of a holding-company system soon to be revamped under the Act said this to me recently, with reference to Section 11:

> Integration of generation, of natural trade areas, and diversity factors are a very sound background upon which to reset the operating companies of the nation. The electric power industry has only one reason for existence and that is to render dependable service as cheaply as possible. To do this the capital invested must have reasonable certainty of return. The corporate form that it takes should be simple and understandable and workable. The management should be as close as possible to the territory served.

And the staff of the New England Power Association recently laid on my desk an interesting analysis and justification, from an operating and engineering point of view, of the philosophy of Section 11. Their paper [2] said in part:

> The development of the electric power industry in the United States has brought about the existence of four broad classes of electric utility units. One is the small and constantly decreasing number of isolated local units, isolated as to electric connection with their neighbors and local in their management. Another is the group in which the units are under common management but which are not physically connected each to the other. The third class comprises those units which are physically interconnected but are under separate management. Finally there is the integrated unit, or system, consisting of completely intraconnected units, located in a single area and whose development and operation are coördinated through common control but which, on account of state laws and local conditions, cannot be combined or consolidated into a single corporate entity.

2. "Public Utility Integration," F. J. Dunn and Associates, *Harvard Business Review*, Spring, 1939.

The benefits which accrue from group management have for many years been widely discussed. Similarly the economies resulting from interconnection are so well appreciated that further explanation of them is unnecessary. The integrated system receives more completely the benefits arising from group management and interconnection and in addition enjoys certain advantages not available through either alone and is free from many of the weaknesses inherent in each.

The proper limitation to the area served by an integrated system, while difficult to establish, is very real. It is determined generally by the availability of suitable markets and sites for major hydro or steam developments, all within economical transmission distances of each other. The major part of the load should be located within the outer boundaries of these sites, such remaining load as lies beyond this outer boundary must be located within economic transmission distance of it. These economical transmission distances generally depend upon the size of the load or of the sources of power. For average conditions the area served by a single integrated system would probably extend over not more than a few hundred miles, but under special circumstances it might be economical to go much further in order to obtain a proper balance of fuel and hydro-generating capacity to supply the base and peak loads. Such a balance having been established, the operating advantages due to further extension become less important.

In general, however, though the technically practical extent of the interconnection may be considerable, other considerations operate to limit integration to something like the radius mentioned. Benefits accrue from integrating the power facilities on a reasonably broad scale but unlimited extension serves no useful purpose.

We have stated that geographical limits of successful integration are usually smaller than the technical limits of practical interconnection. Our discussion of the benefits which are unique to the integrated system makes these additional limits more clear even if we cannot measure them in miles. All the benefits we have discussed stem from a single root: The close contact which gives a vital knowledge and appreciation by the central service organization of the conditions peculiar to the area within which the system operates.

So long as additional area can be included without decreasing that knowledge and appreciation, integration has not reached its most effective extent. Thus we see that in regions of large homogeneous area, whose sections are quickly and easily reached, integration can be extended over a broad territory. When due to distance, natural barriers, and absence of quick and certain communication, that local intimacy with conditions diminishes, the most effective size has been passed. Then the design forces become consulting engineers for the units of the system. The operating staff becomes a central bureau supervising in only a general way the local forces by whom the decisions resulting in the day-to-day economy of the system are determined. The central maintenance organization loses the intimate character of a family physician and becomes merely a consulting specialist. The management becomes an absentee landlord in place of a resident supervisor. The whole system becomes unwieldy and the far-reaching advantages of integration vanish.

The combination of these philosophical and practical considerations gives Section 11 of the Act an extremely firm foundation. Aside from the way in which extremists think the Act *might* be administered, do any sound objections to Section 11 remain?

A committee of executives of disintegrated parts of the industry has urged that "the principle of diversity of investment, represented by both geographic location of operating properties and character of business served by them, is a very important factor in the raising of additional capital and that such principle should be preserved in the public interest."

Let me restate what I think is meant by this statement: It is important, it is contended, in order that holding companies may attract new capital, that they should have control over properties which are more scattered geographically than is permitted under the restrictions with respect to integrated systems imposed by Section 11. Freedom from these geographic restrictions, it is argued, will permit the operating companies of the system to serve different types of customers and different economic areas and thereby to lessen the tendency of the revenues of the system to rise and fall with the business cycle. Because of this, it is argued that investments in the securities of a diversified system are more stable and secure and hence more attractive to capital.

But, in my opinion, facts, history, and reason bear witness

against the theory that *mere diversification*—that is to say, mere scatteration of properties and investments—has promoted stability or security of earnings. As to facts, we have collected figures showing comparatively the results obtained by various scattered, conventional holding-company systems and by various integrated, regional companies and systems over a period of years. A fairly comprehensive study was made of one typically scattered or "diversified" system (American Power and Light Company), one integrated electric utility system (American Water Works and Electric Company, Inc.), and one large integrated company (Pacific Gas and Electric Company). A study was also made of a few types of data with respect to eight scattered, nonintegrated systems * and ten integrated companies and systems.† In all, the book value of the assets of the companies and systems covered is about 60 per cent of the assets of the entire industry.

It should be noted that this was a mere statistical sample, subject to a more comprehensive survey. I also want to make clear that I realize that the utility industry is affected by an almost infinite number of human and economic factors which are difficult, if not impossible, to evaluate in terms of comparable statistical data. Yet these statistics do furnish some criteria for judgment. It is impossible for me in this paper to give you the detailed results of the study. But there was an amazing uniformity of results. Let me give you a few samples.

We took the gross operating revenues of eight scattered, "diversified" systems and of ten integrated, regional companies or systems for the years 1929 to 1934, inclusive. We ascertained

* These eight companies were: American Gas & Electric Co.; American Power & Light Co.: Commonwealth & Southern Corporation; Engineers Public Service Co.; National Power & Light Co.; The North American Co.; United Gas Improvement Co.; and United Light & Power Co.

† These ten companies were: Boston Edison Co.; Commonwealth Edison Co.; Consolidated Edison Co.; Detroit Edison Co.; Pacific Gas & Electric Co.; Public Service Co. of New Jersey; Public Service Co. of Northern Illinois; Niagara Hudson Power Corporation; Southern California Edison Co.; and Consolidated Gas, Electric Light & Power Co. of Baltimore.

the highest annual revenues for this period, and the lowest, with respect to each company. The gross operating revenues of the eight scattered systems showed an aggregate decline of 18.4 per cent; the ten integrated companies or systems showed an aggregate decline of only 11 per cent. Only two of the ten integrated companies showed a decline of more than 15 per cent; one of these showed a decline of 15.6, the other of 26.9 per cent. All except two of the eight "diversified" systems showed a decline of more than 15 per cent. The six showing such decline revealed a drop of 15.9, 16.9, 18, 21.3, and 25.9 per cent, respectively. Certainly, it cannot be urged in the face of these figures, that diversification, in and of itself, has promoted stability of earnings—or has prevented hard times from cutting the heart out of the income of a diversified public-utility system.

Let me cite to you some more figures leading to the same conclusion. This time I shall take my figures from our more comprehensive study of one "diversified" system, one integrated system, and one large integrated company. The "diversified" electric utility system (American Power and Light Company) * is itself a subsidiary of one of our largest holding companies (Electric Bond and Share Company). It operates in Texas, Kansas, Florida, Iowa, Nebraska, Minnesota, Montana, Washington, Oregon, and Arizona. It serves large cities, small towns, and rural areas. It serves industrial and farming regions. The integrated electric utility system (American Water Works and Electric Company) † operates in West Virginia, Virginia, Maryland, Pennsylvania, and Ohio—a fairly compact territory. It serves industrial and agricultural areas, cities, towns, and rural

* American Power & Light Co.; Central Arizona Light & Power Co.; Florida Power & Light Co.; Kansas Gas & Electric Co.; Minnesota Power & Light Co.; Montana Power Co.; Nebraska Power Co.; Northwestern Electric Co.; Pacific Power & Light Co.; Texas Electric Service Co.; Texas Power & Light Co.; Washington Water Power Co.

† American Water Works & Electric Co., Inc.; West Penn Power Co.; Potomac Edison Co.; Monongahela West Penn Public Service Co.

consumers. The integrated operating company (Pacific Gas and Electric Company) operates on the Pacific Coast and likewise serves a well-diversified compact area, with a balanced urban and rural domestic, commercial, and industrial load. We studied the electric operating revenues of each of these for 1930, 1933, and 1936. Both of the integrated systems were better able to stand the adversities of fortune between 1930 and 1933 than the "diversified" system; and both responded better to the upturn reflected in 1936 revenues of electric operations. Here are the figures:

We took the year 1930 as our base of 100 for each company. In 1933, the electric operating revenues of the "diversified" system declined to 82.1 per cent; those of the integrated system dropped to 86.3 per cent; those of the integrated company, only to 92.3 per cent. Similarly, when 1936 brought an upturn in the electric revenues, those of the "diversified" system rose only to 103.3 per cent, while the integrated system showed a rise to 112.1 per cent, and the integrated company to 104.1 per cent.[*]

These figures indicate that the integrated systems were *less* vulnerable to business depression than the scattered or diversified system, in terms of revenue from sales of electricity. The same is true with respect to breakdowns of this revenue. Revenues from residential customers, from small light and power customers, and from large light and power customers—each showed the same type of behavior. With respect to each, the record of the integrated system shows that there has been more resistance to the downswing of the business cycle and greater response to its upswing than was true of the "diversified" system.

From the point of view of the investor, what was the result? The "diversified" system earned its fixed charges and preferred dividends 1.28 times in 1930; it did not cover them in 1933,

---

[*] The figures which I have cited for Pacific Gas & Electric Co. are the consolidated figures published by Moody's *Manual*. They have been adjusted by Moody's to reflect acquisitions and mergers during the period and are therefore comparable.

earning only 84 per cent of fixed charges and preferred-dividend requirements, and earned them only 1.02 times in 1936. On the other hand, both integrated systems earned more than fixed charges and preferred requirements in all three years. The integrated system covered them 1.32 times in 1930; 1.13 times in 1933; and 1.21 times in 1936. The large integrated operating company covered them 1.88, 1.45, and 1.77 times in each year, respectively.

Taking the eight "diversified" systems and the ten integrated companies, which I have already mentioned, we computed the decline in earnings available for common stocks between the highest annual figure and the lowest, during the period 1929 to 1934, inclusive. The "diversified" systems' earnings available for common stocks dropped 72.4 per cent; while the earnings of the integrated companies showed a decline of only 52.3 per cent. It is doubtless true that in some of these diversified systems a high degree of recklessness characterized financial practices with the result, among other things, that they were overcapitalized and had top-heavy capital structures. Such factors doubtless contributed to a degree to the volatile nature of the latter statistics. But they cannot tell the whole story. And furthermore, is it a mere coincidence that the recent parade of receiverships and reorganizations was made up essentially of these diversified systems? To mention only a few which come to mind: American Gas and Power Company; Arkansas–Missouri Power Corporation; Central Public Utility Coporation; Commonwealth Light and Power Company; Inland Power and Light Corporation; The Middle West Corporation; Midland Utilities Company; Peoples Light and Power Company; Standard Gas and Electric Company; United Telephone and Electric Company; Utilities Power and Light Corporation. Which of these companies was developed as an integrated system in accordance with the standards of Section 11? Is it merely a coincidence that disregard of such sound standards has resulted so often in financial disaster?

Now these figures speak for themselves. At the least they are a red light to those who argue that diversification of public-utility systems is necessary or desirable. They cast grave doubts on the validity of the contention that diversification, as contrasted to geographical integration, has meant stability of earnings and increased safety of investment. On the contrary, they indicate that in fact and truth diversification—that is to say mere scatteration—has meant increased sensitivity to downward spirals and less response to upturns of the business cycle. I do not claim greater probative value for these figures than they deserve from the most cautious point of view. Some may say that too few companies were included; that the integrated and diversified companies included in the figures are not truly comparable because of differences in the areas served, the character of their business, and so on; and that the more favorable record of the integrated companies may be accounted for by factors of various sorts too numerous to mention. I recognize the possible justification of such criticism. I do not claim that these figures *alone* show that an integrated system is more stable or more profitable than a "diversified" system. But I do assert that they demonstrate that no one can properly contend that a diversified system, *because of its diversification,* has been more stable, more productive, or more deserving of investors' money than an integrated, regional system.

To argue that the pattern of present-day holding-company systems should be maintained because of a "principle of diversity of investment" is to beg a basic question. Holding-company systems have not been organized upon any such scientific-sounding "principle." As I have mentioned, in the roaring 'twenties and before, they were slapped together merely on the theory of putting together every utility property that the dominant interests could acquire. Diversity of risk was merely a slogan for the security salesman and not a standard for the promoter. Where it did exist, diversity of investment was frequently the more or less accidental result of a policy of acquiring properties, wherever located, mainly for the purpose of promoting the sale of equipment, of profiting from the sale of securities, or of realizing fees for financial, construction, or management services.

No one can study some of our largest public-utility systems and discover any rational diversification of investment. The dominant interests in such systems were not interested in diversification; they were interested in pyramiding control and in the power and profit incident to control. Some of the holding companies which have most loudly proclaimed the advantages of diversification to investors show the effect of such expansion. In this mad pursuit of bigness, they resorted to wild financial practices to such a degree as overwhelmingly to offset any possible advantages of diversity. When these companies argue for diversity, they argue only for bigness and for geographical and economic disunity.

The argument, therefore, that the widespread holding company which we see today must be preserved in order to secure diversification of risk does not accord with the facts. Moreover, recent experience has demonstrated the relative unimportance of the location of properties in different portions of the country in achieving stability of earning power. With the rapid extension of transportation and communication facilities, the interdependence and homogeneity of all parts of our economic structure have increased. As a result, cyclical conditions have a much more uniform effect upon the level of business in different sections of the country than formerly.

Unquestionably there is still some appeal in the theory of diversification. It is urged, for example, that an investor might not want to have all his funds tied up in a holding company which derives most of its income directly or indirectly from merely one segment of the industry. But on the other hand, investors know that merely because a holding company controls utilities both in California and Maine, true diversification is not obtained. True diversification depends upon a distribution of risk factors resting upon an analysis of elaborate economic facts. And more important than this, investors have come to realize that diversification of risk is an investment function, not the job of management. They have learned, from bitter experience, that so many extraneous factors enter into the decision of management to invest as to make management diversification dangerous, in most instances. They have learned that if an investor wants diversification in his utility investments, he can best get it by direct investment in a number of companies. Diversification of risk is a matter of investment judgment to be undertaken by the individual investor or by an objective investment institution, not by those controlling or managing operating companies. As the President has said, "Investment judgment requires the disinterested appraisal of other people's management." *

The losses suffered by holding-company investors in recent years, despite the relative stability of operating-company earnings throughout the country, has strikingly demonstrated how relatively unimportant is the factor of geographical diversification; how vastly more important are the integrity of management and the soundness of the financial structure. The excellent credit of soundly capitalized local operating companies today indicates that lack of geographical diversification is no real handicap to obtaining capital on favorable terms. As a matter of fact the best securities even in the large nationwide holding-company systems have not been "diversified"; they have been the senior securities, the bonds and the preferred stocks, of the subsidiary operating units, which offer no geographical diversity of risk to the investor. As the Senate Committee on Interstate Commerce in reporting out favorably the Holding Company Act stated:

The giant holding companies, by and large, have not drawn money into capital improvement and expansion of the industry but have utilized their investors' funds for the purchase of utility properties

* *Monopoly Message* (1938), p. 3.

already built. Even after the holding company became a dominant factor in the utility industry, credit and investment were obtained for the industry directly through the operating companies rather than through the holding companies. It has been in the securities of the operating companies that insurance companies and savings banks have placed the bulk of their utility investments. They have wisely chosen the tested and secured obligations of the operating companies, and not the so-called "diversified securities" of the holding companies based on slender and speculative equities.*

It seems clear from these facts that the case for diversification, as it has been known in the utility industry, carries with it a burden of proof that has not been satisfied to date. But perhaps some who urge the theory of diversification mean something different from diversity as it has been practiced. It is true, as a theoretical matter, that if a holding company were restricted in its investments to *integrated systems,* a degree of stability would be obtained which is not present in the *existing diversified systems.* So the gravamen of the complaint may be, not geographical integration itself, but the limitation on the number of integrated systems to which one holding company is limited. If that is it, the answer seems clear. To limit these holding companies to geographically integrated units but to allow them to develop in such unrestricted manner would involve the grave risks which I have previously enumerated. It would run counter to the whole theory of regional growth and development. It would be a negation of the desire of communities in this country to keep their businesses at home. It would perpetuate the untenable practice of absentee management and remote financial control. It would work for pyramiding of an important segment of our economic life in the hands of a few. But the disadvantages are not purely social and economic. They go deeper than that. They embrace all of the disadvantages from the operating point of view which I have mentioned earlier in this paper. To paraphrase and adapt the observation of the staff of the New England Power Association which I have pre-

* "Senate Report No. 621," 74th Congress, 1st Session, p. 15.

viously quoted, it would follow that under such a system the central maintenance organization would lose its intimate character of a family physician and would become merely a consulting specialist. Management would become an absentee landlord in place of a resident supervisor. The whole system would become unwieldy. The far-reaching advantages of integration would vanish. Due to distance, natural barriers, absence of quick and certain communication, local intimacy with conditions would diminish. And by that test the most effective size would have been passed. These considerations make for the heaviest presumption against any such diversification and seem wholly to justify the ban which the Congress has placed upon it.

In belittling the importance of extreme geographical diversification, I do not wish to be misunderstood. The obvious operating advantages of having a balance between rural and urban, industrial and residential, customers also contribute an element of investment stability. This, however, is a matter which the Act not only permits but positively encourages. An integrated system, as defined in the Act, essentially depends upon engineering and economic facts. Basically, it is an aggregation of units which may be economically operated as a single coordinated system in a single area or region, whether or not that area or region is in more than one state. This is not a Procrustean, arbitrary definition. It depends upon demonstrable economic facts. Certainly, the Act does not contemplate that an integrated system shall be so restricted as to make impossible its adequate, economical operation and financing. Precisely the contrary is true.

There is no need for theoretical discussion of the workability of these prescriptions. It is sufficient to point to some of the regional systems already in existence which have had a strong appeal to the investor. I need only mention the financial experience of such regional or local systems as Pacific Gas and Electric, Public Service Corporation of New Jersey, Consolidated Gas, Electric Light and Power Company of Baltimore, among others. It is unreasonable, on its face, to concede the economic and business advantages of regional integration and organization, and then to argue that investors will put their money only into national, disorganized, and disunited systems. Investors will realize that organization upon a regional, integrated basis will contribute vastly to the stability and earning power of public-utility systems; and it follows that investment capital will find such systems more attractive than ever before.

CHAPTER XV

CONSERVATIVE FINANCE AND THE HOLDING COMPANY ACT

This talk was given before the Harvard Club of Boston in November, 1938, eight months after the Supreme Court had upheld the con- stitutionality of the registration provisions of the Holding Com- pany Act. By this time virtually all the holding companies had registered with the Commission, after having resisted the law since its enactment in 1935. Thus there had been a delay of nearly two- and-a-half years before the Commission and the industry could begin to tackle the many technical problems of administration.

D URING the heat of battle over the Public Utility Holding Company Act of 1935 the picture was fre- quently drawn of its destructive qualities. But since then there has been greater and greater recognition that that Act calls only for conservative practices—for practices and standards designed to protect the industry itself and the in- vestors and consumers against financial wizardry, indiscretion, and excesses. This has come about as a result of the fact that emotionalism has been on the wane and business judgment and technical considerations have been on the ascendancy. A few examples will illustrate what I mean.

We need not have elaborate statistical or financial studies to know that write-ups of property accounts or of investments have been the sand upon which some holding-company struc- tures have been built. We know that in times of stress and strain some of those structures have collapsed or have become dangerously top-heavy as a result of such practices. Under the Act the matter of write-ups is hereafter the concern of the Se- curities and Exchange Commission. It arises in several ways. Thus on the issuance of securities by registered holding com- panies or their subsidiaries the Commission must be satisfied that the security is reasonably adapted to the earning power of the issuer. It is also its duty to prevent the payment of dividends out of capital, to prevent the payment of dividends which will impair the financial integrity of companies in the holding-company system. As a result of these and other provisions of the Act the detection of write-ups is a continuous necessity; the elimination of write-ups is frequently essential. The work which the Commission and the industry have done on this problem has led to extremely significant results. The elimination of write-ups by voluntary act of the industry has become truly fashionable. Published results to date tell only a fraction of the story. In many utility offices today elaborate plans are under way to restate these accounts along conservative lines. This will entail the elimination of many millions of dollars of water from utility structures. Many of these efforts will bear fruit soon; others will take longer, since in some cases delicate operations are necessary. But greater progress is being made. And one utility executive recently told me: "Give me time, and the elimination of write-ups is not only theoretically sound, it is desirable as a cold practical proposition." And another company official called us up on the telephone and said: "We want to eliminate some write-ups in our system. Will you show us how to do it under the Act?" So when the elimination of write-ups becomes, as it has, the "fashionable thing to do," we can rest assured that the practical men in the industry have found in the letter and spirit of the Act provisions which appeal to the judgment and instincts of conservative financial men.

Another example of conservative practices instilled through the Act relates to the creation of debt by holding companies. Under the Act holding companies can issue bonds only under exceptional circumstances. The purpose of the restrictions is clear. They were partially designed to eliminate unsecured bonds which had behind them only a portfolio of common stock or other securities and hence by conservative standards did not warrant the normal connotation of that term. Furthermore, they were designed to protect the holding company itself from unsound capital structures; they had as their purpose creation of capital structures of holding companies composed essentially of stock, preferably common stock, so that the ups and downs of cyclical trends could be more readily weathered. The other day a prominent holding-company executive was in my office. He had caused his holding company many years back to issue debentures. He was relating to me the headaches which those debentures had caused him. In times of great prosperity, he said, the enormous leverage in the stock which was in the holding-company portfolio made those debentures seem as strong as Gibraltar. But when markets declined and earnings fell, those debentures with their promise to pay and with their heavy interest requirements became the bane of his existence. Only by Herculean efforts could he save his entire holding-company structure from complete collapse. On the basis of that experience he vehemently pounded my desk, saying, "Never let any holding company issue any debt." Here was an executive of broad experience adopting on the basis of his own experience a conservative standard of finance—a conservative standard which the Congress wrote into the Act in modified form in 1935.

That Act is replete with similar examples. Thus there is the provision which makes it possible for a holding company to have children and grandchildren but not relatives of a more distant relationship. Men of the world of finance approve that general standard. They approve (at least all to whom I have talked do) because they know on the basis of experience that once a top-heavy holding-company structure is created, with tier upon tier of companies, it takes not only a higher mathematician but a magician as well to figure out what the third preferred stock (not to mention the fourth preferred or the common) in the top company really is worth. The technical men and the policy men in the industry silently approve in practice as well as in theory such examples of conservative financial practices.

And aside from the normal conservative practice which the Act instills there are other provisions which reduce the risks of extravagant practices in which the occasional financial genius has reveled. Two of these are noteworthy of comment. One was presented to me impressively by an operating company only a few weeks ago. This operating company had had a good record. It operated exclusively in one state. It was proud of its intrastate character. Its securities were largely held locally. Years ago it suddenly awoke to the fact that a far-distant and foreign holding company was silently acquiring its stock for purposes of control. The management was startled at the prospect and saw happening to them, if the foreign raider was successful, what had happened to other local companies; namely, a siphoning off of their assets to some distant financial center. Working feverishly, it and its lawyers worked out an elaborate scheme to prevent such control from being acquired. Without going into details, suffice it to say that they created a holding company of their own with an elaborate voting trust as well, and sought deposit of the outstanding securities. With that legal paraphernalia, too elaborate to discuss here in detail, the contest was on. The local company moved with sufficient dispatch substantially to thwart the plans of the foreign holding-company raider. But the complicated holding-company structure which was created to accomplish the result remained, piled on top of this operating company and making cumbersome its every act. In fact, that top structure was viewed by the company itself as somewhat of a monstrosity. To those who are proud of their local companies, who desire to keep them local, who desire to prevent them from becoming overnight a mere pocket in a foreign holding-company system, the Act is a great comfort. For the Act places great restrictions on such acquisitions. They can be made only after public hearing before us with opportunity for interested parties to be heard and then only on our approval.

From the viewpoint of those who desire to keep their utility industry at home, or in many cases to bring it back home, the Act holds great promise of comfort in other respects. As you know, the Act contains standards for geographical integration of holding-company systems. As a general rule—there are exceptions—it provides that a holding company must confine itself to a single, geographically integrated system. The Congress discarded the "scatteration" theory which would permit far-flung scattered properties to be pulled together into one huge utility empire. The Congress decided in favor of integrated local or regional systems, closely knit, compact, and confined geographically. I personally think Congress decided wisely. But whatever may be any one person's view as to the soundness of that decision, that mandate is the law of the land. And it is gaining enormous practical appeal to numerous local or regional interests or groups. Local leaders, including investment bankers, are fast awakening to the realization that here is a superb opportunity to free their home or regional enterprises from remote control. Responsible citizens from a number of states have conferred in my office during the last few months on their paper plans to reconstruct various utility properties along state or regional lines. Many who have been seriously intent on bringing control of home industry closer to home now see a way of doing it. How these tentative plans will work out is too early to predict. Certainly, we are going to give a right of way to the plans, desires, and programs of the industry, so far as is reasonably consistent with the standards of the Act. I merely emphasize at this point the opportunity, now being realized for the first time, for those who desire to keep their basic industries at home.

And I might add, parenthetically, that the realization on the part of investment bankers of the enormous underwriting and distribution job involved in all these programs is beginning to provide something of a profit-motive spark plug in the whole process. At least wherever that realization has appeared, the wheels have begun to turn.

These matters are, as I have said, illustrative of the conservative business and financial standards which pervade this statute. They point up and illustrate one of the real reasons why a genuine business and financial leadership is not guilty of supine submission to "crack-pot" theory, but rather displays the conservative stewardship of old-fashioned standards when it puts its shoulder to the wheel with us to make these statutes going concerns.

So much for the will on the part of business and finance to assume a position of leadership. Now as to *modus operandi*. Perhaps, after the comments which follow, I should make a slight apology to my lawyer friends. For my formula on *modus operandi* is to leave the lawyers out of it. At one of our hearings a few years ago the late Grayson M. P. Murphy with his usual sparkling humor commented from the witness stand that the surest way of producing a real case of the jitters was to give a New York lawyer a few minutes to confer with a New York banker. However that may be, I can state the following indisputable facts of record. In the first place the progressive program worked out between the New York Stock Exchange and the S.E.C. and now in process of being consummated was done without benefit of counsel. In the second place, the rapid strides being made by the utility industry to work constructively with the S.E.C. in developing a holding-company act program was likewise accomplished without any intermediary in the form of lawyer or otherwise. That is fact number one. Fact number two is this. Once the lawyers disappeared from the holding-company scene and the executives of those companies sat down for direct conversation with me and my colleagues, peace and harmony began gently to settle over the entire scene. That in turn may be nothing but a coincidence. But to those who are thinking in terms of *modus operandi,* I do not think it is entirely irrelevant.

There is no magic formula for bringing together conflicting interests and enabling them to sit down together around the table and resolve their differences. Those who seek such a formula bring to mind the portrait of the ancient Chinese physician of the fifth century B.C., who was the great healer of his day. The portrait shows him girt with ropes of herbs and minerals which he had collected from various parts of the earth for their medicinal qualities. But they had failed him. And deep in thought he walks beside a placid lake upon whose unruffled surface the moon's reflection rests. He reaches out his hands toward the mirrored image and exclaims, "Ah, if only I could gather up the healing properties in the moon as well, I would cure all of man's ills."

As ephemeral as the reflection of the moon on the water are the qualities which will fuse the energies of Government and business. Yet, wherever the search for those qualities may lead, I am convinced that their discovery will be a positive force for democracy and capitalism. For by their discovery, we will have placed deep in the national consciousness a philosophy whose curative qualities may have almost mystic effects. That is why this new enlightened business leadership, accepting the philosophy of the new legislative program, holds such great promise.

PART IV
REFORM OF CORPORATE REORGANIZATIONS

In the Securities Exchange Act of 1934 Congress directed the Securities and Exchange Commission to investigate the functioning of protective committees in connection with the reorganizing of bankrupt companies. Previously, there had been a number of surveys of the need for reform in bankruptcy law. At Yale, Mr. Douglas, then Sterling Professor of Law, had conducted a study of bankruptcies in collaboration with the Department of Commerce. It was logical that the newly formed S.E.C. should invite him to take charge of its study of protective committees.

The Commission's investigation lasted two years. Extended public hearings were held on such famous reorganizations as Kreuger and Toll, St. Louis–San Francisco Railway and Paramount Publix Corporation. The reports to Congress covered eight volumes.[1]

These reports were the basis for legislation for reform of corporate reorganization practice; namely, the broad revision of Section 77B of the Bankruptcy Act, sponsored by Congressman Chandler and enacted in 1938, and Senator Barkley's Trust Indenture Act adopted in 1939.

1. *Report on the Study and Investigation of the Work, Activities, Personnel and Functions of Protective and Reorganization Committees.* Part I: "Strategy and Techniques of Protective and Reorganization Committees." Part II: "Committees and Conflicts of Interest." Part III: "Committees for the Holders of Real Estate Bonds." Part IV: "Committees for the Holders of Municipal and Quasi-Municipal Obligations." Part V: "Protective Committees and Agencies for Holders of Defaulted Foreign Governmental Bonds." Part VI: "Trustees under Indentures." Part VII: "Management Plans without Aid of Committees." Part VIII: "Conclusions and Recommendations." These are cited hereafter as "S.E.C. Report."

CHAPTER XVI

THE NEED FOR REFORM IN CORPORATE REORGANIZATIONS

This is an address delivered in June, 1937, before a convention of the National Association of Credit Men in Chicago. Although it is primarily a discussion of the various reforms embodied in the then-pending Chandler Bill,[2] it constitutes in effect a brief summary of the findings of the Protective Committee Study with respect to corporate reorganizations.

FROM the viewpoint of investors, reorganization is a critical process. By that process values are either salvaged for investors or appropriated, in whole or in part, by reorganizers. As a result of that process, the business is subjected to a healthy reconditioning influence and launched on a sound and conservative basis, or the new business emerges carrying within it the causes of the breakdown of the old. The integrity and efficiency of that process are the investors' only protection. They are largely helpless to help themselves. They need minimum assurances that those who actually, though perhaps not legally, determine their fate are held to fiduciary standards. These matters are important not only from the viewpoint of prevention of capital exploitation and waste; they are also important in restoring confidence in the integrity and honesty of the reorganization process and in the credit structure of corporations. These are especially important in view of the aura of disappointed hopes which surrounds the average reorganizations. There is, to be sure, no magic formula in law or in business to restore or create values where none exist. But there are constructive measures which can go far toward curbing excessive practices, which can prevent racketeering

2. "House Report 8046." A bill to amend the National Bankruptcy Act. Enacted June 22, 1938. (Public No. 696—75th Congress, 3d Session.)

groups from seizing on reorganization chaos to exact tribute, which can create confidence in the integrity and honesty of the reorganization procedure. Investors will not be satisfied with less. Government cannot meet its responsibilities with less. In final analysis it is government which creates the courts whose imprimatur reorganizers eagerly seek for their plans. The least which government can do is to require that the instruments of government not be exploited for the benefit of reorganizers and to the detriment of investors. Until that challenge is met, government has not done its task. Until that challenge is met, legitimate business continues to suffer from the disintegrating influences of irresponsible reorganizers. The effects on our capital markets and on our financial processes are profound.

For these reasons, it is important for us to consider the pending proposal, in the form of Section 12 [3] of the Chandler Bill, to amend Section 77B of the Bankruptcy Act.[4] Section 77B, as well as the pending amendment, was drafted primarily for the corporation which is publicly owned—that is to say, which has securities outstanding in the hands of the public. The Chandler Bill makes it clear and unambiguous that businesses which need to be liquidated, or which can obtain adequate relief by composition proceedings under other provisions of the Bankruptcy Act, cannot seek reorganization under Section 12. These provisions are generally adequate to take care of the small or individually owned business in financial distress and should go far toward eliminating the so-called "hot dog stands" from the shelter of this complicated reorganization statute. But increasingly within the past generation, the publicly owned corporation has preëmpted the fields of manufacturing and wholesaling; and it has made substantial inroads in other fields including the retail field. The protection and preservation of

3. Now Chapter X of the Bankruptcy Act, as enacted June 22, 1938. (Public No. 696—75th Congress, 3d Session.)

4. The Securities and Exchange Commission had submitted a series of recommendations for amendment of Section 77B. S.E.C. Report, Part I at 898–903.

the public stake in these enterprises are of chief concern to the health and well-being of our national economy.

The Stake of Business in Sound Reorganization

Business has a stake in the conservation of investors' funds. Business is concerned that investors' funds be available in abundance to supply it with capital for development and growth. And business has a direct and selfish concern that management be efficient and that its stewardship of corporate assets be honest and prudent. Efficient and prudent corporate management, sensitive to its high obligations, is essential to success and progress. If the management of corporations is conducted in accordance with the highest traditions of trusteeship, the result will be increasing vitality. The all-important sources of capital—necessary food for such vitality—will be conserved and multiplied; capital will not be squandered in reckless schemes or in operations profitable only to a few insiders. Investors will get a square deal—and getting a square deal, they will continue to invest, and their funds for investment will multiply. At the same time, investors will have the wherewithal to pay their debts and to make new purchases of the goods which invested funds produce. Efficient, far-sighted, and faithful corporate management will also result in a square deal to labor. And in turn labor will have the funds to pay its debts and purchase more goods. This may be an oversimplified statement. But in its simplicity lies an abiding truth, that the integrity and competence of management are a *sine qua non* of our national vitality.

A Thorough Appraisal of Management

The proposed amendment of Section 77B should have an effective influence within its limited scope, in encouraging and promoting efficient and faithful management of corporations. Primarily, it is directed toward obtaining fair and thorough reorganizations of distressed corporations—reorganizations which will salvage for creditors and investors, in fair proportion, whatever there is of value in the enterprise; reorganizations which will not be oppressive to those who have devoted themselves to its success; and reorganizations from which the corporation will emerge with new health and vigor under a management which either has accounted fully and has been found not wanting, or has given way to a new management. Secondarily, this amendment, by providing for a thoroughgoing process of reorganization, under judicial supervision, in which an accounting must be made for stewardship and in which an opportunity is afforded to all interested in the enterprise—investors, labor, creditors, and others—to be heard, will exert a generally beneficent influence upon corporate management. This amendment, if it becomes law, will constitute notice to corporate managers that when reorganization comes, they will stand or fall upon the basis of their record. Honest and competent management will have nothing to fear; but those who have played recklessly with other people's money will. The Chandler Bill requires that in every reorganization proceeding a disinterested trustee shall inquire into and report to the court upon the past conduct of the business, including the activities and achievements of the management. No longer will management be able confidently to rely upon the unlikelihood of inquiry and the likelihood of perpetuation in control through many defaults and reorganizations.[5] On the contrary, throughout the life of the corporation, they will have to conduct themselves prudently and faithfully, so that if default comes and they seek reorganization their record will bear detailed scrutiny.

Under Section 77B as it now stands, there is no duty, and no real opportunity, to make an examination and appraisal of the management of the debtor. The debtor may remain in possession of the property; or one of its officials may be appointed trustee for the debtor. As a matter of fact in over a

5. S.E.C. Report, Part I, section i; Part II, sections ii, iv.

majority of cases the debtor remains in possession, a strange and novel privilege for debtors in a bankruptcy proceeding or even in a receivership proceeding. The debtor may propose a plan without conference or negotiation with any of the persons whose money is involved. No other person is so privileged. Investors must get 25 per cent of a class and not less than 10 per cent of all classes of security holders in order merely to propose a plan. If the debtor can get the consent of 66⅔ per cent of each class of creditors and of a majority of each class of stock, and approval of the court, its plan becomes effective and binding upon all interested parties. By use of this machinery, perpetuation in control of the company's assets, absolute power over the funds of investors and the fate of creditors, is relatively easy for the debtor, with the aid of its investment banking and other allies, to gain.[6] With the debtor so securely in the saddle, there is no possibility of genuine appraisal of the management's virtues or shortcomings, of its honesty or culpability, or of the desirability of continuing it in control. Anything that a creditor can do in a 21(a) examination [7] of the affairs of a large, publicly owned corporation is apt to be superficial and ineffective. By use of the present machinery, reorganization can be effected, with sacrifices perhaps only on the part of investors. The debtor continues in power perhaps without sacrifice or change in personnel or policy, and with practical immunity, whatever be its acts of omission or commission.

Now what is the debtor? The legal answer is simply a person known to the law as a personality separate and distinct from those whose money is invested in it and those who manage it. But however necessary and useful this legal answer may be, it cannot blind us to the fact that for purposes of reorganization the debtor is the management. To give the debtor a status is to give it to management. To allow a debtor to propose a plan

6. S.E.C. Report, Part I, at 290–312.

7. Section 21(a) of the Bankruptcy Act provides that, upon order of the court, the debtor's officers may be examined at a hearing concerning its acts, conduct, and property.

is to allow the management to do so. To place barriers in the way of proposals of plans by investors and to place none in the way of the debtor is to give management a special privilege and prerogative over investors. Why should management *qua* management receive this preference? The company having failed, it would seem more natural and equitable, if special privileges are to be awarded, to award them to the real owners of the enterprise.

To be sure, there are occasions upon which this procedure of leaving the debtor in possession may work and has worked without hardship or injustice. The corporation may have been overwhelmed by misfortunes beyond the control of its management. We all know that there are honest and nonculpable failures, where the management has been efficient, prudent, and faithful. The plan of reorganization which it proposes may be fair and wise. But there are no fixed criteria by which these matters can be determined. Such issues can be resolved only *after,* and not *before,* study and investigation. They cannot safely be assumed. Or again, the debtor may find itself in that rare sort of reorganization where the creditors and stockholders may be organized in effective, *bona fide* groups. In these comparatively rare cases, changes in the management's plan may be secured or imposed by the court or at the instance of groups of creditors or investors; or what is still more unusual, the record of the management may be carefully examined. It may be made to account for its past activities; and its qualification to continue in control may be closely appraised.

But, generally, this is not what happens. Management usually remains in dominance of the situation during and after reorganization, as before. It meets only casual scrutiny, at most; its plan is adopted; it does not account. Good, bad, or indifferent management continues in the saddle. It is beyond question that in many cases which are matters of public record this state of affairs has resulted in hardship and loss. And I believe it equally beyond question that the present method promotes and induces superficial, surface reorganizations which leave uncured dangerous diseases in the corporate body; and that this superficiality of method thwarts the objective of reorganization—the production of a fair and equitable plan and the launching of a vital business enterprise under able, faithful management.

The importance of this problem of management is difficult to overemphasize. A corporation cannot exceed in quality the character of its management. This is the reason why reorganizers commonly insist that management should not be disturbed even on the advent of default or insolvency. They urge that the paramount importance of management makes it essential that all efforts be made to have management free from the practical limitations and restrictions of supervening bankruptcy. That philosophy is premised on the theory, more often than not born of selfish interests and desires, that those in control should stay entrenched, so that the least possible disturbance will result. But from the viewpoint of investors it is paramount that those in control stay entrenched only where they are competent and faithful stewards. This latter philosophy requires that reorganization provide for a careful scrutiny and appraisal of management. Since management is so all-important, a reorganization, which does not inquire into the quality and character of corporate management, is indeed superficial. It is then not rehabilitation; it then falls short of dealing with the fundamental, all-important part of the corporation—its management.

Let me emphasize that genuine opportunity for appraisal of management, and for displacing it if it is unacceptable, usually comes, if at all, only upon reorganization. Management is by and large self-perpetuating due to its undoubted monopoly over the proxy machine. Furthermore, in the ordinary history of a corporation, investors are likely to get only formal information, if they get anything. They frequently lack information upon the basis of which they can form an intelligent judg-

ment of the policies, good faith, and skill of the management.
They are the abject subjects of an authoritarian government
which has virtually complete control of the information they
get, and against which they can accomplish little. Generally
speaking, it is only when this authoritarian government admits
defeat and appeals to government—i.e., the courts—for reorganization, that an opportunity is afforded for examination of
its policies and practices, and for an intelligent, informed, and
effective decision to continue it in office or replace it.

It is not a simple matter, under the existing system, to make
sure that in reorganization there will be this examination and
appraisal. The management and its investment bankers exercise control over the sources of information; and they are in a
strategic position, directly or indirectly, so to dominate the
court proceedings, the activities of protective committees, and
the reorganization plan, as to make thoroughgoing examination
and appraisal difficult, if not impossible.[8] It is for this reason
that examinations under Section 21(a) of the Bankruptcy Act,
though sometimes salutary, have so frequently proved inadequate. The quality and integrity of management cannot be
discovered by asking the corporate officers about it. Generally,
it cannot even be discovered by an audit of the company's
books. To make an intelligent judgment concerning it, one
must have complete and unhampered access to all its records;
and one must become thoroughly familiar with its business
details. So long as the management is in control, it is futile to
expect that a genuine accounting for its past activities can be
had, or that its record can be thoroughly analyzed and appraised.

The Independent Trustee

The Chandler Bill remedies this deficiency. It makes it certain
that in every reorganization under its provisions there will be
a thorough inquiry into the quality of the corporation's man-

8. S.E.C. Report, Part I, section ii.

agement. It makes it certain that investors will have access to
all facts relating to the corporate management and to the administration of the funds which they entrusted to it. It accom-
plishes this by requiring the appointment of an independent,
disinterested trustee in every case. This trustee, an officer of
the court, becomes upon appointment the nominal and legal
head of the corporation. He has free access to its books and
correspondence; as nominal head of the corporation he can
become thoroughly conversant with the details of its business;
he can become acquainted with its employees. He can, with
permission of the court, institute suit. He can, both theoretically and practically, check on the policies, contracts, and
practices of the company and require changes where changes
appear necessary. He is, in short, in a position to become thoroughly familiar with the business—not by a hit-or-miss process,
but through daily association in a position of responsibility, and
through the study and analysis which he is required by the bill
to make. And on the basis of such familiarity he must report to
the court and the investors, facts and judgments upon the basis
of which they can intelligently decide the future of the company.
All these are old powers which have always been vested in the
trustee by the Bankruptcy Act. Nothing here is novel. In fact,
to any bankruptcy student it is extremely novel not to have a
trustee appointed but to leave the debtor in possession.

There are tasks to be done in reorganization which it is absurd to ask the management to undertake. It is absurd to expect
the management to require itself to account for past acts; to
investigate itself; and to appraise its own fitness to continue.
A management—no matter how reckless—cannot be expected
to oust itself from power. And it is absurd to expect that if the
debtor or one of its officers is made the appointee of the court
to do these things, that they will be well and thoroughly done.
Elementary knowledge of human nature and only a casual
acquaintance with reorganization history would carry conviction of the truth of this observation. Similarly, it is idle to expect

that a trustee, affiliated with any one set of interests in the debtor
—such as a class of stockholders or creditors, or the underwriter
—can or will do a job that is thoroughgoing and impartially
fair to all. A trustee who is a stockholder or a creditor, for example, can hardly be expected to take action which may result
in invalidating or impairing the worth of the stock of the debtor
or of his claim against it, regardless of the advantages of such
action to the estate as a whole. A trustee who is affiliated with
special interests cannot be expected to recover for the estate
assets which those interests have wrongfully diverted or appropriated or to destroy or impair the other stakes which such
persons may have in the enterprise. The record of reorganizations in the past decade and before bears ample witness to these
propositions. In short, a trustee charged with the exacting duty
of discovering and recovering all assets of the estate—in the
form of causes of action or otherwise—must be disinterested.
The obvious soundness of this conclusion cannot be obscured by
generations of practice embracing a contrary theory.

The Chandler Bill does more than require an investigation
of the antecedents of the failure. It goes further than merely
requiring that the plan of reorganization contain provision for
fair selection of management of the new company. The Chandler Bill, by reason of the requirement for the appointment of
an independent trustee will make these mandates possible of
attainment. In other words, it not merely provides that reorganizations shall be thoroughgoing and fair; it sets up machinery and conditions to enable achievement of these objectives.

The objection has been made that the provision for an independent trustee in every case will deprive the estate of the
benefit of an experienced management familiar with its problems. This criticism indicates a misconception both of the
purpose and of the effect of the independent trustee requirement. The Chandler Bill does not prevent the retention of
worthy members of the old management to assist in the conduct

of the business while the reorganization proceedings are going on. It expressly provides that the trustee may employ officers of the debtor at a rate of compensation to be approved by the court. All that it says is that the old management shall not be vested with fiduciary powers and duties which it is not shown to be qualified to fulfill. If the members of the old management do not find sufficiently attractive the opportunity to serve their real principals—the creditors and stockholders—at a fair salary fixed by the court, unless the additional opportunities are afforded of covering up possible causes of action against themselves, of controlling the reorganization process, of insuring their retention by the reorganized company (and these are the only opportunities of which the members of the old management are deprived by the requirement of an independent trustee) they certainly have no claim to act in a fiduciary capacity.

The foregoing supply one reason why the provision for mandatory appointment of an independent trustee is the keystone of this program for improvement of reorganization procedure in the interests of investors. But there is another reason, equally, if not more important, which makes the independent trustee provision the most important aspect of the Chandler Bill. By terms of the bill the independent trustee will serve as the focal point for formulation and negotiation of a plan of reorganization. This important function under the present system has been left to the inside few. That normally has meant leaving it to the management and the investment bankers. It should no longer be left in these hands, since those persons too often have interests conflicting with those of the investors. The content of the plan is the all-important item in the whole proceeding. Its preparation and negotiation should be carefully scrutinized and supervised. Placing this function in the hands of the independent trustee also means that greater opportunity for investor participation in the preparation of the plan can be afforded. Under the bill proposals of plans are not restricted to the favored few; it forsakes the tradition of leaving all of these

matters to the insiders. By its provisions any investor can pre-
pare, or submit proposals for, a plan. Thus greater democratization in these proceedings is assured; and more of the investor
point of view is injected into them. At the same time the dangers
of "town meetings" are avoided by placing on the trustee the
duty to head up the formulation of a plan and to report out a
plan to the court within a reasonable time. That is to say, the
Chandler Bill is designed to cause the independent trustee, as
a representative of the court, to play an active role in the formulation and negotiation of plans and to supply scrutiny and control thereof in the interest of creditors and stockholders. The
provision for the independent trustee would provide a forum
where creditors and stockholders could be heard. In handling
the suggestions of proposals for plans, the independent trustee
would act in an informal administrative manner. He is made
the active head of the reorganization process. In short, vital
functions which in the past have been performed by inside
groups, or by protective committees seeking personal profit, will
be vested in the trustee—with the advice and consent of creditors
and stockholders and subject to court supervision. No longer
will the basic, all-important phases of reorganization be performed by groups which have a selfish interest to protect and
promote. Heretofore these groups have thrived because they
have provided leadership for investors where otherwise there
would be anarchy; because they have seized the reins and produced action and provided direction—regardless of their desti-
nation. Under the Chandler Bill, these functions will be performed by a disinterested person appointed by the court with
the opportunity to interested persons to express their views on
the appointment.

This unquestionably means that the responsibility of the
independent trustee under the Chandler Bill will be great; and
unquestionably his power will be substantial. With such power
and responsibility, it would be an enormity if the trustee were
not required to qualify as impartial. Any less requirement

would be a violation of that rule of elementary decency which requires that a fiduciary be free of any interests competitive with those of any persons toward whom he bears responsibility. A disinterested person, fully qualified to act as an officer of the court, can alone be entrusted with such responsibility. Any other conclusion involves approval of the proposition that the debtor can act as trustee for the creditor; and that a man interested in one side of a transaction should be armed with the power of the court in his dealings with persons on other sides of the bargain.

The wisdom and necessity of placing these greater powers and responsibilities upon the trustee is, I believe, beyond question. The record of corporate reorganizations of the past—and particularly those of the recent depression—is not pleasant. It shows the absolute control exercised over reorganizations by the inside few; it shows the financial well-being of investors, and the public sacrificed to the insiders' desires for protection and for further profit. It shows corporations struggling to reorganize for many years; returns denied to investors; labor injured, and business damaged by the resulting uncertainties and instability. It shows that these delays, these futile prolongations of the agony of reorganization, were frequently due to deliberate sabotage by a group which had something to gain and was unwilling to compromise, or to the lack of motive power necessary to draft a feasible plan and procure its acceptance. The record also shows, with overwhelming proof, that plans of reorganization were frequently dictated by a single interest—by a closely knit inside group; primarily in the interests of that group and of dubious wisdom so far as interests outside the inner circle were concerned. These conclusions have indeed become so generally accepted and so widely known as to be commonplace. These conclusions indicate that something must be done to provide impartial, capable control over reorganizations; to produce impartially fair and sound plans of reorganization; and to provide effective motive power which will lead to the production and consideration of reorganization plans. The Chandler Bill is designed to do these things for bankruptcy reorganizations; and it does them for the most part through a disinterested trustee appointed by the court.

These functions of the independent trustee are difficult to overemphasize. They have profound philosophical and practical aspects. To summarize briefly: In the first place, the trustee would be required to assemble the salient facts necessary for a determination of the fairness and equity of a plan of reorganization. He would assemble the necessary ingredients, so to speak, of a plan. For the first time such information would be available to the court and the investors as a routine matter. On the basis of such information, the court and the investors could intelligently decide whether or not proposed plans were fair, equitable, and sound—whether assets were being wasted or overlooked; whether there was a complete accounting for the old venture before the new one was launched; whether the old management should be restored to power; whether the allocation of assets, earnings, and control was fair. Through an impartial trustee, such facts could be assembled and appraised. Only through some such method could the court be in a position to exercise an informed judgment and to afford a critical scrutiny and supervision of the estate at all times. Without its own agent being fully informed the court would remain too much at the mercy of the competence, vigilance, and integrity—or lack of them—of those who happened to be active in the case. In sum, the independent trustee would put the court in a position to perform its functions adequately.

In the second place, it is necessary to have an arm of the court perform the functions which the Chandler Bill places on the independent trustee, if there is to be greater democratization in these proceedings. That the trend toward democratization is essential and desirable in the interests of investors, few will deny. But no significant progress can be made toward that end unless machinery is provided in these proceedings whereby investor participation can be provided, the investor viewpoint can be articulated, and the investor interest be represented. It would be idle for example to provide that any *bona fide* investor may propose a plan without likewise providing machinery for handling those proposals when they are made. It would be idle to provide that protective measures be adopted without likewise providing the means whereby such protection can be afforded. It would be futile to profess a desire to return these bankrupt estates to the real owners without providing the mechanism whereby the real owners could come into possession and power. In other words, democracy in reorganization cannot be expected to work unless there is power and responsibility in the hands of a qualified representative of investors. Otherwise chaos and disorganization would result. To state it otherwise, any endeavor to effect greater investor participation and opportunity will remain largely idealistic and academic, until and unless the investors are afforded a "focal point" for organization. In the words of reorganizers, there is an essential need in these cases for a "spark plug." Investors, no more than reorganizers, can function without one. Such a device as the independent trustee furnishes them with one. Without it, the desired power will not lie in investors' hands; it will rest where it always has, outside the proceedings in the hands of reorganizers. For that reason, if there is no requirement for an independent trustee the other parts of the Chandler Bill begin to crumble.

In the third place, the device of the independent trustee gives assurance that the great power hitherto exercised *outside* the proceedings will be exercised *within* the proceedings by and for the benefit of investors. There are great increments of value inherent in that power.[9] Those who have possessed it in the past have been able to employ it advantageously to serve their own ends. That power means control; control means profits. There is not only the business patronage incidental to every

9. S.E.C. Report, Part I, section i.

reorganization; there are also valuable emoluments within reach of those who emerge with control over the new company. This is not theory; it is a fact. Those who have shared the spoils of reorganization know how valuable such power is. The central problem in reorganization is to see to it that that power is not exploited by reorganizers but appropriated for the benefit of investors. With that power resting *outside* the court, the difficulty of employing that power for the benefit of investors is increased many fold. So long as it can be governed by the conventions of a few dominant parties, there is great likelihood that that power will not inure to the benefit of the estate. There is greater assurance of its being done if it is placed where it belongs, in the court. It then becomes an asset, so to speak, of the estate. No such shift in power has resulted without a great effort. It will always be bitterly opposed. But I suggest to you that such a shift in power, inherent in the device of an independent trustee, is basic and fundamental if the reorganization system is to be reconstituted in the interest of investors. These are the profound philosophical and practical aspects of the Chandler Bill. In comparison the other proposed reforms are and can be only indirect toward protection of investors.

The Opportunity to Appraise a Proposed Reorganization Plan

I have discussed these provisions of the Chandler Bill at such length because I sincerely believe in their great importance. I do not wish to leave with you the impression that this is the sole modification of importance which the bill proposes. In many other respects, the bill embodies provisions which I believe will be a great boon to business and investors alike. It is impossible for me to discuss all of them in the short time left to me. I think it is important, however, to comment briefly upon a few.

In a variety of ways, the bill seeks to make it possible for courts and investors to exercise more intelligent and better-informed judgment concerning the merits of reorganization plans. Under the present system, the situation is so completely controlled by the insiders that the hands of persons whose money is at stake—and often even the hands of the court—are tied. No matter what an investor may suspect, or what facts he may know, he often has little opportunity to act upon them. Likewise, the amount of information the court may have, and its own opinion of the inadequacies of the plan of reorganization may be of little practical use. Reorganization plans are frequently presented to the court after a long period of negotiation, and after time, effort, and money have been spent in obtaining the necessary consents from creditors and stockholders. Courts are then extremely reluctant to withhold approval of a plan—or to require its modification. If the court disapproves the plan or requires substantial amendment, the time, effort, and money of the reorganizers may have been spent to no avail. A new plan may have to be negotiated; creditors and stockholders may have to be resolicited. Waste and additional expense result.

Experience and the decisions of the courts themselves show this to be true. When a plan of reorganization is presented to the court with the approval of two thirds of the creditors and a majority of the stockholders, that plan is virtually approved. The act of approval by the court, in such cases, is likely to be little more than a formality. The court is reluctant to cause additional delay and expense; it cannot, under the present scheme, be sure of its judgment concerning the plan, because it has not the time or facilities to make the necessary detailed inquiry. Therefore, it accepts the fact that a large percentage of creditors and stockholders have approved it, as raising a strong presumption of fairness. Now, most courts probably realize that the consent of creditors and investors to a reorganization plan is frequently not the expression of a considered, matured judgment; that sometimes it is approval obtained in an oppressive way or merely the evidence of a habit of executing proxies to the management; and sometimes merely the result of bitter realization of the futility of opposing the program of the insiders. But the stage has been so set in favor of the insiders that the court is content or under great practical compulsion to approve the plan to which the necessary consents have been obtained.[10]

The Chandler Bill seeks to change this. It seeks to vitalize the consent of creditors and stockholders and the approval of the court. It seeks to make them more significant. It seeks to make it possible for these acts which put the seal of approval on a plan of reorganization, to be the expression of informed judgment freely exercised.

In the first place, it prohibits the solicitation of consents to a plan until *after* the court has approved it as fair and equitable and feasible. The court will not be asked to put its imprimatur on a plan which comes to it only after it has already been approved by creditors and stockholders. It will have a real opportunity to consider a plan which has been reported out by its trustee and to compare that with plans submitted directly to the court by stockholders or creditors. It will then approve for submission to creditors and stockholders such plan or plans as it finds to be fair and sound. Free from any artificial presumption of fairness; free from the overpowering disinclination to reject a plan at a late stage in the proceedings; and aided by full information, a court can make and put into effect careful and frank judgments on the merits of plans. In this respect the Chandler Bill is designed to free the judiciary from shackles which our reorganization procedure has placed upon it. It will liberate the courts to use their power and judgment in favor of investors. It will put an end to streamlined proceedings which sacrifice thoroughness and honesty for speed.

The Right to Be Heard

Further to enable the courts more effectively to perform their functions, the bill enlarges the right of parties in interest to be

10. S.E.C. Report, Part I, section ii.

heard. The debtor, the trustee under an indenture for any securities of the debtor, any stockholder or creditor is given the right to be heard on all matters. They may appear before the trustee or the court; they may give information; they may comment upon a reorganization plan. In short, they are given the right to appear either in defense or in promotion of their own interests and to assist the trustee and the court. Labor unions and employees' associations, representative of employees, also are given the right to be heard on the economic soundness of plans and on provisions thereof affecting the interests of labor. The advisability of this provision is clear. Just as the management has an interest in the enterprise which the reorganization plan may vitally affect, so labor is concerned with the soundness of plans. Their jobs, their livelihood depend upon a sound capital structure and a healthy business structure. They often receive the direct impact of default, for that often means labor displacement. The employees are likely to be primarily concerned with the economic soundness and feasibility of the plan, so that the current reorganization will not be the forerunner of another disastrous collapse. Consequently, it is highly desirable that the court and the trustee have the benefit of the suggestions and criticism of representatives of employees with respect to the reorganization plan. And, it is only simple justice that these groups, which are vitally affected by the collapse of business and which are essentially concerned with the stability of business, should have an opportunity to express their opinion on the economic soundness of plans and other aspects which affect their interests.

The Place of the Securities and Exchange Commission

There is another important feature of the bill which I wish to mention briefly. This is the provision vesting the Securities and Exchange Commission with advisory power in reorganizations. Its functions are those, so to speak, of an expert, administrative agency which acts in an advisory capacity to the court and thus indirectly to interested parties in the reorganization. It can intervene in and become a party to any bankruptcy-reorganization proceeding. In any case, the court may refer proposed plans of reorganization to the Commission for report; and in cases of national importance—cases in which the scheduled debt exceeds $5,000,000—the court is required to submit such plan or plans as it regards worthy of consideration, to the Commission for investigation and report, before the court approves or disapproves the plan. The report of the Commission on any plan is advisory only; it does not bind either the court, the trustees, or any interested party. There is thus avoided the possible attendant delay and confusion if the power of the courts was shared with an administrative agency. By reason of these advisory reports and intervention of the Commission the court will have the benefit of expert and disinterested advice to aid it in the solution of the complicated financial and legal problem involved in the typical large reorganization. This should fill a long-felt need and be welcomed by both courts and investors. It should provide a further check on the exercise of reorganization powers and give additional assurance that the interests of investors will be served.

"Shopping Around" for Jurisdictions

There are other important aspects of the bill on which, if there were time, I would dwell at greater length. One such is the provision which, in my opinion, will bring an end to the pernicious practice of "shopping around" for friendly jurisdictions in which to initiate and consummate the reorganization proceedings. The wide latitude which the present Section 77B gives to reorganizers in this respect has little justification, in practical necessity. And it is susceptible of great abuse. The only valid criterion for jurisdiction seems to me to be the company's principal place of business, or the place of location of its principal assets. Selection of any other jurisdiction usually means conducting the reorganization at great distances from the place or places where the corporation does its business. It means putting investors to great expense and difficulty if they wish to appear and participate in the proceedings. It means, as I have said, that inside groups who may be in control of a reorganization are able to search around for the jurisdiction in which they estimate it is least likely, for a number of reasons, that their conduct of the corporation will be examined; that they will be exposed to liability, and their perpetuation in office endangered. These abuses and defects have been met and corrected by the Chandler Bill, in limiting the venue of reorganization proceedings to the principal place of business or the location of the corporation's principal assets, for the greater part of the six months preceding the filing of the petition.

Speculation in Certificates of Deposit

Another significant provision in the Chandler Bill is the one which gives the court power to deny compensation to persons in reorganization proceedings who use the advantages of their favorable inside position to buy and sell securities and certificates of deposit, of the debtor corporation. This has been an evil particularly characteristic of protective committee members. These persons, supposedly acting in a fiduciary capacity as representatives of security holders, have frequently taken advantage of inside information about the affairs of the corporation, which they are in a strategic position to obtain, to speculate for their personal profit. They are in a position to know the course of negotiations with respect to a plan; the favorable or unfavorable developments impending; the likelihood of liquidation on the one hand, or of successful reorganization on the other. They may themselves create these developments. Trading in the securities by these persons, and those in similar positions, is undeniably a violation of their duties and responsibilities to security holders. In penalizing those who indulge in such practices, the Chandler Bill moves toward a much-needed reform.

A New Emphasis

The essence of the amendments to Section 77B incorporated in the Chandler Bill constitutes, first and last, a recognition that reorganization is not solely a legal but a business and administrative problem calling for greater power and more express and specific mandates to the courts. Our reorganization procedure in the past was conditioned by the fact that it took place in court. The fact that the typical reorganization plan was merely an incident of—a sort of appendage to—a conventional receivership had important results. The courts were too prone to regard the reorganization receivership as a lawsuit or litigated matter. Issues of fact and law were from time to time presented to the court; the court would hear argument and make its decision. The legal issues presented in this fashion, though numerous, were restricted. The courts did not assume broad administrative control over these estates. Some state courts to this day do not feel called upon or entitled to pass upon the fairness of a reorganization plan. The courts, after they began to pass upon reorganization plans, frequently seemed to take the view that if there were nothing illegal or oppressive in the plan, they would approve it. As to the subtler questions of fairness and of soundness and feasibility of a plan, they would frequently make no decision. To the activities of committees and other agencies purporting to represent security holders they would be apt to give scant or only superficial attention. They acted preëminently in a judicial role; administrative functions were rarely assumed. This is no criticism of the courts. The machinery was so geared and the procedure so designed that the courts could hardly do more than attempt to prevent illegality or the grosser forms of inequity.

Under 77B there was something of a shift in emphasis. The

court was given broader and more express powers. But the improvement was slight, although clear. The court was still largely the judge and arbiter of issues, carefully selected and nicely framed so as to present a justiciable matter. The life, the essence of reorganization flowed in other channels. It did not come to the court. What came to the court were particularized, desiccated problems. The debtor frequently remained in possession of the property. No method was provided for conveying to the court a vital impression of the corporate situation and problems. The reality of reorganizations was something that took place out of court. It was dealt with by the groups in control—generally the management and its investment bankers— who frequently had their own interests to serve.

With this system in operation, the courts could do very little. They could offer investors and creditors little protection. They were crippled by a reorganization system which was based upon the theory that reorganization was a procedure wherein the legal matters were left to the court, the business matters to the reorganizers. Obviously reorganization is not strictly a legal problem. It is a business and administrative matter of great complexity. And even though the courts wanted to exercise a broader conditioning influence over the whole process, they frequently were in no position to do so, since they did not have nor were they in a position to get the facts. The Chandler Bill recognizes this weakness in the system. It makes it necessary for the courts to deal with the business and administrative problems of reorganization. It makes it possible for the courts to do so by giving them administrative and expert assistance. In that way it vitalizes the role of the courts. In a variety of ways it brings the court into association with the facts of the business; it assures that the court will be fully informed; it places in the court power to give impetus to a reorganization—to see that a plan is drafted and that moves are made to get the support of investors; and it gives the court genuine power to see to it that the reorganized company is provided with good management and a sound capital structure. These are necessary and important changes if confidence in our reorganization system is to be restored. In the public eye the courts already have the responsibility; what the courts need are ample powers commensurate with their actual or ostensible responsibility. It would be error to conclude that these powers are adequate by measurement of them in terms of a procedure designed for simple litigated matters.

In the ways I have mentioned, and in others which there is not time now to mention, the Chandler Bill provisions on corporate reorganizations will, in my opinion, promote abler, more intelligent administration of estates in reorganization and at the same time make for greater democratization in these proceedings. They give for the first time in reorganization history, full and definite recognition of, and a significant status to, the widespread and national investor interest in such proceedings. And they supply assurance that the new venture—the ultimate end of the entire process—will be soundly, economically, and expeditiously launched.

CHAPTER XVII

PROTECTIVE COMMITTEES

This statement was made before the Interstate and Foreign Commerce Committee of the House on June 8, 1937, during consideration of the Lea Bill to regulate protective committees. It summarizes the principal findings of the Protective Committee Study with respect to protective committees and their practices.

THERE is at present the problem and the necessity of affording to the individual investors of this country protection against a type of abuse and exploitation with which existing legislation cannot cope—the abuses on the part of protective committees in reorganization. That problem is not precisely a new one; but its importance has been given renewed emphasis as a result of the vast reorganization experience born of the depression. The present need for regulation has been more than amply disclosed by recent governmental investigations, including those by a Select Committee of the House, a Special Committee of the Senate, and by the reports of the Securities and Exchange Commission, which in Section 211 of the Securities and Exchange Act was directed by the Congress to undertake a study and investigation of work, activities, personnel, and functions of protective and reorganization committees.[1] At the direction of Congress the Commission submitted in its recent reports a series of recommendations [2] with respect to the regulation of such committees. The facts enumerated in those public records afford a firm foundation for the desirability of and need for the Lea Bill.

1. "Report on the Study and Investigation of the Work, Activities, Personnel and Functions of Protective and Reorganization Committees." The various parts of this report are listed above at page 172.

2. S.E.C. Report, Part I, at 903–907; Part II, at 528–534; Part V, at 738–741; Part VII, at 412–415.

The years just past have seen thousands upon thousands of corporate debtors (issuers of millions in securities purchased by every segment of the American public) arrive at the stage where they have been unable to meet their obligations. Often in these cases, liquidation and a distribution of assets to security holders have been impracticable if only for lack of buyers. Often, too, it has been unwise, where sound business judgment pointed out that a hope of greater salvage lay in restoring the distressed corporation to the status of a going concern. This could be accomplished only if its creditors agreed to a moratorium on its debts, or consented to an extensive scaling down of its obligations. And in a thoroughgoing readjustment of its financial structure, fairness and equity required of stockholders that they give up at least as much as the sacrifices called for from creditors. It is this process of extensive financial readjustment, commonly called reorganization, which has given rise to the problems with which the Lea Bill deals.

In these reorganizations the individual investor has come to play an anomalous and insignificant role. In every case it is his investment which is at stake, yet the processes of reorganization have so evolved, or have consciously been so fashioned that he is usually given recognition only when his consent is necessary to the consummation of a plan, whether it be a voluntary plan or otherwise. Even then this recognition has at times been of the most perfunctory kind. In other respects the security holder is largely helpless to help himself, or to join with others in his position in an effort at joint action. The impact of this is felt when we consider the existing obstacles in the way of individual action by the investor. Merely by reason of the fact that he is one of many security holders involved in an intricate, difficult situation, and the fact that his average holdings are small, he cannot undertake the burdensome expense of active participation in court proceedings for reorganization or in the negotiations that lead to a completed reorganization. Apart from the question of expense, which might well cost him more than the value of his investment, the average investor does not possess the training, the experience, or the skill which these complicated problems demand.

The problem of protection of investors in these situations has many angles to it. Part of it relates to the adequacy of the reorganization machinery in the Federal courts to protect investors against the reorganizers. This phase of the program, insofar as reorganizations under Section 77B of the Bankruptcy Act are concerned, is in my judgment adequately covered by the Chandler Bill (House Report 8046) [3] presently before the House Committee on the Judiciary. Another phase of the problem concerns the representative role of the corporate trustee who, all agree, should assume more active duties in defending and promoting the interests of bondholders, noteholders, and debenture holders in these default situations. That phase is in my judgment adequately covered by the Barkley Bill (S. 2344) [4] presently before the Senate Committee on Banking and Currency. Other phases of the problem are covered by the Lea Bill which in conjunction with the Chandler and Barkley Bills presents an integrated and pervasive treatment of the whole, though each bill is independent of the others. The two phases of the Lea Bill which should be noted involve (1) protective committees; and (2) a limited participation by an administrative agency (the Securities and Exchange Commission) in certain types of reorganization proceedings. I will deal with these two phases of the problem in that order.

As I have indicated, the helplessness of the average investor to help himself has led to the necessity or at least the desirability of some kind of group action. This need has been supplied usually by protective committees. These committees are usually composed of three or more individuals, though occasionally a corporation has served as a committee. These committees may be formed as a result of meetings of security holders. This is

3. Enacted June 22, 1938 (Public No. 696—75th Congress, 3d Session).
4. Enacted August 3, 1939 (Public No. 253—76th Congress, 1st Session).

rather uncommon. They usually have come into being, self-constituted and self-appointed, with an announcement of program and purpose and with a plea to security holders for support. Their sponsors are usually the management of the debtor company and its investment bankers, not security holders or their authorized representatives.[5] These committees may merely communicate with security holders without attempting to obtain powers of attorney from them. Customarily, however, they seek a power of attorney. This may be in the form of a revocable proxy or in the form of an irrevocable deposit agreement. The proxy is a simple instrument listing such specific or general powers as the committee desires or deems useful or necessary; the deposit agreement is a more complicated instrument. Usually deposit under the deposit agreement means loss by the security holder of effective control over his securities as well as a grant of broad powers from him to the committee.[6]

Within this broad framework committees have operated. They have had important functions to perform, although committees are, in many situations at least, not necessary parts of the reorganization paraphernalia.

These functions can be outlined briefly.[7] For one, united action on the part of investors is sometimes necessary, under the provisions of trust indentures, in order to induce action, such as foreclosure, by indenture trustees for the protection of bond-holders. Experience and investigation have shown that recalcitrant, inactive trustees need the spur of a vigilant committee, representing substantial numbers of bondholders, if such trustees are to be made to take steps for their protection.

Again, the mobilization of security holders is necessary if they are to exercise a continued and careful scrutiny over the administration of the debtor in those cases where receivership

5. S.E.C. Report, Part I, at 341 *et seq.*
6. S.E.C. Report, Part I, at 585–670.
7. S.E.C. Report, Part II, at 1–8.

or bankruptcy occur. Another function is the investigation and enforcement of claims against managements and their affiliates, with the consequence that assets may be added to the estate and all security holders aided. There may also be claims running to security holders individually which result from misrepresentations in the original sale of the securities. Committees may perform this signal function at much smaller cost than could individual investors, thoroughly investigating these claims, and laying the basis for their enforcement. Or there may be certain types of class suits which committees can bring.

Further, in the negotiations and compromises over the terms of the readjustment that are an indispensable part of all reorganizations, committees have in the past been able to supply a service which scattered, disorganized, security holders could not undertake because of its complexity, difficulty, and time-consuming nature. In these negotiations the aid of experts, engineers, attorneys, and the like, may be needed; only group action made it possible in many cases to put such facilities within the reach of the average security holder.

It is the function, also, of committees, able to commandeer expert knowledge, to subject all plans to critical appraisal and examination from the point of view of, and in the interests of, the security holders whom they ostensibly represent. And, since confirmation of a plan of reorganization, in the last analysis, depends on the consent of the creditors and stockholders, it is the function of committees to marshal consents to proper plans, and lead opposition to those believed to be unfavorable to the class of security holders for whom they are acting.

I have mentioned above the fact that customarily committees have been sponsored by the management of the debtor company or by the investment bankers, not by security holders or their authorized representatives. This has been due to several circumstances.[8] Over and above the inertia and lack of leadership

8. S.E.C. Report, Part I, section ii; Part III, section ii; Part IV, at 67–73.

among investors is the fact that if the individual security holder attempts to organize his fellow investors, he will find himself faced at the outset with an insuperable obstacle. He does not know who are his fellow investors, nor can he find out. The lists of security holders are the exclusive possession of the debtor or of the investment bankers for the debtor, and in the main they will deny access to these lists or their use by the individual security holder. Furthermore, they have had inside knowledge of impending default and so have prepared in advance of public announcement of default a solicitation campaign in support of their own committees. The result has been that they have been first in the field with all of the advantages which that means. As a consequence the debtors (which, in any realistic sense, means the corporate management) together with the investment bankers for the corporation have been able to control the effective formation and operation of protective committees. The individual investor has had little choice but to throw in his lot with committees sanctioned and sponsored by banker-management groups. These groups have been able to prevent the effective operation of committees by others; and they have been able, out of motives and for purposes on which I shall enlarge, to set up their own committees and in practical effect to dominate the vehicles supposedly representing the security holders.

I cannot emphasize too strongly that committee members are fiduciaries. As such they owe exclusive loyalty to the class of investors they represent. They owe that class diligence, efficiency, and single-minded devotion. But these fiduciary standards have been frequently flouted to the ultimate detriment and distress of countless numbers of investors. This condition has prevailed, not exclusively in case of management-investment banker committees, but conspicuously in such cases. In the welter of conflicting interests, ulterior objectives, and self-serving actions which flow from investment banker-management dominance over committees, these committees have lost sight of their essential functions which they can perform to advance the interests of investors.

There are two aspects of the manner in which committees have violated these fiduciary standards. The first relates to conflicts of interests; the second to the exercise of the fulsome powers which committees have taken unto themselves.

1. *Conflicting Interests.*[9] As to conflicting interests, the Lea Bill supplies an effective check to the conditions described in our reports. It provides some assurance that those acting in fiduciary and representative positions will be free from conflicting interests. The Securities and Exchange Commission has pointed out at length in its reports the evils and abuses that have flowed from the disregard and violation of this fiduciary principle. The manner in which these conflicts have inhibited proper performance by committees of their functions can be best illustrated in case of committees dominated by the management [10] and the investment bankers.

Where committees have been dominated by such groups, the question of legal responsibility of the management for its acts of omission and commission has rarely been raised by those committees. Though assets may be brought into the estate by the investigation and enforcement of all claims against officers and directors, it has obviously been to the self-interest of managements to resist their assertion and enforcement. This they have been able to do by virtue of the control they have obtained over protective committees. Again, although in many cases no legal responsibility can be spelled out against existing officers and directors, their conduct of the corporation's affairs has been so reckless or so inefficient as to justify the installation, in whole or in part, of a new management. On the other hand, it is to the self-interest of the management to stay entrenched in the business, for the sake of fees, salaries, and bonuses which come to them from their positions, and for the other important patron-

9. S.E.C. Report, Part I, section i; Part II, *passim.*
10. S.E.C. Report, Part II, section ii.

age which can be dispensed to their affiliated interests. Incompetence and questionable activities on the part of officers and directors will tend to be a closed book if the management can control the protective committees in the situation.[11] As a result, the very causes of failure are often perpetuated in the new and reorganized business. The searching investigation of management that is of primary importance in every reorganization is blocked and prevented. The harm to security holders from such practices is incalculable. The only remedy is to insure, so far as practicable, that persons with such conflicting interests are not members of, and do not control, protective committees.

Adverse interests have frequently arisen also because of the connection of investment banking firms with reorganizations.[12] They, together with managements, have had a virtual monopoly over security-holder lists; they have had inside knowledge of impending defaults; they have had great familiarity with the techniques and strategy of reorganization. These, and other factors, have given them a position of dominant importance in the processes of reorganization. Though they have explained their participation in terms of the "moral obligation" which they profess toward those who purchased defaulted securities from them, the Securities and Exchange Commission's investigations and reports have demonstrated that this obligation is more often than not merely an excuse for the investment banker to be active in the situation.

Their active participation in reorganization has been rife with conflicting interests. Their control or influence over protective committees, though shared with the management of a corporation, inevitably leads to the suppression of claims which may exist against both. The diligent investigation into the possible misrepresentation and fraud in the sale of securities, which I mentioned earlier as a notable function of committees, goes by the board when committees are subject to the influences of the

11. S.E.C. Report, Part I, at 157–160.
12. S.E.C. Report, Part II, section iii; Part III, section iv.

very persons who sold those securities. Further, the very close connections between the investment bankers and the management have led to mutual support in the perpetuation of their positions. Partners in the banking houses are frequently directors of the corporation. Often, too, they are a part of the management, though they or their representatives hold no official position as officers or directors. The management's liabilities may frequently be their liabilities also. And just as in the case of managements, so do investment bankers desire to continue their connections with the company for the sake of the emoluments to be derived from such connection. The latter means to the underwriter getting the business of originating and distributing the corporation's securities, inside information on the course of its business, profitable market operations, and a veritable host of other business patronage. In sum, if control of the corporation is shifted to the new group, the prospect, apart from liability for past misconduct, is one of loss of future profits because the banker's connection with the corporation has not been continued.

Then, also, underwriting houses may have an existing financial stake in the securities of the corporation, in the form of outstanding short-term credits, or securities of the corporation other than the securities which committees controlled by them ostensibly represent. Their self-interest in such cases has made them poor fiduciaries.[13] Through control over committees they have been able to reduce the risk that such claims would be excluded from the reorganization plan, or in other ways given treatment which they consider unfavorable. Over and above all else is the desire to "save face," a factor which in my judgment has done more to produce unsound reorganization plans than any other single factor.

All these factors combine to make the representation on, and control over, committees by houses of issue an undesirable, and in many ways, a definitely harmful practice. This observation

13. S.E.C. Report, Part II, section v; Part III, section iv.

is equally applicable to all types of reorganization situations whether foreign or municipal debt rearrangements, voluntary readjustments, or reorganizations in court proceedings.

The foregoing conflicts of interest are largely *sui generis* so far as the management and the houses of issue are concerned. There are others which are applicable to all types of committees. Thus not infrequently stockholders are found serving on bondholders' committees and bondholders on stockholders' committees. The result has been that the pecuniary self-interest of the committee members has been opposed to the pecuniary interests of the beneficiaries of these trusts. As a consequence representation by the committee has not been vigilant and aggressive in the cause of the security holders. The loyalty of the committee has been diluted by the incentive to serve their own selfish ends first.

Further, members of the committee have at times acquired their securities at such low prices as to create a grave conflict of interest. A committee which has purchased bonds at 10 cents on the dollar can make 100 per cent profit by effecting a settlement at 20 cents. But investors who had purchased at or near par would under those circumstances be suffering grave losses.

Out of such circumstances are serious conflicts of interest born. These are merely illustrative. They indicate the nature of one important problem with which the Lea Bill deals.

2. *Activities of Committees*. One type of conduct by committees and their affiliates which has resulted in injury to security holders is trading in the securities of the corporation undergoing reorganization.[14] By reason of inside information, committee members have frequently been able to profit from their position of trust by buying or selling securities. This practice has permeated the whole field. It has been incompatible with the ancient standards for trustees. But committees have attempted to legalize it by virtue of contractual provisions in their deposit agreements, whereby the depositing security holders are pre-

14. S.E.C. Report, Part II, at 315–351; Part III, at 132–152.

sumed to waive the legal disabilities which the committee members otherwise would have.

Another serious departure from fiduciary standards has been common in connection with the charges for fees and expenses of protective committees.[15] By and large, committee fees constitute a substantial source of revenue; they may at times be the major motivation in the organization of committees. The striking fact has been that, with such exceptions as allowances under Section 77B of the Bankruptcy Act, committees have been able to fix their own fees, without independent supervision or review. They are themselves the arbiters of the value of their own services. This shocking lapse from the standards of fiduciaries would no longer be possible under the Lea Bill.

Another phase of committee activities which requires thoroughgoing regulation is their solicitation practices. One item of this is the use of paid solicitors in the marshaling of assents to plans, or the solicitation of proxies or deposits authorizing the committee to act generally on behalf of the security holder. Special solicitors employed on a commission basis contact security holders; almost inevitably this practice results in "high pressure" tactics. In other ways, too, pressure is frequently exerted on uninformed investors, as, for example, by threats of discrimination and undesirable consequences if they fail to assent or deposit their securities with a committee. A catalogue of tricks and dodges utilized by committees to exert pressure upon security holders is set forth in the recent reports of the S.E.C. to the Congress.[16] I will not stop at this point to relate these; it suffices to emphasize again that they involve innumerable departures from the proper standards of conduct for fiduciaries. These standards the Lea Bill will enforce, and security holders would under it be relieved of the indefensible pressure tactics of committees.

Another source of oppression of investors is the one-sided

15. S.E.C. Report, Part I, at 195–210; Part II, 351–394.
16. S.E.C. Report, Part I, at 457–485.

contract known as the deposit agreement.[17] These are complicated documents which the average investor would rarely understand even if he saw one, which he seldom does. These agreements fix the authority and the powers of the committee. Since they are prepared by committees and their counsel, their terms inevitably give to the committee almost complete dominion over deposited securities and at the same time immunize them from any real responsibility. But there is no mutuality in these agreements. The security holder, once he deposits his bond or stock with a committee, finds withdrawal either impossible or difficult and expensive. By and large, committees through the vehicle of deposit agreements exercise an arbitrary power over the investor's right to withdraw, and over every other right that the investor would otherwise possess by reason of his ownership. For example, a committee controlled by a house of issue may succeed, if it obtains deposit of securities, in effectively cutting off rescission rights of depositors. The form and content of such agreements and the occasions for their need must be carefully regulated in the interests of the investor rather than of the committee. Too long have they been employed as instruments of oppression.

Such conditions as I have enumerated have not been isolated and infrequent—they have been persistent and widespread and of a truly national nature. They have permeated the whole reorganization field from real-estate cases to foreign-debt rearrangements. They have meant that the functions of protective committees have been perverted if not destroyed. As a result, the investor has been at the mercy of self-constituted and self-appointed committees whose objectives are frequently incompatible with the objectives of investors. They are interested in concealing claims for fraud or mismanagement; investors are interested in collecting on those claims. They are interested in keeping the past a closed book; investors are interested in examining the past to determine whether or not the management

17. S.E.C. Report, Part I, at 585–670.

has been so incompetent or faithless as to be discharged rather than restored to power. They are interested in reorganization profits; investors are interested in economy and fairness. They are interested in effecting a reorganization which will "save face" for them; investors are interested in thoroughgoing reorganizations. For such reasons, the interests of reorganizers and the interests of investors are often incompatible.

Existing law is not adequate to deal with these situations. Large numbers of protective committees do not come under any regulation or control. So far as the states are concerned, few adequate controls exist; and in view of the *interstate* complexion of most protective committee activities, *intrastate* control is of necessity limited in effectiveness. The solicitation of proxies, deposits, and assents, by use of the mails and of agencies of *interstate* commerce, is likewise free of regulation to a great degree. Existing *federal* control and supervision over such solicitation are both limited and inadequate.

At the present time some committees are required to register under the Securities Act of 1933, as amended, but such registration requirements are applicable, by and large, only to committees seeking deposits of securities. Committees which seek powers of attorney or proxies are, by and large, exempt from that Act. This result flows from the fact that only in some circumstances are proxies so constituted as to come within the definition of "security" under that Act. Nor is the application of the registration requirements at all pervasive in the case of committees seeking deposit of securities, by reason of the many exemptions of which protective committees may avail themselves under the Act. For example, under section 3(a)(2) of the Securities Act there is included within the category of exempted securities the certificates of deposit for any security issued or guaranteed by any state or by any political subdivision of a state. This means that the Act cannot be brought to bear upon committees acting for the holders of municipal obligations, committees which, as indicated in Part IV of the S.E.C.'s report to the Congress, are sorely in need of regulation. Similarly, the disclosure of full and material information from many other types of committees has been inhibited by the exemptions provided in section 3(a)(10) of the Securities Act. Under this provision certificates of deposit receive an exemption where the terms and conditions of their issuance and exchange for outstanding securities are approved by any court, or official or agency of the United States, or other governmental authority expressly authorized by law to draft such approval. My observation is that too frequently such approval has been *pro forma*. Courts, overburdened and unacquainted with technical details of these situations, have not afforded the measure of scrutiny to be desired. They have not been given a sufficiently specific and adequate standard against which to apply the legislative mandate. Further, under section 3(a)(9) of the Act, solicitation activities on the part of corporate managements seeking to effectuate so-called voluntary plans for reorganization may be free of desirable requirements for full and adequate disclosure. Furthermore, the power of the Securities and Exchange Commission under the Securities Exchange Act of 1934 over the solicitation of proxies, consents, and authorizations is applicable only to certain securities registered on national securities exchanges, while the powers of the Commission over committees under Sections 11 and 12 of the Public Utility Act of 1935 extend only to securities and reorganizations of registered holding companies and subsidiaries thereof.

This brief examination of the narrow scope of existing Federal regulation over the solicitation of proxies, deposits, and assents indicates the first conclusion to which the Commission was led in its study and investigation of protective and reorganization committees under Section 211 of the Securities Exchange Act of 1934. (1) In the first place, the present controls must be given a broader base. Methods must be designed to bring within the Federal system of regulation and control the many committees presently exempt and immune from any supervision. In practical operation, it is our belief that this can be best achieved by an extension of the presently limited supervisory power of the Securities and Exchange Commission. But this step alone will not suffice. (2) Even where the Commission today possesses jurisdiction over the solicitation activities of committees, its powers need to be strengthened materially. This will be equally true in the event of the extension of the Commission's present jurisdiction. Its administrative control and supervision needs to be implemented so that more effective and pervasive supervision over those who are engaged in such solicitation may be had.

This is necessary because if committees are made to meet merely registration requirements they will be forced to disclose only the truth as to their organization, and affiliations, and their plans. But in reorganization situations mere disclosure is hardly sufficient for the protection of investors. To the ordinary prospective purchaser of securities disclosure of the pertinent facts surrounding an offering is of great value, since by and large he may buy or not, as his whim or judgment indicates. But upon default investors in these reorganization situations, for the most part unorganized and to a great extent incapable of self-help, have little freedom of choice. Their only choice, and it is not a real one, is to go along with those who by virtue of long tradition and practice in corporate reorganizations have come to possess dominance over the organization and operation of protective committees, or to proceed by themselves. The latter course is a futile one. Hence the investor is in effect forced to throw his lot in with those who, self-constituted and self-appointed, announce themselves as his protectors. Disclosure of all the pertinent facts concerning the committee will be of small comfort to the investor; his choice is hardly expanded though he knows that those who control the destiny of his investment are incompetent or faithless fiduciaries. In other words, the basis for administrative regulation must be broadened so as to require not only the disclosure of relevant facts but also to permit some restraint on the conduct and activities of committees and some check on their personnel at the time of their formation and during their existence. There is required the power to refuse to qualify as committees those who have palpably conflicting and adverse interests. There is need to curtail and restrict in the public interest and for the protection of investors the powers which committees may take unto themselves, and the unconscionable practices which may persist in spite of full disclosure. This is not a wholly new departure for congressional action. The beginnings of such type of control over committees are to be found in Sections 11 and 12 of the Public Utility Holding Company Act of 1935 where the Commission is given powers to make rules and regulations governing the solicitations by committees and others in case of registered holding companies and subsidiaries thereof. With the benefit of the rich experience born of the depression and of the experience under the present statutes, a broader program should be undertaken.

Such a program should be built on the firm foundations of the other Acts. It should be envisaged as an evolutionary development of present controls, not as a radical or revolutionary development. It entails a separate statute dealing with solicitation of proxies and deposits. Such a statute is conceived as an extension and evolution of the regulatory acts now administered by the Securities and Exchange Commission. Committees acting in reorganizations would be required to qualify under such statute, in lieu of registration under the Securities Act of 1933, as amended, or compliance with the pertinent provisions of the proxy rules of the Commission under the Securities Exchange Act of 1934 or comparable rules under the Utility Act. Furthermore, exemptions presently provided committees under the Securities Act of 1933, as amended, would be restricted in their application to the new statute. This system of control must be sufficiently broad to cover committees operating in connection with voluntary reorganizations, foreign debt rearrangements, municipal debt readjustments, and the solicitation of proxies, deposits, and assents by use of the mails or agencies of interstate commerce in connection with reorganizations in state or Federal courts.

Such administrative control would provide a greater degree of assurance that those who are acting in a fiduciary or representative capacity will be free from adverse interests and will take unto themselves only those discretionary powers necessary or appropriate for protection of investors. But in view of the fact that committees are not always an essential or necessary part of reorganization paraphernalia, some minimum control over the solicitation of assents to, or acceptances of, plans should be devised. Otherwise, groups or individuals not soliciting discretionary powers but only assents to, or acceptances of, plans might do all the essential work of reorganization without subjecting themselves to the conditioning influences of such new regulation. This would not be desirable, since conflicts of interest may be as important in connection with solicitation of assents as in case of solicitation of proxies or deposits. This condition is apt to be particularly acute in case of voluntary reorganization plans [18] which are free from scrutiny or supervision by any agency. Furthermore, committees are not a customary or usual part of voluntary reorganization procedures. In such cases, the management commonly solicits assents to plans directly. In view of the frequent appearance of conflicts of interest in such solicitors, a minimum degree of control over solicitation of such assents is necessary. Accordingly, at least in the voluntary reorganization, the same degree of control over solicitation of assents or acceptances should be provided as in case of solicitation of proxies or deposits. Furthermore, assents to and acceptances of a plan subject to the jurisdiction of a court or other agency which has power to pass on the fairness

18. S.E.C. Report, Part VII, section vi.

of the plan should in general not be allowed until the plan has been carefully scrutinized by the court or agency and its submission to investors authorized.

In summary, such a statute would give renewed emphasis to the fact that representatives of security holders in reorganizations occupy a fiduciary position. The standards of fiduciaries require that neither they nor their lawyers should possess dual or multiple interests. Likewise, they require that neither committees nor their lawyers should be permitted to be the sole arbiters of the value of their services to security holders. Such a statute would eliminate the abuses which have characterized the strategy and techniques of reorganization. It would not permit the use of deposit agreements in oppressive and undesirable ways. It would break the virtual monopoly which the inside groups made up of bankers and managements have over lists of security holders. It would control high pressure salesmen, so that security holders would be assured of an honest and complete portrayal of all material facts affecting their investment. In other words, it would give investors protection on a national scale against the abuses which the recent depression has portrayed in such flagrant fashion.

Participation in Reorganization Proceedings by the Securities and Exchange Commission

Control over the reorganization process in the interests of investors entails more than the foregoing supervision over committees. Some strengthening of the reorganization proceedings themselves is necessary. Insofar as reorganizations under Section 77B are concerned, the Chandler Bill makes significant and noteworthy reforms. Some elements of those types of reform are needed in other counterparts of the reorganization system. They are appropriate to incorporate in an amendment to the Securities Act of 1933, since they pertain to the power and functions of the Securities and Exchange Commission.

The present reorganization system is composed of a variety of procedures. In the first place, many different sorts of debtors utilize that system. It is not only the industrial, real estate, utility, and commercial corporation which has sought reorganization. Many municipal corporations have endeavored to work out debt rearrangements.[19] Numerous foreign governmental obligations, widely held by American investors, have gone into default and these have needed readjustment.[20] In the second place, the methods and techniques of reorganization have varied widely. The hard-pressed domestic corporation may seek a haven in equity receiverships or the bankruptcy courts, and thereby stay the efforts of creditors to collect upon their individual debts while the effort at over-all readjustment goes on. Or while yet able to meet their obligations, domestic corporations have sought to forestall impending receivership or bankruptcy by effectuating so-called voluntary plans of readjustment.[21] In the case of domestic corporations, these voluntary plans may run the gamut from mere moratoria, primarily affecting claims of creditors, to consolidations, mergers, and sales of assets, primarily affecting stockholders. The latter have been made possible (if security holders consent in sufficient numbers) by corporate-charter or trust-indenture provisions, or by statutory authority granted by the debtor's state of incorporation.

From the standpoint of regulation of security holders' committees, these *voluntary* reorganizations present an anomalous situation, for it frequently happens that no committees appear in such reorganizations. The plan is commonly formulated by the management and bankers of the corporation, and is directly submitted by them to the security holders for their assent. In such circumstances, some minimum control over the solicitation of assents or acceptances by the debtor corporation is necessary. And even more important is the fact that such voluntary

19. S.E.C. Report, Part IV, section iii.
20. S.E.C. Report, Part V, section i.
21. S.E.C. Report, Part VII, *passim.*

plans are not subjected to any scrutiny or review as in the case of reorganizations in the Federal courts. The management alone is the arbiter of the fairness of the plan. As a consequence, great inequities have been done to security holders. A management, heavily interested in the common stock, has foisted on the preferred stock by means of divers threats and practices, plans of readjustment which have been unfair and inequitable. A management, faced with the dire threat of being ousted from power by means of receivership or bankruptcy, has by high-powered tactics and by transforming the company's treasury into a war chest, coerced senior claimants into receiving junior interests. These and like cases have been of frequent occurrence in the voluntary field. State corporation laws afford little protection to investors. Those who dissent may obtain a rather tenuous appraisal right. They may, if they have adequate funds, resources, ingenuity, and perseverance, be able to obtain injunctive relief from the courts. But there is no large or substantial measure of protection in these ways. The states have provided no system of administrative supervision over those readjustments. And it is unlikely that they can effectively do so, in view of the orgy of competition among the states for the corporate business.

These are compelling reasons for a Federal administrative agency such as the Commission to assume a more important role in such cases. A signal and important function, however, which such an agency may perform in this type of case, is to undertake for the benefit of investors (or at least to have the power in necessitous cases to make) a careful scrutiny and examination of the plans which managements and bankers seek to have consummated. At least a modest advance toward this objective can be made by vesting such power, if not the duty, in the Securities and Exchange Commission. As I have said, the investor in this type of case lacks the protection which an honest and qualified protective committee might give him; and since the reorganization takes place out of court, he lacks the protection ordinarily supplied in some measure in judicial re-organizations by the judge's scrutiny and approval of submitted plans of reorganization. The ordinary investor, left in such cases to his own devices, has been easy prey for self-seeking managements and bankers. Administrative review of these plans in the form of reports to security holders on them can go far toward amelioration of that prevailing condition.

This recommendation is equally applicable to reorganizations in the courts, even though protective committees participate actively. In the last analysis, however worthy and necessary are the other functions which I have already enumerated, the ultimate objective of most protective committees' activity should be the accomplishment, expeditiously and economically, of fair and equitable plans of reorganization. In the achievement of this objective, the assistance of a qualified administrative agency can be of enormous service, both to the courts and to investors.

This administrative assistance, as I have just said, should take its most important form in the work of preparing advisory opinions on the merits, the fairness, and the feasibility of suggested plans of reorganization. Apart from so-called voluntary plans, the work of preparation of such plans; the arm's-length negotiations over their terms between representatives of conflicting classes of securities; the "trading-out" of disputed claims —all these repose traditionally in the hands of security holders and their representatives. In another connection, i.e., the Chandler Bill, the Commission has recommended that an officer of the court, an independent trustee, be made an active participant in these processes in order to supply to them the presence of a disinterested, objective guardian of the interests of all the security holders. That is a matter which goes beyond the scope of the Lea Bill. But it seems altogether consistent with the purposes of the Lea Bill to make provision for the close and careful scrutiny and examination of reorganization plans—the end product of any committee's activities—in order to supply a double-barreled assurance that committees have done their work effectively and honestly.

It is only after an objective determination of the merits of a plan that it can be said that a reorganization has or has not fulfilled its purposes. The identical determination is the decisive factor in deciding whether or not protective committees have sufficiently performed the functions which give them their only excuse for being. In this way the administrative analysis of plans and advisory reports thereon would give to investors increased assurance that their representatives have or have not done their work well; it would give them also protection at the stage when protection is most sorely needed; i.e., before they are compelled to vote upon the plan.

In those cases where reorganization takes place under the aegis of a court, provision for such administrative assistance should be of immeasurable benefit to the courts also. For the growing need for such administrative assistance is the result, from another angle, of the flood of reorganization cases which engulfed the courts in the period of the recent depression. They made unprecedented demands upon the experience, skill, and judgment of judges in complex and intricate financial and business matters. Judges, however, are not, and do not profess to be, financial experts. However great their legal training and native intelligence, they are not always in a position to discharge completely the responsibility which is theirs, to see that only those plans are approved and consummated which are fair in their allocation of assets and earnings and which, among other things, give adequate assurance that honest and competent management will assume control of the reorganized company. This is not to say that the courts have done an inadequate job; frequently they just do not have the necessary time to spend on these complicated questions. Rather, an even better job than they have done could be accomplished if they could avail themselves of expert administrative assistance in unraveling the intricate complexities of the many financial matters that enter into every plan of reorganization for larger corporate enterprises.

Such assistance would not usurp power from the courts, but it would strengthen and implement them in the performance of their onerous and burdensome reorganization functions. Such reports would deal with the fairness and equity of the treatment accorded to various classes of security holders and claimants by the terms of the plan, and the adequacy of the steps taken to discover, disclose, and collect all assets of the corporation or of individual security holders. This would include all causes of action against officers and directors of the corporation and the underwriters of its securities. Such reports could treat also of the reasonableness and propriety of the fees and expenses of the reorganization; and would examine carefully into the provisions made in the plan for the management of the reorganized corporation in order to ascertain whether such provisions are in the interests of the security holders. It could examine into any other material and significant phases of the plan.

A similar provision is embodied in the Chandler Bill, of which I made mention earlier. That provision, however, deals only with reorganizations under Section 77B of the Bankruptcy Act. A large area of such administrative assistance may remain in Federal equity receiverships, a field equally deserving of attention and in the past, equally, if not more, susceptible to the abuses which I have already discussed. The two provisions need to be carefully integrated, and, in combination, should effectively cover all occasions on which there is resort to any Federal courts in the course of effecting a reorganization. In addition, should a state court or agency wish of its own initiative to call upon the Commission for its aid in the scrutiny and analysis of reorganization plans, provision should also be made empowering the Commission to render advisory reports when it is requested to do so by such state court or agency.

As a companion measure, the Commission should be given

the power to intervene in reorganization proceedings, so that as a party in interest it could perform additional advisory functions in the courts.[22] There have been in the past necessitous cases where throughout the whole proceeding security holders have not had the benefit of able and disinterested advice and representation. That is to say in many proceedings there has not been an articulate, well-informed investor point of view. The Commission on intervention would not be representing any particular class of security holders. It would be present in the case in the public interest and in the interest of investors to see that unfairness or inequity was not done, that honesty in administration took place, and that reorganizers were not engaged in exploitation. The right of the Commission to intervene and to be heard on all phases of many of these cases would, in my judgment, supply a conditioning influence over the whole proceeding and supply the court with counsel and advice which in many cases have been sorely lacking.

In conclusion, the existence of widespread and persistent abuses in the reorganization field calls for vigorous and aggressive action—action as constructive and as progressive as that which produced the Securities Act of 1933, the Securities Exchange Act of 1934, and the Public Utility Holding Company Act of 1935. There is such a national investor interest at stake in these reorganizations that mild or temporizing remedies will not suffice. The necessary reforms call for revisions in the present system along the evolutionary route made apparent by the experience of the last four years.

22. The Commission now has this power, subject to the approval of the court, in proceedings under Chapter X of the amended Bankruptcy Act.

CHAPTER XVIII

MUNICIPAL DEBT READJUSTMENT

The Protective Committee Study took Mr. Douglas deep into the field
of defaulted municipal debts and their readjustment.[1] This paper,
read before the United States Conference of Mayors at Washington, D.C., in November, 1936, is based largely on that experience.

FOUR years ago local government defaults had once
again become so widespread as to assume the proportions of a Federal problem. I say once again, for it will
be recalled that during each of our previous periods of local
government default—of which there were several during the
last century—the United States Government was called upon
to protect through its judiciary the interest of municipal security holders. When the defaults began to recur a few years ago,
the sole governmental mechanism for dealing with them was
the judicial machinery, comprising the device of writs of mandamus which had been developed by Federal courts for this purpose during the last century. This judicial machinery was primarily designed for cases which might be termed "wilful repudiation." Hence these writs had limited utility.[2] In the first
place, where the debtor was insolvent, these writs had no magic
in them which permitted creditors as a whole to collect. And
for the most part local government defaults of the present era
reflect not repudiation but inability to pay, due to either temporary or more deep-seated conditions. In the second place, the
role of litigation will always be simply ancillary to the main
process of negotiation.

Hence, when the present era of defaults arrived, it was speedily recognized that voluntary negotiation of readjustment plans

1. S.E.C. Report, Part IV, *passim.*
2. S.E.C. Report, Part IV, section iii.

under circumstances as peaceable and free from the irritant of litigation as possible was the only practicable procedure. But a local government default is more often than not an extremely complicated situation. Groups with great diversity of interest are involved, each with a different stake in the situation. Bargaining power is unequally distributed as between groups, and even within groups. In the typical situations, moreover, the outstanding securities are scattered throughout a large part of the United States and sometimes throughout the world. Many of the holders are small investors in no position to take independent legal action or even to inquire into the situation. Furthermore, even though plans of debt readjustment are worked out by the debtor and representatives of the creditors, there is no effective way to bind minority or dissenting creditors to the plan. The necessity of dealing with the minority effectively but nonetheless fairly gave rise to a demand for a Federal bankruptcy law applicable to such debtors.[3] This, as you know, resulted in 1934 in the National Municipal Debt Readjustment Act, which was held to be unconstitutional by the Supreme Court in the spring of this year.[4]

The end result is that these problems remain for the most part unregulated and free from supervision. No effective machinery has been supplied by the states. The matter rests where it always has—for the most part in the hands of debtors and creditors.

The common pattern for these current debt readjustments has been negotiation between creditors and debtors. Normally, the creditors have been represented by protective committees.[5] Last year, 1935, there were in existence or had recently been in existence over two hundred such committees. These committees have been self-constituted and self-controlled. In their hands

3. S.E.C. Report, Part IV, section vii.
4. As subsequently revised this Act, now Chapter IX of the Bankruptcy Act, was held constitutional by the Supreme Court in *Lindsay-Strathmore Irrigation District* v. *Bekins;* 304 U.S. 27 (1938).
5. S.E.C. Report, Part IV, section v.

rested the fate of thousands of bondholders. Vested with broad powers, they proceeded to negotiate debt-readjustment plans with no check or restraint except their own consciences. They proceeded to fix their own fees and expenses without the scrutiny or supervision of anyone—certainly not of the bondholders. At times they were in positions irreconcilable for fiduciaries— representing their own adverse interests on the one hand; purporting to represent the bondholders on the other. To conclude that committees in this field should be regulated and controlled in the interests of investors is not to deny that these committees have and should continue to perform important functions. It emphasizes that the functions which they perform are so important and so essential that precaution should be taken lest these functions be perverted. I am confident that no fair-minded student of the subject—that is, one who has no special interests to serve—can effectively dissent from the decision that independent supervision, scrutiny, and control over these committees are necessary if investors are not to be exploited. The issue is not whether there should be any such regulation; the issue is the kind and degree of supervision which are necessary and adequate.

Although this problem is of interest and importance to municipalities, it is essentially an investor's problem. I stated that normally protective committees had been used to represent creditors in negotiations. But negotiation is not always present. Not infrequently the debtor attempts to consummate a plan through the good offices of a fiscal agent,[6] without negotiation with representatives of the creditors. Such fiscal agent is likely to be a bond house which either originated the security issue in the first instance or at least participated in its retail distribution. One reason for the prominent position of such bond houses in such plans is that they have access to the lists of purchasers of the security. They also have the coöperation of other dealers, in tracing and contacting such holders.

6. S.E.C. Report, Part IV, section iii.

Complete data with respect to such fiscal agents and their activities do not exist for the nation as a whole. But enough is known to render it certain that no program for insuring adequate representation to holders of defaulted securities through supervision and control over protective committees would be complete unless it included as a component part some provision for the regulation of the activities of these fiscal agents. The activities of fiscal agents which require regulation are activities approaching fraudulent practices, which unless checked also work to the ultimate detriment of municipal debtors.

The undesirability of neglecting this phase of the problem becomes clear if we consider the very real potentialities—indeed, probabilities—of abuse which inhere in the fiscal agency practice. It is, in the first place, very difficult in any given case to tell for whom the fiscal agent is working in the absence of full disclosure. Ostensibly the interests of the agent may lie with the investors; actually, they may be with the debtor. The agent is usually a bond house. Where a committee for the bondholders is formed, such a bond house is usually found supporting the committee, indeed taking some initiative in its organization, if not serving as a committee member. Even in cases where no committee is formed such a bond house is often found working with an informal creditor group in an endeavor to negotiate, on behalf of the creditors, interim collection on account of interest and eventually a final plan. Such activities the bond house justifies on the grounds that it owes a moral obligation to the security holders to render this kind of service. Furthermore, some of the holders of the obligations are customers of the bond house, who may expect the bond house to look out for their interests. Preservation of its good will may thus be the actual or ostensible reason why the bond house becomes very active.

But in the fiscal-agency arrangements now under discussion the bond houses are retained by the debtor taxing district and urge the debtor's plan of adjustment upon the creditors. It is then in the hire of the debtor. Its commission in part, and frequently in the entirety, is dependent upon its success in inducing the great majority of the creditors to accept the terms of composition offered. Yet the more intensive the independent inquiry, if any, conducted by the fiscal agent into the capacity of the debtor to pay, the greater its expenditure and the less its net profit on the transaction. There are, furthermore, only conscience and integrity to prevent the fiscal agent from trading in the securities affected. The market value of these securities will have dropped with announcement of default. Once a plan is put through their value will rise. The temptation will always be strong for these agents to capitalize on their inside information by buying at default prices and selling when the plan is put through. Furthermore, a plan may be grossly unfair to the investors even though the fiscal agent doubles his money on such purchases and sales. A settlement at fifty cents on the dollar may be vicious from the viewpoint of those who have purchased at or near par. But for those who have purchased at twenty-five cents on the dollar, the settlement will be inordinately favorable. A fiscal agent who is in such a position as a result of his purchase of bonds at default prices has a distinct conflict of interest as respects the investors. If he purports to represent them without disclosure, he has perpetrated a fraud.

Surely these circumstances point to a need for full and free disclosure by bond houses acting as fiscal agents if the ordinary run of customers of the bond houses are not to be victimized. But instances have been reported wherein a fiscal agent has in one such transaction collected its commission from the debtor for effecting the refunding, made a profit from its own trading in the securities affected, and has even taken commissions from some of the bondholders who were under the impression that the bond house was representing them. These are not merely fraud upon the investor. Some of the examples I have cited may even be violations of the fiduciary duty which the fiscal agent owes to the municipality, its principal, and for which the agent might be held accountable. Taken together these cases are, furthermore, illustrative of practices that can result only in ultimate disillusionment on the part of investors, with the consequence that the credit standing and borrowing abilities of municipalities whose fiscal agents indulge in such practices may suffer permanent impairment.

There are other forms of abuse, which can only be described as out and out rackets. Unscrupulous dealers have at times been known to propose default to low-grade taxing districts for the sole purpose of earning a fee by effecting a refunding on a scaled-down basis. The incentive held out to the taxing district in such cases is, of course, the prospect of a reduced debt and, in consequence, lower taxation. Such proposals have, moreover, been accepted; and an exchange of bonds on the basis of questionable representations has been successfully negotiated by the dealer with its customers.

The vicious potentialities of the fiscal agency when it is subject to no supervision or check stand out in bold relief. These are accentuated by the difficulties in any attempt to evaluate the fairness of any plan. The capacity of a debtor municipality or taxing district to pay, which is the supposed basis of any fair plan, is at best a matter of very technical estimate based on a great many problematical future variables. Even assuming possession of all the facts as of a certain date bearing on this capacity to pay, there is nevertheless always room for a very wide difference of estimates when that is projected over a future period of years. The ordinary investor whose adherence to a compromise plan is solicited cannot have all those facts, and could not evaluate them if he had. There is the impossibility of ascertaining the fairness of any plan solely by examination of its terms. The percentage of consent obtained is a poor criterion of fairness. In the absence of complete disclosure of the qualifications and interests of the several parties to the negotiation, and of the methods whereby the consents were obtained, such criterion may be wholly false and misleading. In the interests of investors the least which can be done is some check over the manner and method by which such consents are obtained.

Much of the mischief inherent in the conflicting position of the fiscal agent is obvious. Indeed, the mere circumstance that a commission from the debtor is involved affords an incentive to bond houses to negotiate hasty refundings without adequate assurance that they will stand up. There are instances where municipalities and local subdivisions had, during the few years prior to their open defaults, staved off the evil day through a series of exchanges of maturing obligations, which could not be met, for new short-term refunding bonds. It soon transpired that those, in turn, could not be met at maturity. Hence there was an open default. But for each of these exchanges a bond house acting as fiscal agent received a fee from the debtor. Yet the fiscal agent later admitted that at the time of negotiating some of those exchanges it did not expect that the debtor would be able to meet maturities on the new bonds. Investors, however, were led to believe quite the opposite.

Some instances of refundings carried out in bad faith by fiscal agents have been reported. These involve obligations of municipalities deriving their major source of revenue from a municipal utility or from the proceeds of special state taxes allocated to local subdivisions. Debtors and their agents have been known in some such cases to proffer refunding bonds which could never be paid without the proceeds of the special tax, and, at the same time, lobby for repeal of the tax law. Or to make the plight of the debtor look sorrier, the fiscal agent may be tempted to encourage concealment or diversion of these assets. Where the major source of revenue is from a utility, there may be nothing to prevent the disposition of the utility. In any event, its revenues could not be reached by mandamus. But these matters are carefully concealed from the investors by the fiscal agents, who, in fact, may purport to be protecting them. Though these episodes have doubtless been only occasional, they nonetheless emphasize the need for some check and restraint.

The problem of control over fiscal agents, like the problem of control over protective committees, is, therefore, in large measure a phase of the problem of control over the fairness of municipal debt-adjustment plans. It should be remembered that the great bulk of the taxing districts still in default are relatively small units. Protective committees are less likely to be organized in such cases. Hence, much of the field is in consequence left open to the fiscal agent. The timeliness of this problem is therefore apparent. I am certain that no municipality will disagree with the conclusion that there is proper place for regulation designed to check and control fraudulent or near-fraudulent practices of fiscal agents.

What kind of control over these fiscal agents should be provided? The first step seems clear.

The minimum which should be required is complete disclosure by such fiscal agents.[7] They should be under a duty to disclose to investors the terms of their agency, including compensation; their own holdings and trading in the securities affected; and their interest, if any, in any plan which they sponsor. Underwriters of other types of securities are required to make comparable disclosures when they go to the public with offerings of securities and penalties are imposed on them by the Securities Act of 1933, as amended, for false and misleading statements of material facts. No one can deny the value and prophylactic effect which these requirements have had on our securities markets and thus on investors. Such requirements of disclosure insofar as they deter fraud and overreaching and bring to investors material facts concerning the issue offer some

7. The Securities Act of 1933 does not apply to municipal securities. While some of the earlier drafts of the bill had included municipal securities, there was considerable opposition to such a provision, and this class of securities was ultimately exempted from the provisions of the Act.

assurance that the high functions performed by underwriters will not be perverted, as they frequently were before 1933.

Basically the same considerations apply to the private fiscal agents in these municipal default or refunding siuations whether or not actually or technically these agents are underwriters. There is no reason why we cannot move immediately toward the objective of requiring from these agents complete disclosure of their own activities.

Such disclosure should produce beneficial results. It should tend to protect investors and debtors alike by deterring these fiscal agents from fraud and from self-seeking impropriety. In such a constructive program investors and debtors have a community of interest. For the large number of refundings worked out conscionably and fairly, such disclosure would entail no burden. But recognition of this principle in municipal financing would afford some assurance that exploitation would be curbed.

CHAPTER XIX

LAWYERS AND CONFLICTS OF INTEREST

This talk was given before the Eastern Law Students Conference at the Catholic University of America in Washington, D.C., March 20, 1937.

THE importance of the role of the lawyer in reorganization is difficult to overestimate. This is true whether his client is a trustee, protective committee, the reorganization managers, a receiver, or the debtor. Here more than in other situations the lawyer is the strategist, technician, and economic adviser. He not only tells the client what he may lawfully do; commonly he decides what may be wisely, properly, and profitably done. The lawyer will often deny this. He will insist that he is only an amanuensis, a boss draftsman, or a clearing house of ideas. But this denial may be attributed either to professional modesty or to a desire to cultivate or perpetuate the fiction that his judgments and opinions are limited to the law. The fact remains that in reorganizations the lawyer reigns supreme. That supremacy may be partly due to the fact that reorganization strategies and techniques, involving as they do complicated legal machinery, call for the participation of lawyers much as ordinary litigation does. And it may in part be due to the fact that in these reorganization situations either the questions of law and business fact are subtly blended or the distinctions between them are blurred and indistinct. Whatever may be the cause, the result is that the lawyer is the determinant influence over the whole debt-readjustment process.

I mention this fact not to bear evidence against the profession nor to criticize it for performing such important roles in reorganizations. Rather I emphasize the matter for substantiation of my theme that the quality of reorganization practices is in large measure dependent on the lawyer.[1]

Counsel for the debtor commonly selects the forum for and method of reorganization. In the case of equity receiverships, he often prepares the papers long in advance of default, ready to be filed by a fictitious adversary lawyer on behalf of a fictitious hostile creditor. Upon default he causes the papers to be filed and receivers to be appointed. He also can—and does—exert influence upon the choice of the receivers. Upon this choice, plus the choice of counsel to the receivers, depends in a large measure a great many issues of paramount importance—the character and administration of the estate; the perpetuation or discontinuance of contracts; the investigation of and suits against management, bankers, and their allies; and other such vital matters. In other words, if he succeeds in his plans and outwits hostile creditors, counsel for the company is able to keep the old management in the saddle and in control of the reorganization.

Before or concurrently with the institution of receivership or bankruptcy proceedings, the management and the bankers normally form protective committees. Perhaps it is not well known or clearly recognizable that many committees have been selected

1. The part played by lawyers in corporate reorganizations received careful scrutiny in the Protective Committee Study directed by Mr. Douglas. A novel feature of the hearings was that lawyers as well as their clients were called on to testify. Mr. Douglas once described the role of the lawyer in reorganization as follows:

"And back of the whole scene sits the lawyer. He is not only the director of the play—he is in charge of stage settings, he writes the dialogue, he selects and trains the actors. He is responsible for the tone, the quality, the finish of the play. It is his production, and so it is that you cannot study reorganizations without studying him. To study protective committees without him is to study them *in vacuo*. To study reorganization plans without him is to reduce the question of fairness of such plans to a mathematical formula. To attempt a diagnosis of committee policy without him is to eliminate the policy formulator. Around him the whole reorganization process revolves. He supplies the initiative, the drive and in part the profit motive that gives the reorganization procedure momentum and power." Talk before the Duke Bar Association, Durham, N.C., April 22, 1934.

to a great extent by counsel to the management or the bankers. But, indeed, the history of protective committees clearly shows that more commonly than not the attorney has become the focal point for their organization and activity. He also has played a dominant and often determinant role in the formulation of the policy of committees. One familiar with the operations of protective committees is led to the conclusion that counsel commonly are more important in determining policies than are members of a committee. He who selects committees and determines or is influential in determining their policies can condition and perhaps control the whole reorganization process. He can pervert these processes to the selfish ends of those whose interests do not lie with the security holders; or he can bring into a position of dominance and power those who are genuinely interested in protecting the security holders rather than themselves.

The work of committees commonly entails preparation of proxies, deposit agreements, and solicitation literature. Whether or not particular provisions should be included in proxies or deposit agreements has been the decision of the attorney. He may insert in these agreements such a broad sweep of powers as to vest in the committee almost unlimited control and dominion over the deposited securities with few residual rights for the security holders. Furthermore, he may design these agreements to afford the committee members and their affiliated interests protection against the normal incidences of fiduciary obligations. In spite of the fact that courts have treated committee members as trustees, he may attempt to give the committees complete freedom to trade in the securities, to profit from the trust, and to act as freely as if they were launched on an entrepreneurial rather than a fiduciary venture. Or he may take steps to provide the security holders with protection against the overreaching or greed of the committee members by providing for independent review of their fees and expenses, by outlawing trading activities, and the like. The strategist and technician in all such matters is the lawyer. He can, if he likes, insulate his immediate client, the committee, from his ultimate client, the security holders; or he may provide his ultimate client with real protection.

Similarly in case of the solicitation material, the lawyer has been both draftsman and editor. If that literature has been illuminating and fair, it is the result of his scrutiny and supervision. If it has been false or misleading, or if material facts have been hidden in fine print, or the truth has been told in such devious ways as to be incomprehensible—and such examples are numerous—the blame may likewise be placed on him. He has disclosed what he deems wise, necessary, or expedient for the objectives of his client. These examples are merely illustrative. The prominence of the lawyer extends down to the close of reorganization and includes the negotiation and consummation of a plan of reorganization. He is in large measure responsible for its honesty, efficiency, and thoroughness. That is not to say that committee members, receivers, trustees, and the like do not have their own ideas. But the lawyer has given those ideas force and direction and has molded them to meet the immediate objectives of his client. And at times the client has abdicated, so to speak, leaving the lawyer in sole command.

I know of no reason why the lawyer should not take or assume this heavy responsibility. As an officer of the court he is accustomed to act in a fiduciary role. The traditions of his profession likewise make him peculiarly fitted for this exacting stewardship. But there has been a degeneration of the bar in these situations. Conflicts of interests have had their corroding influence. One of the foremost canons of professional ethics reads:

It is unprofessional to represent conflicting interests, except by express consent of all concerned given after a full disclosure of the facts. Within the meaning of this canon a lawyer represents conflicting interests, when in behalf of one client, it is his duty to contend for that which duty to another client requires him to oppose.

If the letter and the spirit of this canon were consistently observed, there would be little need for thoroughgoing reorganization reform. To state the matter otherwise, observance of the
letter and spirit of that canon would in and of itself constitute
the one most important and basic reorganization reform.

This is not to imply that a committee, receiver, trustee, or
creditor is not entitled to representation, though his motives
not be noble. Nor does it imply that there is not due a client
all the protection that the law affords him. A lawyer for a committee who outwits the lawyer for another committee by use of
legitimate reorganization strategy may not be deserving of a
gold star for public service. Neither is he subject to condemnation. But when as lawyer for one committee he outwits himself
as lawyer for another committee the process of degeneration
has set in.

I speak somewhat crudely. But these situations are not uncommon. At times, to be sure, the conflict is more tenuous and
subtle; it concerns itself with the spirit, not the letter of the
canon. A few illustrations will suffice.

Thus, where a house of issue has undertaken to discharge its
"moral obligation" to security holders by forming a protective
committee, we often find its counsel has become counsel to the
committee. It may seem at first blush to be a noble and laudatory
move on the part of the bankers to set up committees to espouse
the cause of those to whom the bankers have sold securities. And
as a concomitant it may seem wholly consistent for counsel to
the bankers to become counsel to the committees. But the vice
of the situation is that the objectives of the bankers are not
always compatible with the objectives of the investors. In fact,
we frequently see that one of the grave risks of the bankers is
that security holders may sue them in fraud and rescission for
misrepresentations on the sale of the securities. Bankers in control of a committee may be able to suppress or thwart such attempts. They may do so, for example, in case of rescission claims
by getting the securities deposited under agreements which

make withdrawal impossible except on such terms and at such times as the committee desires. Counsel to the bankers who is also counsel to the committee is thus in an ambiguous position. On the one side are the security holders; on the other side are the bankers. He cannot genuinely protect one without sacrificing the other. It is not difficult to see which client will receive the more conscientious treatment. After all, the committee is a transitory thing; the bankers are more or less permanent. Aggressive action against the latter, or failure to afford them adequate protection, may mean the loss of future retainers.

The consequences are similar where the management of the company forms a creditors' committee and counsel to the debtor becomes counsel to the committee. The conflict here may often be more acute and basic. In the first place the officers and directors may be legally responsible to the corporation for their wrongful acts. In the interests of the security holders represented by the committee it will be desirable and beneficial to have those claims asserted and collected for and on behalf of the estate. From the selfish viewpoint of the management it will be desirable to have any investigation or suit stifled. The lawyer in this dual position cannot serve both masters with undiluted loyalty. In fact we see, at times, counsel to the committee defending the officers and directors in suits brought against them by representatives of the estate. In the second place, the management, though not legally liable, may have been so incompetent or reckless as to make their ouster from the corporation not only desirable but necessary for the future protection of investors. In negotiation of a plan it may be that the interests of the investors would be served only by providing for a new management. But if counsel to the old management is negotiating the plan for the investors, it is easy to predict that that course will be unlikely.

It may be that in particular situations of this sort the transactions complained of were consummated as a consequence of the advice of this selfsame lawyer. Or the lawyer may have been one of those officers or directors. This of course aggravates the situation. In such cases he is beyond all doubt unqualified to represent security holders. But even though the attorney may not have been so directly associated with the particular transactions, his intimate relations with the management frequently give him a definite disability to represent security holders with vigor and undiluted loyalty.

We frequently find the former counsel for the company acting as counsel to the receiver or trustee in bankruptcy. The result of this position carries the gravest dangers to investors, since the attorney occupying this position determines the diligence with which assets will be collected, claims scrutinized, and causes of action prosecuted. If, as I have said, there are claims against officers or directors or their affiliates, the investigation of these claims may be stifled and assertion of them suppressed. This will be to the interest of the management; it will be against the interest of security holders.

The obvious and direct nature of these conflicts often makes counsel for the company or the bankers hesitant to appear formally as counsel to committees or to the receivers or trustees in bankruptcy during reorganization. In such instances, the attorney for the company or its banker is more likely to work backstage and refrain from appearing for these other parties as a matter of record. From this comparatively inconspicuous position he may be wielding great power in the formulation of policies. The distinction between this type of representation and formal appearance as counsel is purely technical. The conflict is not eliminated by refraining from appearing publicly as counsel to a committee or the receivers or trustees in bankruptcy. That is merely nondisclosure of a highly relevant fact.

At times lawyers undertake to represent both junior and senior interests in reorganizations. Thus, attorneys for short-term creditors or junior security holders will not infrequently be found representing first-mortgage bondholders. Such dual representation of conflicting interests means that the dominant client will receive protection; the subordinate client will suffer. The chances are that the latter will not receive that portion of the assets, earnings, and control of the new company which they justly deserve. The lawyer cannot press for a larger share for the junior interests without diluting the position of the senior claimants. Nor can he exact a full measure of protection for the senior claimants without putting the junior interests at a great disadvantage.

We find lawyers in reorganizations in still other conflicting positions when counsel to trustees under indentures permit themselves to become associated with other groups in the reorganization. Being the party who put into operation the machinery of foreclosure after a corporation defaulted upon its bonds, the indenture trustee was an essential cog in equity reorganization proceedings. For the foreclosure cleared off all liens and claims so that a reorganized company could start afresh, burdened by no obligations except those which the plan of reorganization expressly preserved.

This same indenture trustee would have had a number of duties before any need of reorganization arose. He may have had the duty to guard the release and substitution of collateral securing the bonds issued under the indenture. He may have had the duty to oversee the application of the moneys raised by the bond issue. For generally the offering circular describing an issue of bonds to prospective investors specifies the use to which the proceeds will be put. Control over application of the proceeds is essential in order that the investor shall obtain what he bargained for. But the investor cannot do this himself; it is a job for a single agency. And it is in the course of things a function which only a trustee can perform.

If a trustee has been derelict in performing these duties, and a number of other important obligations which the indenture may impose upon it, it is the duty of the protective committee representing the bondholders to compel the trustee to make restitution. This will not happen if counsel to the committee and to the trustee are identical. The result may be seriously prejudicial to the holders of the securities issued under the indenture. This is not an academic matter, for at times we observe counsel to the trustee, who is also counsel to the committee, in court defending the trustee in suits brought by the security holders represented by the committee.

Furthermore, the trustee owes duties to all bondholders. A committee commonly represents only a majority of the bondholders. The history of reorganization demonstrates that majorities are not adequate champions of the interest of minorities. The trustee who has thus become affiliated with the committee by virtue of counsel to the trustee becoming counsel to the committee, has thrown its weight on the side of the majority and is no longer an effective representative of those who have not deposited with the committee against the oppressive or unreasonable actions of the committee. Thus, in case of foreclosures, the committee will be interested in cutting down the bid upon foreclosure so as to give minorities a bare minimum. Nondepositors on the other hand are interested in a high bid to increase their distributive share. If the trustee is affiliated with the committee through common counsel, it is likely to accede to the committee's desires. And indeed, if such counsel gave the trustee an opinion that the committee's bid was unduly low, it would be acting in a manner prejudicial to its other client—the committee.

In a sense the matters which I mention are purely ethical ones. But they also have broader implications, since this frequent duality of the role of the lawyer in reorganizations has a definite impact on our social and economic life. Furthermore, it is symptomatic of a condition which pervades the field of finance. Thus, throughout the entire field there is a discernible trend for a few to move into a position of command and domination over financial empires. Lawyers have been their professional tutors. This is not necessarily grounds for condemnation of lawyers from a narrow professional point of view. It may merely indicate that the lawyers are serving assiduously the interests of their clients. But in view of the kind of system which has been created, it suggests that frequently the lawyer has been not a constructive but a corroding influence.

Throughout the entire field of finance one sees a system designed by lawyers, whereby persons win their profits by reason of the fact that they are on both sides of the bargain. This is the easy route to financial success. He who dominates the company can dictate the terms on which he will do business with it. There has been in large segments of business a contest to get that control because it means profits. The self-serving transactions out of which these profits are made are often involved, intricate, and mysterious. Their legal garb often is awe-inspiring or baffling. Only an analyst or lawyer may be able to fathom them. Actually, however, the fundamental problem is neither intricate nor involved. It is not one reserved for analysts, financiers, or lawyers. It is so simple that he who runs may read and understand. It is basically nothing more or less than a man serving at least two masters—security holders on the one hand; himself on the other. I say it is nothing more nor less than a man serving *at least* two masters, because more often than not finance has a plurality rather than a mere duality of interest. When that plurality or duality of interest enters, history has it that one of his several self-interests will be served first.

It is disturbing to see this condition in the field of business and finance. It is a danger sign to all those who are genuinely interested in preserving capitalism. It is particularly a dangerous trend because the lawyers, who are officers of the court, not only participate in it; they are at times its guiding and controlling influence. Those whose courage and vision might well carry the day in public interest and in the interests of investors are subservient to their dominant clients. They are willing not only to become, as Mr. Justice Stone has said, "the obsequious servant of business," [2] they have neglected the element of public trust inherent in their profession.

In sum, not only finance but also the bar needs reëducation on the simple and obvious principle that no man can well serve, directly or indirectly, two or more masters.

2. "The Public Influence of the Bar," an address delivered at the dedication of the Law Quadrangle, University of Michigan, June 15, 1934, published in the *Harvard Law Review*, Vol. XLVIII, No. 1 (November, 1934).

PART V

ADMINISTRATIVE GOVERNMENT

Americans like to think of their government as simply executive, legislative, and judicial. But it is not always so simple.

When the governing problem becomes complex, when a high degree of specialized technical knowledge is called for, as in the regulation of railroads, radio, stock exchanges, or public utilities, we find Congress resorting to a more modern device. A measure of legislative power, a measure of executive power, and a measure of judicial power are welded together in a single agency and assigned to the specialized task. We call the agency administrative because its task is to administer a law in which there are set down for it its basic policies, its duties, and its limitations.[1]

In the three branches of government the administrative agency finds not only the source of its power but its destiny as well. It obtains its authority and funds from the legislature, its performance is conditioned by the executive, and its decisions are reviewable by the judiciary.

Though its origins lie many years back, the administrative agency has attracted much notice in recent years because of its extensive use in dealing with regulatory problems. Thus "administrative government" becomes a new technique. Its nature and its problems are discussed in the following three selections.

1. "In terms of political theory, the administrative process springs from the inadequacy of a simple tripartite form of government to deal with modern problems. It represents a striving to adapt governmental technique, that still divides under three rubrics, to modern needs and, at the same time, to preserve those elements of responsibility and those conditions of balance that have distinguished Anglo-American government." *The Administrative Process*, James M. Landis (Yale University Press, 1938).

CHAPTER XX

VIRTUES OF THE ADMINISTRATIVE PROCESS

This talk was given before the Eighth Annual Forum on Current Problems sponsored by the *New York Herald Tribune,* October, 1938.

MOST of the issues of human and social relationships are not of the black and white variety. Right and wrong, sound and unsound, are elusive in the complexities of modern business and finance. For the Congress to endeavor to provide definite and precise formulae to govern many of the complex and intricate activities of business and finance would be as difficult as to endeavor to state what is a reasonable rate of speed for an automobile under any and all conditions. There are two sides to most of these problems. Several divergent interests are always pressing at least ostensibly plausible claims. These various and diverse interests can seldom be neatly balanced against the standard of the common good by means of a precise and inflexible formula. If such an attempt were made, the Congress would be faced with the choice of a strait jacket of outright prohibition on the one hand, or a do-nothing policy on the other hand. Both of these are un-American in their philosophy. It is the American tradition to insist on keeping to an irreducible minimum regimentation in any form, particularly a "thou shalt not" regimentation. It is likewise the American tradition that our government be a responsive, as well as a responsible agency—ready, willing, and able to assume a position of leadership at those points where self-help would lead to chaos. For these reasons the Congress has merely isolated, not solved, many important problems. Their solution has been delegated to administrative agencies such as the S.E.C.

It is true that if the Congress did more than isolate these

problems, business and finance would have certainty; but it would frequently be certainty so arbitrary as to be loathsome. But when the Congress isolates a problem and sets up standards for its solution, it leaves play for discretion. Discretion, tempered by fairness and reasonableness and protected by constitutional safeguards, permits elasticity and flexibility. Case by case, group by group, problems can be solved with particular reference to the merits of each. Property rights and—even more important—liberty and freedom can thus be more readily protected.

Take the case of the stock exchanges. Theoretically Congress might have provided in the Securities Exchange Act of 1934 prescriptions for every phase of their activities. That would have entailed spelling out the minutiae of regulation in the statute. But such a step would have been a legislative blight. To avoid that, Congress wisely left many important problems for future solution. It permitted the S.E.C. to deal with the problems of exchanges on an hourly or daily or weekly basis; to move forward with speed where haste was necessary; to meet changing financial and economic conditions at whatever rate the exigencies of the situation demanded. The same philosophy persists under the Public Utility Holding Company Act of 1935, which empowers us to administer in detail the broad mandate laid down by Congress over utility holding companies and their subsidiaries; and under the Securities Act of 1933 which is aimed at requiring those who make public offerings of securities to tell the truth about their wares.

Much of the shirt-sleeve work of government is done by administrative agencies, such as the S.E.C. Much of the responsibilities of government is carried by them. Under democratic forms of government, they have been increasing in importance and dignity. They have become more and more the outposts of capitalism; they have been given increasingly larger patrol duties, lest capitalism by its own greed, avarice, or myopia destroy itself.

The virtue of the administrative process is its ability to deal with technical, debatable, undefinable, or imponderable matters in a discretionary manner. It provides a realistic and sound alternative to hard and inflexible rules which proceed on the false assumption that right or wrong, black or white constitute the only choice. But beyond that it permits of action not only case by case but by rules. A rule can be expanded, contracted, or repealed in light of changed conditions or new experience. A formula fixed by legislative act tends to become more difficult to dislodge. Furthermore, the power to make rules means the power to deal with emergency situations, directly and with dispatch, in terms of minutes or hours rather than months or years. In a dynamic, fast-moving economic system responsible government must have a reserve of such powers if it is to save capitalism from its own complexities.

Wise government exercises such powers hesitatingly; intelligent business makes a free exercise of such powers both unnecessary and undesirable. With the Old Guard philosophy dominating stock exchanges, a fulsome exercise of such powers under the Securities Exchange Act of 1934 was an imminent necessity. But with a new management recognizing by deed, as well as by word, that such exchanges are public institutions impressed with a public trust, a fulsome exercise of such powers would not be necessary. Likewise, with a utility industry quickening to the great possibilities for healthy and sound reconstruction under the Public Utility Holding Company Act of 1935, opportunities for individual initiative should and will be accorded first place; governmental propulsion second place. In the American way of life, individual initiative will always remain preëminent. But in the American way of life, governmental fiat plays its important role—where self-help breaks down or where inaction thwarts the popular will. Fulsome powers of administrative agencies are reserved for those occasions.

In all of this there is no specter of unbridled discretion, no

element of dictatorship. Congress in all of these situations specifies the standards which are to be applied. The administrative
agency has no powers but the powers granted in the statute. Its
rule-making power is circumscribed by the law itself. And the
action of these agencies is quite properly subject to review by
the courts. Furthermore, these agencies are not only responsive
to the Executive, they are responsible to the Congress from
which comes not only their powers but their appropriations.

But administrative agencies have mandates as well as discretionary powers. Under the Securities Exchange Act of 1934, it
is our bounden duty to stamp out pools and manipulation.
That has been our constant endeavor. Under the Public Utility
Holding Company Act of 1935, we have no discretion but to
enforce what the President properly called not the "death
sentence" but the "health sentence." That in effect says (1)
that holding companies must be restricted geographically, thus
permitting state or regional development; (2) that holding
companies can have "children and grandchildren" but not
more distant relatives. Our job is to administer these laws as
they are written, not to nullify them by inaction nor to trade
out at the conference table decisions made in legislative halls.
This is the mandate required by the trusteeship of public office.
The fact that I personally agree with the philosophy of the
"health sentence" under the Holding Company Act is wholly
immaterial. The task of the administrator is to offer fairness and
reasonableness in fulfilling his oath of office. To ask for that
should be unnecessary; to ask for more than that should be
effrontery.

Administrative government is here to stay. It is democracy's
way of dealing with the overcomplicated social and economic
problems of today. The fact that it is here to stay presents two
important challenges for the future. In the first place, it offers
a challenge to business and finance to provide the progressive
leadership which must go hand in hand with administrative
government. For it is already clear that if these administrative

powers are to be exercised sparingly, enlightened business need only take the lead. And if these powers are to be exercised wisely, enlightened business must work at the round table rather than in the courts. Some cartoonists to the contrary notwithstanding, these agencies are designed not to twist the tail of business but to aid business in assuming a new position of leadership. There is no reason why the men of action and idealism in business and in government may not jointly forge the destiny of our economic system on the anvils of reason and in the fires of national ambition. There is no reason why the heat of controversy cannot be taken out of the business-government relationship. Neither side can make the progress which the nation demands unless the task of creating issues is discarded and all energies are devoted to the solution of problems.

The permanency of administrative government presents secondly a challenge to America to place the public service high in its scale of values. For the character and rate of our progress depend upon the quality of men in public service. It demands a development along the lines envisoned by President Roosevelt of a new American career service, reorganized along sound business lines and creating the profession of administrative government. A prominent businessman recently told me that his one fear was that the quality of these administrative agencies would be no better than the quality of business management. We all know the difficulty of keeping any institution—whether public or private—free of internal decay and institutional paralysis. For administrative agencies the need is a constant infiltration from the ranks of youth. America has the tradition of sending its sons into business and the professions. It does not have the tradition of sending its sons into government. Other countries can afford to take a few years of the lives of their sons for military purposes. Democratic government can afford to ask its sons, who by training and tradition can assume a position of leadership, to give at least a few years of their lives in times of peace for the task of preserving capitalism and democracy.

CHAPTER XXI

PROBLEMS OF ADMINISTRATION

This talk was given before the Yale Club of Washington, D.C., in April, 1936.

A LIBRARIAN of one of the Western states was recently telling of her difficulties in keeping intact a 1,000-volume library which she had installed in the state prison. She had designated as prison librarian one of the inmates—an ex-minister. On one of her trips of inspection she discovered that 500 of the 1,000 volumes had disappeared. She remonstrated to the prison librarian and told him frankly of her disgust at his negligent supervision of the library. He apologized profusely and then stated, "Madam, whenever you get several hundred men together you are bound to find among them a couple of crooks."

It was not precisely on that theory that Congress, in pursuance of its considered and informed judgment, enacted the Securities Act of 1933 and the Securities Exchange Act of 1934. Had the problem been one of dealing solely with crooks, it would have been a simpler problem. But the task was not merely to catch crooks. In dealing with the fundamental problems of corporation finance the technique required was to establish in financial practices higher standards of ethics and morality to the end that investors might be protected and the public interest served. It had become clear to all attentive observers of finance, including the better element of business, that those higher standards of conduct were essential if the capitalistic system was to survive. Those engaged in manipulation were using other people's money; those managing corporations were managing other people's money; those seeking new capital were seeking other people's money. The demand was insistent that the activities of such persons be conditioned by the standards of fiduciaries or trustees. To that end the Securities Act and the Securities Exchange Act make measurable progress. They supply for the first time standards of conduct, welcomed by those who never desired or who certainly no longer desire to sacrifice ethics for expediency, but who in the competition and pressure of high finance drifted into the loose habits of the market place.

The Securities Act of 1933 calls for the full disclosure of material and relevant facts concerning the issuer before securities are sold. The Securities Exchange Act of 1934 sets up administrative machinery over stock exchanges (and to a lesser extent over the over-the-counter markets) with a view of supplying reliable and current information concerning securities traded in on the exchanges and also with the view of preventing manipulative practices in such securities. It also requires adequate and truthful disclosure in regard to the solicitation of proxies and transactions by officers, directors, and large stockholders in the stock of their corporation. Through the disclosure requirements of these statutes and of the rules and regulations thereunder, the Commission has started on the task of policing the securities markets and of establishing standards for officers, directors, bankers, accountants, and other experts who make or contribute to the representations which are made about securities.

The new codes of conduct established by these laws are not exclusively or essentially for crooks but for the run of the professions of banking, management, accountancy, and the law. Successful administration will be measured not by the number of crooks who are incarcerated but by the number of leaders of the professions who either through compulsion or conversion respond to the insistent demand that those who have the powers of fiduciaries likewise assume the responsibilities. As a matter of fact, it is not too much to expect that if the first hundred of each of these professions seriously undertook to make permanent the fundamental changes in codes of conduct which this legis-

lation envisages, the most difficult of the problems of administrative control over finance would be solved. For it must be
remembered that they are the ones who not only handle the
bulk of the most important financing but also set the fashion
which those of lesser lights follow. Until that transformation
takes place, administrative control over finance will not have
been successful. And until such transformation takes place,
one of the greatest hazards to any administrative agency in this
field is that it will expend its energies and resources in pursuing
the lesser lights whose importance is chiefly in the fact that
they, like the poor, will be ever with us.

The factors that impede such transformation are numerous.
Only two need be mentioned. In the first place morals in the
field of finance have been too frequently determined by what
actually prevails in practice. Once the tradition becomes established, lawyers, bankers, accountants tend to bow to it without
question or hesitancy. It becomes the proper thing to do because
it has always been done or because everyone else is doing it.
The conventions of the various professions are too often accepted without inquiry as to their social or economic consequences. The accepted way of doing things becomes the proper
way of doing them. The ethics of the situation are subtly adjusted to conform to the requirements of the tradition. These
traditions are chains which bind fast these professions to the
ancient order of finance. They constitute one of the most potent
imponderables which promises to delay the advent of any new
era either in practices or in ethics.

In the second place concessions to any new order which are
made will tend to be made solely in the interest of expediency.
It is idle to say that the requirements of business are constantly
going to be determined in light of the requirements of the
public interest. The history of business reveals no such paramount importance of the public interest. Concessions to the
public interest are frequently made. But the immediate requirements of management will tend to bow to the larger public

interest only when necessary and to the extent that is necessary. It would be against all experience with psychological facts to expect sudden and permanent conversion. This in turn means that the bare minimum required by the recent legislation may be the maximum to be expected. This in turn means that once those bare minima are established they will tend to become a routine and hence a mere formality. They will serve as the offering at the altar of the public interest. Thus, once professional scriveners are developed it would be no great step to be able to make disclosure of material facts so blurred and so obtuse as to carve the heart out of the Securities Act. That is to say, when disclosure of truth becomes an art and when avoidance of disclosure becomes a game, the essence and spirit of the new legislation will have become subverted although the formalities may have been fully satisfied. The immediate requirements of business will frequently make that objective seem to be a desirable one. For that reason no sudden transformation to any new era of finance can be confidently expected.

These matters are of importance in any administration of these acts. They mean that since social change is slow, an administrative agency would be innocuous rather than effective should it succumb to reduction of its requirements to mere routine and formality. Nowhere as in the field of finance is the requirement of flexibility of administrative action more clear. There are several phases of this problem.

In the first place, financial practices are not standard. They are varied and complex. They change constantly. They cannot be reduced to simple formulae. The requirements of business prevent it. The ingenuity of man forestalls it. It will be only the aggressive administrative agency which can keep pace with these developments. When it comes to disclosure of the truth about securities, forms get outmoded. What was adequate for investors under the original situation becomes inadequate as a result of evolution of financial practices. Somewhat the same thing is true of practices involved in the distribution of securities. New and different types of manipulation appear, more subtle in influence, more effective in result than older and grosser forms which we are quick to denounce. Alertness and vigilance supply the essential ingredients of thoroughgoing administration at this point.

In the second place, effective control calls not for the slower and heavier method of judicial decision but for the more subtle and more sensitive control of daily administrative direction. This is not to say that studied efforts should be made to prevent parties from having their rights established by the courts of the land. Rather it means that adequate and effective methods of administration have never been and can never be fashioned through the judicial process. The residual group of cases susceptible of control by that process is insignificant. The battle will be lost through the fearfully cumbersome and indirect processes of the courts even assuming judicial approval or indulgence. Pools are run in weeks or months. Quick and immediate action is necessary. The most effective procedure will commonly be immediate investigation and disclosure with all the pressure which pitiless publicity entails, before the public is mulcted. That is to say, the battle will be won only by constantly progressive administrative standards quickly and surely applied and delicately adjusted to requirements of particular cases. Lawsuits and prosecutions will supply the final chapter to the story. In the interim preventive administrative action will reduce the losses to a minimum. The judicial process can thus be reserved to mark those significant milestones of achievement or those crossroads that indicate the direction in which constitutional control may be found. Thus it is that the most significant victories which will be won for investors will be found in those unheralded and perhaps unknown administrative sorties which prevent the happening of events which prove to be so disastrous to investors.

In the third place, this slowness of adaptability calls for administrative control which is constantly testing the validity of the fundamental hypotheses upon which our financial practices and our financial organization rest. All of us are prone to accept the validity of the normal and traditional manner of effecting financial transactions. The institutional method becomes the proper method. We are slow to question its adequacy or propriety.

The administrative task involves, at least in part, constant inquiry into the validity of these underlying assumptions. This is necessary (1) so that we may be certain that the traditional methods are not harboring a host of evils and abuses which an uncritical eye would fail to see; (2) so that we may be constantly ahead in the program of progressive reform to the end not only that we may be prepared for further change but also that we may anticipate change and pave the way for it by easy but direct steps. Such an approach not only gives vitality to our whole enforcement machinery, but also prepares us for the exigencies of the years which lie immediately ahead.

I need not multiply examples of the things I have in mind, for you are all familiar with them. Margin trading is one. A thoughtful student of the subject cannot fail to be impressed with the naïveté in the common assumption that margin trading is as essential to our welfare as is the Constitution. It may be. But it is an open rather than a closed question. The ramifications of that subject have never been adequately studied. I am confident that any administrative agency will be face to face with that problem ere it goes far in advance of the solution to the problem of security speculation and security manipulation. Constant and attentive consideration of the incidences of abolition of margin trading becomes essential for the immediate and long-range program of control in this field.

Another instance is the problem of the corporate trustee. We are prone to accept the validity and adequacy of the trust indentures under which bonds, debentures, and notes are issued and pursuant to which the duties and obligations of the trustee are defined. The customary habit of thought precludes any serious questioning of the adequacy of that instrument from the point of view of investors. Such instruments are manufactured in law offices out of the traditional legal boiler plate which generations of lawyers have made standard. They are drawn with neatness and precision. They are administratively effective. Corporate trustees can do business under them. In other words, the system seems to work. But trustees acting thereunder can hardly be called trustees. They are stakeholders with immunity clause after immunity clause insulating them from liability and divesting them of responsibility. Yet the tradition that this is the proper way of doing it is so strong that the question, "Why should not a corporate trustee be a trustee?" is stilled, and the question, "Can we not devise a system where the investors under such instruments will have a real guardian and protector of their interest?" is seldom asked. Such questions are not asked because the traditional manner of doing things tends to foreclose critical analysis.

One further instance is the conventions of accountants. These tend to become fixed and ritualistic. They are likely to degenerate into shibboleths. Instead of being descriptive tags, accounting terms too often become vague and indefinite words of art, not pungent with meaning, not vital with significance. Instead of accurately reflecting the true financial condition of the company and the state of its accounts, they too often result in devitalizing the facts by forcing them into a mold which only traditional and conventional practices can justify. Accountancy at times may seem to be faced with a choice of two equally undesirable alternatives. The one is to standardize practices into a fixed and inflexible formula. The other is to forsake all conventions and make the formula fit the facts. Neither of these is the desirable alternative. But up to date, little attention has been given by accountants to the problem of determining what the minimum or maximum acceptable accounting principles really are and what guides should be left for the residual cases which cannot be forced into any fixed mold. In this connection, certificates of accountants have tended to be accumulations of weasel words—evasive, general, and meaningless. The true function of the public accountant—to subject to an impartial mind the accounting practices and policies of issuers—has too often been lost sight of. The consequence has been that protection to investors which might be afforded by the certificate has been sadly lacking. To be sure, some improvement has been made since the advent of these statutes. But the easy course is to succumb to the insistent demands for certainty and simplicity and to reduce the accountants' conventions to ready-made and fixed formulae. It is this course which an administrative agency must resist. Effective resistance must take the form of constantly reappraising and testing the soundness and propriety of those conventions which tradition and practice have fashioned but which experience in the protection of investors shows to be frequently not only meaningless but misleading.

There are those who feel that there can never be effective social control over finance. They can cite in support agencies which started with promise but which became innocuous or ineffective either as a result of ineptitude or as a consequence of being captured and controlled by those whom they were supposed to control. But with the growing public and professional recognition of the permanent importance of these programs of reform and with the measurable progress already made, effective social control over finance becomes more than a possibility. If it ends in failure, I am confident of one thing—that it will not be due to lack of persistent, honest, and aggressive efforts.

CHAPTER XXII

ADMINISTRATIVE GOVERNMENT
IN ACTION

This speech was given before a public-relations group at the Lotos Club in New York in November, 1938.

ONE can easily recall the time when government was synonymous with red tape, delay, chairwarmers, and the inefficiency of officialdom. Nor did we expect anything different. Some were wont to say that government was our great public futility. And many were more or less content to have it so. The notion of a government official was something like the ostrich who, coming across six other ostriches with their heads buried in the sand, exclaimed, "Where is everybody, anyway?"

Now I think we all can detect a change, subtle and imponderable as it seems at times. A change in attitude toward government; a change in attitude in government.

The tidal waves of intense nationalism, the explosions of racial and class emotions, the violent economic swings which swept the world enlisted all of us in the common cause of making democratic government work, of making it an increasingly vital force for order and unity, a servant of a free people, an active working partner (not a sleeping partner) of capitalism and private enterprise. That led to a real demand for adequate power in democratic government to deal daily or even hourly with pressing problems. The relentless pressures of modern times demanded that government do a streamlined job. It meant no sham performance which might create confidence through the illusion of progress. It meant action—not as an end in itself, but action which was constructive and curative. And for those ends it meant men of training and ability who were willing to take chances of being wrong; who were willing to assume a position of leadership along with business in finding hardheaded solutions to practical problems; who were willing to apply new regulations in the spirit of reasonableness so that restrictive rules would prove to be constructive influences.

The vehicle for performance of this daily work of government has been more and more the administrative agency—that thing which lawyers and publicists sometimes delight in painting as some sort of three-headed legal monster. Such agencies are the repositories of much of the workaday powers of government. Partly because of the newness of their form, partly because they had thrust upon them in so many instances pioneering jobs, the administrative agencies are most critically judged. Today a thousand critical eyes appraise the performance of each of these agencies on the basis of their daily routine.

In important segments of business and finance these agencies, such as the S.E.C., now share with private management certain definite responsibilities. I have spoken often of the trusteeship of management to the stockholders, of dominant groups to minority groups in business. And I have spoken often of the fiduciary responsibilities of the elders in business and finance, responsibilities that were inherent in their powerful positions of leadership. That type of trusteeship is as real as the trusteeship of public office. But it is only fitting, perhaps, that in discussing the business of government I take a moment to define those standards of trusteeship which must prevail in public office. The trusteeship of the public official is something beyond the simple honesty of spurning such subsidiary emoluments as may go with the office or of avoiding exploitation of the circumstances that may attend the performance of official duties. In the administrative agency, particularly, the standard of trusteeship goes beyond these elementary concepts. It demands a strict devotion to the law both in letter and spirit. It demands a fearless respect for facts, regardless of pressures or consequences. It requires a mastery of technicalities. It demands complete independence of—yet intelligent, official sympathy for—the group being regulated. It demands dispensation of reasonableness and fairness to all alike. It entails a high order of law administration so that the statute being administered becomes a constructive force for progress.

Both the trusteeship in business and the trusteeship in government have high standards of performance. Both have a responsibility not only one to the other but to the public. Jointly they can provide a constructive, dynamic influence in the cause of capitalism and the profit system.

The responsibilities of administrative agencies and of business demand statesmanship on both sides. Thus, in the case of stock exchanges, the point where self-determination should cease and direct regulation by government should commence must usually be determined not by arbitrary action but by neatly balanced judgment and discretion on both sides. The administrative agency plays a singularly important role in that process. It may be the propelling force for action where institutional paralysis of business has set in. Or it may be quietly and unobtrusively performing merely a residual role with its presence felt but not seen. The latter is ideally the role; the former is too frequently the necessity.

But whichever may be the role of the administrative agency it is constantly operating at the technical level. In fact the administrative agency is the technician of government. The job of administrative agencies like the S.E.C. is for the most part a technical job. Although much of its language and nearly all of its actions are necessarily the language and actions of the law, the agency's thinking is in terms of accounting, engineering, finance, and business. This follows, of course, from the place of these administrative agencies in our scheme of things. Their roots lie really in the problems that flow from the great industrial development of the country. They find their origin in public recognition of the fact that a national problem exists in connection with such industries as railroads, stock exchanges, radio, telephone and telegraph, public utilities and aeronautics, to name only a few. These matters do not suggest lawbooks or litigation. They suggest, rather, active businesses, nationwide industries, dynamos, transmission lines, rights of way, bond issues, mergers, annual reports, independent audits, payrolls, salaries, employees, and a host of others which taken together constitute American business and finance. They are the day-to-day work of administrative agencies.

Performance of this technical job involves two functions—first, finding of facts; second, determination of policy. Factual inquiries constitute the leg work of these agencies. In their results lie the real bases for administrative action. Those inquiries are usually quiet and unobtrusive. Frequently, however, they entail stepping on another's toes. Relentless search for facts in discharge of official duties is therefore not always pleasant. But pleasant or unpleasant, the test must always be relevancy to official duties. The approach cannot be that of a mere historian who is opening closed chapters of past conduct for purposes of research or idle curiosity. But even the unsavory past frequently has immediate bearing on today's problems. To that extent, the administrative agency often has disagreeable tasks. But without the relentless search for facts, the daily work of administrative agencies would degenerate to arbitrary and capricious levels. Without it, there would be no assurance of technical proficiency.

Some time ago an acquaintance of mine was facing the prospect of being called as an important witness at a public hearing in connection with an investigation being made in Washington. He was uneasy and nervous. He was not sleeping well. He had many advisers who were trying to give him comfort. He had retained lawyers who had polished and repolished statements for his use. But in spite of this great preparation on all flanks, he was still perturbed. And he said, "What shall I do?" To experts, perhaps the advice I gave would seem naïve and amateurish, for I said, "Forget about your lawyers. Search your heart, your mind, your files and then get on the stand and tell the truth."

As respects performance of our official duties, such insistence on disclosure of facts is the keystone to many of our achievements. Without it, we could not have effectively prevented the sale of millions upon millions of fraudulent securities. Without it, we could not have prevented or penalized many manipulations or jiggles of stock on exchanges. Without it, we would be in no intelligent position to ascertain what amount of inflation or water existed on the books of some holding companies. Without it, we could not intelligently pass on reorganization plans which conceal past financial wizardry for which investors are now paying. Without it, we could not have prevented the sheer exploitation in some instances of business by finance. The price of doing these official chores is at times the charge of being a snooper. But the search for facts, surrounded by essential constitutional safeguards and void of vicious practices such as wire tapping or star-chamber proceedings, affords some assurance not only of technical proficiency but of reasonableness and informed judgment on the part of administrative agencies. Equally important, it gives some guarantee to business that facts rather than theories will be the foundation of administrative policy.

The formulation of policy, the second of the functions of administrative agencies, presents somewhat different considerations. In administrative proceedings against, or involving, an individual or a company, the application of the law to the facts is relatively easy. But in broader situations finding the facts frequently is the prelude to intensely difficult determinations of policy. To put the matter another way—we catch a broker jiggling a stock on an exchange. The facts are clear; the law is clear; our duty is clear; the decision is easy. But frequently Congress has not itself laid down a prohibition or prescribed a precise formula for solution of a problem. Rather it has left its solution in the light of prescribed standards to an agency like the S.E.C. Such was the way in which Congress left with us the problem of short sales. The policy back of such delegation by Congress is a sound one both from the viewpoint of government and of business. If Congress supplied in a statutory formula precise answers to many of these problems, it would be placing business in a legislative strait jacket. The statutes would then become legislative prescriptions of black and white, sound and unsound, right and wrong. Many problems of American business cannot be answered in such facile manner. Unsound capital structures of holding companies frequently can be spotted at first glance. But precise statutory definition of sound capital structures would be wholly arbitrary. The precise extent of the geographical expanse of a public-utility holding company might be arbitrarily determined by legislative fiat. But its general application would be most apt to fly in the face of engineering facts. A statutory formula for short selling would be possible. But today I doubt if anyone has the omniscience to defend the ultimate validity of any one formula against all vicissitudes of the stock market under all circumstances. And so it goes for security issues of operating utility companies, for dividend policies of utility companies, for stabilization of prices of securities, for material facts to be disclosed in prospectuses, and the like. If Congress undertook to settle all of these problems by legislative fiat, business would have its certainty and definiteness. But business would also be heavily afflicted by a legislative blight.

And so it is that responsible business cannot join in derisive comments or attacks on what some delight in calling "government by discretion." All realize to an increasing extent that the "elbow room" which administrative agencies have in applying these restraints and controls is a boon to business and to the public alike.

Realization of this fact likewise points to the desirability of business and government working coöperatively at the technical levels of these problems. Where Congress has left instructions to an agency like the S.E.C., there is no alternative but to proceed to carry them out. But where Congress has supplied merely the standards for action and has left elbow room for the nature and extent of action by the administrative agency, practical wisdom can frequently be acquired through a fusion of the energies of government and business on the technical aspects of the problem. For this reason both government and business can profit immeasurably by the use of the "round table" technique. In that way can facts from the laboratories of business be utilized in the government's workshop.

But there is another phase of the problem which has commonly been overlooked. Under our administrative form of government, the preservation for business of the principle of self-determination is both possible and practicable. As I have said, an agency like the S.E.C. has elbow room in dealing with some of the problems which Congress has assigned it. Flexibility and discretion are both provided in, and circumscribed by, the law. For every grant of power there is a compensating restraint on its use. Where abuse of power may creep in, there is opportunity for review or control from existing superior authority. Congress prescribes both the objectives and the standards. We can change neither. If we attempt to do so, the courts quite properly can rebuke us. But occasionally Congress has given such an agency little or no discretion except as to method. In certain instances that discretion offers the choice between direct action by the government or joint and coöperative action by the government and the particular business being regulated. Some have regarded the very existence of such alternatives as alarming examples of "government by discretion." But they are prone to overlook a very fundamental consideration; namely, that Congress by that method has preserved for business a great deal of the democratic principle of self-determination.

We hear that it is good or bad, better or worse. One day there is a "split," the next day a "rapprochement." These are symptoms of transition. They do not describe the permanent level of the business-government relationship. As a matter of practical functioning, business and government cannot remain on a good-or-bad relationship, except as respects violations of the law. I think there has been a growing recognition of the supremacy of the law, a recognition of the fact that once the broad national policies have been embodied in statutory law, the business-government relationship moves out of the realm of controversy and debate. It ceases to be an issue; it moves into the province of the technicians. The problems must be worked out, under the law, but in business terms. They are to be worked out not on the political but on the technical level. That not only can be done, it is being done.

I have already referred to the experience of the S.E.C. with the utility industry under the Holding Company Act. Since the passage of that Act, the S.E.C., in contemplating the objectives of the integration provisions of the statute, has continuously looked toward a broad voluntary program under which the utility industry would, over a period of years and through normal evolutionary channels, reshape itself to meet the standards of the law. But such visions were often obliterated by the cries of "death sentence," "confiscation," and "ruination." And it was not until we had cut our way through a phalanx of protecting legal strategists that we were able to sit down with the operating heads of the companies and work out our joint problems, not as adversaries, but as technicians bent on getting done the job which Congress had prescribed.

I have said this on other occasions and repeat it here with due apologies. It may be nothing but a mere coincidence; yet once the lawyer disappeared as the intermediary between us and business, the job began to roll. Once the business executive and we could sit down across the table and talk, not through an interpreter but directly, things began to happen. Once the phrase "without benefit of counsel" became popular, things began to happen. I say this most hesitatingly because of my respect for my profession. But now that businessmen have moved their engineers and investment bankers up front, the illusion of motion has disappeared and a sense of real progress is present. The business executive, the engineer, the investment banker has no smaller supply of acumen and ingenuity than the lawyer. But he does seem to lack some of the mental qualms of the legal theorists—yes, even as respects the dangers which are supposed to rest in administrative agencies. To business, the administrative agency offers a practical and realistic approach to those business problems which are of national scope and public concern. The businessman is more and more cognizant of the fact that for effective work on at least the policy phases of these problems the best way of avoiding red tape is not to bring it with him when he catches the train or plane to Washington.

To sum up, I have tried to give you some insight into the nature of this new governmental creature we call the administrative agency. It is the mechanism of democratic government whereby capitalism can discipline and preserve itself. It is equipped to meet business on business terms. It is in its infancy, but it is here to stay. And its future development will in large part be molded by business. With joint action it becomes an efficient business force; acting alone it becomes a police force. The choice rests in the hands of business.

Yet, in discussing it, I do not want to be guilty of the same overemphasis that characterizes so many of its critics. I do not want to leave the impression that the development of the administrative agency in any way alters the fundamentals of democratic government. Nor do I want to leave the impression that the administrative agency is the all-important factor in effective government. For government goes far beyond agencies and bureaus and commissions. In the broad sweep of things, the verities of democracy remain. The system by which this country has always run itself rests on the fundamental thesis that the ultimate power is vested in the voting population. That principle is the cornerstone of democracy. It is that principle which we must defend. We hear a great deal about threats to democracy—about the dangers of bureaucracy, the need for effective opposition, the safeguards of vigorous minorities. All of these have their validity but they are all subsidiary to one basic fact. That is that the key man in democratic government is the voter. To protect democracy we must protect the voter, and that is a problem which intimately concerns all of us.

It is an old saying that if the people understand a question, you can pretty well depend upon them to decide it the right way. That is still a sound principle. It is particularly evident when the issue of good government is presented. But the democratic process assumes that the individual voter—the farmer, the factory worker, the housewife, the clerk—will be able adequately to comprehend and grasp the larger questions at issue —questions many times as complicated as the simple question of good government, or the problem of catching crooks. Yet the past twenty years have seen the issues grow in complexity and multiplicity, until they threaten to outstrip the capacity of the voter to evaluate them. The voting population tends to get further and further away from an ability to understand the questions which, under the democratic process, it is called upon to answer. This is a problem which the country's media of information have sought to meet. Witness the enormous amount of space in newspapers and periodicals, and the time on the radio given over to national affairs. Witness the columnists, the commentators, the polls of public opinion. Unquestionably this increased discussion of national problems has been a great service. But there are great portions of the population scarcely reached by the usual carriers of information. These are the segments of the voting population which cause concern. For the voter who has gotten out of touch with the issues of the day is a weak voter. And a weak electorate means a weak democracy.

The danger is not merely that the poorly informed voter will not wield the ballot wisely. It is that he is prey to those who would control the ballot. He is the easy victim of the false issue and the trick slogan. We have all of us seen such efforts—the use of traditional symbols and catch phrases for the purpose of stating—but frequently of misstating—in oversimplified terms complex and vital questions. But we are prone to underestimate the undermining effect of such methods. Yet we have only to look abroad to learn their ultimate stopping place. We tend to forget that every time we fail to clarify an issue for the electorate and use instead the political catchword method we make the electorate that much easier prey for some future political witch-doctor. Enlightenment is the sure antidote for political witchery. Democracy will be as vigorous as it is informed. It is the responsibility of all of us who want to preserve our democratic system to see that the country genuinely understands the issues before it.

The national problems of the future will be economic and business problems. They will lie in the realm of industry and finance. They will be complex, and they will be as difficult for the layman to comprehend as for the expert to solve. But our own resourcefulness can match them. They need not overcome us nor need they destroy our heritage of freedom. To meet the challenge of the future we need to arm ourselves in two ways.

In the first place, we must continuously perfect our methods of transmitting facts, of analyzing facts, of interpreting facts. I speak of facts, not propaganda—elementary facts on basic issues. Only in this way can we have an informed electorate, alive to the issues, aware of the country's need, and sensitive to its dangers. Without such continuous education in terms of facts, democracy cannot continue as a vital force.

In the second place, we must make certain that we continuously perfect a governmental technique which can deal effectively, on a daily or even an hourly basis, with the nation's industrial problems. This means, in part, a professional career service in administrative government. It means, in part, government keeping abreast of the changing problems—indeed taking the lead—not, puffing and panting, strenuously trying to catch up with a problem that has years or even months of a head start. It also means a permanent machinery for meeting industry on its own ground and at the technical level, so that hardheaded solutions of practical problems may be readily had in tune with progressive principles.

In both these steps a progressive administrative agency by development of its traditions can play some part. Perhaps it can demonstrate in miniature the art or technique of coping with fundamental economic and social forces. If it can, it should help build into the national consciousness a confidence in the ability of democracy to be the master of its own fate.

PART VI

EDUCATION IN GOVERNMENT AND LAW

CHAPTER XXIII

CHALLENGE TO YOUTH

In June, 1938, Mr. Douglas received an honorary degree of Doctor of Laws from his alma mater, Whitman College at Walla Walla, Washington. The following statement is from his address at the Commencement exercises.

WHITMAN has an unusual capacity for turning out sentimental alumni. Whitman did that to me and it is about to do that to you. From the viewpoint of the sentimental alumnus the primary objective of his alma mater should be to remain on the pinnacle of educational triumph which it achieved in his days. Its primary achievements were made during his four college years. The members of this class, as duly imbued with the Whitman spirit as I am, doubtless think that Whitman achieved its greatest accomplishments in 1938. But they are in error; it was in 1920. My classmates and I can prove it—which may go to show that as the years roll by the sentimental alumnus becomes more sentimental and hence more of a problem to his college.

But though the rosy mist which envelops the sentimental alumnus becomes denser and denser with the years, the pleasure which it excites increases. It has the neat psychological advantage of obliterating all traces of unpleasant things and of keeping sharply in focus the others. It has a rare capacity for preserving in *status quo* the things that once were. Whitman to me means all of those who were on the faculty in 1920. Those men still teach full time in the Whitman which is mine. In my Whitman there are no new appointments to the faculty; no alterations in curriculum. Gaunt and bleak Prentiss Hall is still inhabited by boisterous, carefree first-year men. Reynolds Hall (inhabited by extraordinarily beautiful women) is still guarded in hawklike manner by an extremely vigilant and efficient Dean of Women. Whitman still stands supreme, even though beaten in football some hundred-odd points by its more professional opponent. Whitman, like life, is exacting. Whitman means heartaches and struggles. But Whitman also means life and hope to those insistent on not being submerged by either economic or social limitations. It also means, to rich and poor alike, rare opportunity for individual development and growth. That Whitman may be nothing but a mirage; but it is mine. Your mirage is doubtless different from mine. But I am sure it is nonetheless pleasant.

As detached observers rather than as sentimental alumni, we can understand why Whitman has such a strong grip on us. It is due to those unique and substantial attributes which this distinguished institution has. Educationally, it is independent. It does not succumb to passing educational fancies. The waves of educational "isms" do not deflect it from its course. When expansion and publicity are popular, Whitman remains quiet and unperturbed, mindful of the fact that the crickets in the field always did make more noise than the ox. When the standard of athletic supremacy comes into vogue, Whitman is not interested.

When the world of education turns more and more to research and begins to measure a faculty by research standards, Whitman is unconcerned. And the reason is simply this—Whitman is interested in teaching. In final analysis that is the real function of the college. Its energies are expended not in the laboratories, not in field studies, not in professional training— but in the classroom. Its aim is to communicate knowledge. Its emphasis lies in teaching men and women to think, to think in the terms of the values of our inheritance; to think in terms of the current, relentless tide of events. Whitman has always understood this basic principle. It has not forsaken it for false gods. And in executing it Whitman has had outstanding success. As a detached rather than as a sentimental alumnus, let me say this: Whitman gave us the best teaching I have either experienced or observed anywhere. And I know that it is still strong in that tradition.

This spirit of independence in education is symptomatic of the attitude which prevails on the campus. That spirit of independence was imparted to us subtly; and it has been imparted to you. It came to us in no formal way. It was part of the climate of opinion; it was a matter of attitude and atmosphere. It created its own sense of values. Those values to us were work— hard, unceasing work. The self-supporting student was the rule, not the exception. Work is not associated with country clubs; and Whitman was no country club. It was a workshop. Self-supporting students were given a social status which made work a thing to be desired. Education, being an opportunity which work created, was for us a serious business.

The Whitman tradition thus gave, and still gives, preference to those who by necessity or choice come up the hard way. Values of this kind are a precious part of our national inheritance. To the extent that educational institutions like Whitman can help preserve them, they are performing a broad national service. Such values are sorely needed in these critical times.

The time was when one in "the Street" was pretty well assured of financial success if he wore the right necktie and belonged to the right club. Such days awaited many on their graduation from college. They do not await you. They may return at a future time. But it will be no disappointment to those strong in your tradition if they do not. For in perilous times it is those (whether rich or poor) who have come up the hard way who have a real contribution to make and who have perhaps the greatest satisfaction in making it. And we live in perilous times. The common enemy of economic forces has invaded us. The lights of reason are getting dimmer and dimmer in other parts of the world. We face the imperative necessity of keeping from our shores the plagues which have descended elsewhere. You who are about to graduate do not want success handed to you; you merely want business and the professions to afford you the same kind of opportunity that Whitman afforded you in education. But the perils of these days may impair your opportunity. Those perils, therefore, become perhaps your foremost concern.

These are not perils just to you. They are perils to capitalism and democracy. In their solution you have not only an opportunity and a duty to coöperate but an opportunity and a duty to assume a leadership. Their solution does not rest solely with government or with labor or with business. The problems call for joint effort and joint action by all. A united front by all of us will solve these problems. Working together we can overcome any problem which besets capitalism and democracy. Working together we can make this profit system work and at the same time not sacrifice humanity for some legal or economic fetish. Our main efforts must lie along the lines of making as certain as possible that opportunity for work exists and that honest business has opportunity to make honest and substantial profits. Freedom of opportunity is as essential to healthy capitalism as it is to healthy democracy. By our joint efforts we can preserve that freedom of opportunity. By doing so we will preserve capitalism and democracy. Let us not be deluded into mistaking personalities for issues. The issues live on, though personalities change. The answer to those problems cannot be found by reliance upon dogma or smugness. They will not be found if groups in this country expend their energies on each other rather than on the issues. They will be found if by joint endeavor we utilize the boundless initiative, the great courage, the brains, and the character which make up this nation's unique heritage.

Youth must bear the brunt of these problems, for many of the most crucial ones will be in balance during the rising generation. And in their solution youth will not be denied. Nor should youth be denied, for its whole stake in the future of America is involved. I have great confidence in youth and that confidence is evidenced by the fact that the S.E.C. is manned by youth. And whenever at the S.E.C. I have entrusted to youth grave responsibility, I have invariably seen youth grow overnight to the stature which the job demanded. It was youth which gained the recent, signal victory over the Old Guard in the New York Stock Exchange. I have confidence in the stability and maturity of youth under the stress and strain of responsibility. I have confidence in the flexibility of youth to adjust itself to change. I have confidence in the sensitivity of youth to the pressures of social evolution. I have confidence in the courage and bold decisions of youth under pressure. These qualities are emerging fast because youth, whether rich or poor, is coming up the hard way these days. All these qualities are essential if we are to preserve our inheritance.

The growing complexity of state and national government over the decade is obvious. The social and economic pressures which have created these increases in governmental activity are not fancied but real. Though their particular forms may change, the advent of these new instruments of government promises to be permanent. That in itself is not a political but an educational challenge. Those who man these agencies of government must be skilled not only in the art of government but also in technical skills which these specialized tasks demand. If we are to receive full service from government, the universities must give us trained men. That means a constant reorientation of university instruction and research not for the mere purpose of increasing technical proficiency but for the purpose of keeping abreast with social and economic change. Universities attuned to this program of change can and will render government lasting service, for government is no better than its men.

There is thus a real challenge to universities to produce men competent and equipped to do the increasingly important tasks of government. The experience I have had in government has to a constantly increasing degree emphasized the importance of this. We have indeed been fortunate to date. But we must provide for future needs. We must at all times be manned by those who are stimulated by a desire to bring order into the administrative procedure and above all to keep government geared to the swift changes of the times.

I spoke of the fact that government alone cannot do the job, but that government working coöperatively with business and labor can. But I do not want to belittle the role of government. It holds great promise not of being a bureaucratic blight but an energizing and directive influence. It can supply a coördination to divergent forces. It can give to states and the nation a cohesive and unifying quality which will defy any foe from within or without. The importance of government has increased with the quantity and rate of change. The growing complexity of state and national government over the decade is obvious. The social and economic pressures which have created these increases in governmental activity are not fancied but real. Though their particular forms may change these new instruments of government promise to be permanent. We cannot turn the clock back. That in itself is not a political but an educational challenge. Those who man these agencies of government must be skilled not only in the art of government but also in the technical skills which these tasks demand. And there must be an increasing number of top men and women who are willing to forsake the glamorous bypaths of the professions and business to dedicate themselves to the state. This means financial sacrifices. It means heartaches, assuaged only by a deep inner satisfaction of service well rendered, by thankfulness for an opportunity to strike at least one blow for humanity and popular government. There must also be on the part of government an increasing willingness to grant to select trained men and women a career service marked by permanency in tenure and by financial security. The President's grossly libeled Reorganization Bill [1] included a constructive endeavor of this kind. Similar improvements in civil service are essential so that

1. S. 2970, 75th Congress, 1st Session, introduced August 16, 1937.

there will be an increasing infiltration of top men and women from our leading colleges and universities into a career service with our national government.[2] It is essential that we obtain this high quality of person, for it must be remembered that government is no better than its men.

So I lay down these challenges to youth. They are challenges to youth whether its contribution is made through local, state, or national government; or through labor, business, or the professions. And I am confident that youth will meet these challenges. I am also firm in my belief that youth imbued with your tradition will meet them successfully. That is not only because you have come up the hard way. It is also because you have caught the spirit of the pioneer, the drive of the constructive liberal, the zeal and perseverance of those who, like Marcus Whitman, are in search not of mere financial rewards but of the lasting satisfactions which come to those who plead at least one cause of humanity.

2. In a brief talk before the staff of the S.E.C. on November 17, 1938, Mr. Douglas said:

"Administrative agencies such as the S.E.C. require, not only in their early stages but during their later development, a continuous inflow of technically trained, competent, imaginative and adventuresome people. . . . Having come from the field of education and having worked with students in class rooms and in research laboratories, I know what the limitations of modern education are as regards training for work of the kind that we do daily in the S.E.C. . . . Realizing that deficiency, I set about two years ago to try to work out on paper a scheme for a graduate school of finance within the S.E.C. . . . I believe if we can do something like that we shall have helped make administrative government increasingly attractive, because we shall have provided a real educational opportunity for the people (young or old, experienced or inexperienced) who come here to work. With such a program I am convinced that we could attract and keep young people who would see here an opportunity for professional advancement through a broader, fuller education."

CHAPTER XXIV

EDUCATION FOR THE LAW

This address on law teaching in America was read at a dinner in Boston of the American Association of Collegiate Schools of Business in April, 1936.

LAW schools are over a generation slow in their educational program. I mean that in several ways. In the first place, there has been only perceptible progress since Langdell some sixty-five years ago deserted the law treatise and introduced the so-called law case in the classroom, and since Ames some forty-five years ago brought that system to the height of its perfection. As a matter of fact, the major effort of most law schools since has been to catch up with Langdell and Ames by perfecting that method and the pedagogical skill which it requires. In that effort almost all the energies have been consumed. In that endeavor most of the imagination has been sublimated. This has meant that the content, drive, and direction in legal education has been toward teaching teachers' law rather than lawyers' law. That is to say, the law-teaching profession has been following the system of Langdell and Ames who taught strictly library law—the sole pabulum of such intellectual activity being the content of court opinions. In the second place, we have been principally engaged (whether consciously or not and whether adequately or not) in preparing country practitioners for the days of the 'seventies and 'nineties. In the third place, we have professedly been concerned strictly with professional law training; yet viewed from that single point of view we have fallen far short of that objective. It is with these phases of legal education that I wish to deal.[1]

1. While on the faculty of the Yale Law School, Mr. Douglas sought to enable his students to study corporation law against the background of

The school of legal education which flourished on the introduction of the so-called case system developed the dialectical method to a high point of perfection. With stern precision were the syllogisms, drawn from the opinions of the judges and applicable to the various issues, worked out. Through use of the Socratic method legal problems were tested by these syllogisms. Those that fitted represented good law; those that did not represented bad law. The analysis was tight and incisive. The intellectual discipline was severe. The system of law which was taught had symmetry and consistency. It likewise had apparent certainty. Though much of it might seem metaphysical, it had little of the imponderable in it. In such a system there would be found no place for the pressure of current social problems on judicial decisions. In such a system there would be found no place for the effect of economic theories of judges on the decisions which they made. The *opinion* rather than the *decision* was the paramount and important matter. This system, however, developed a body of doctrine which, though highly conceptual, was a work of art, and which, though pretty well insulated from the facts of the social and economic problem at hand, had internal logical consistency.

But the case system of study on which this school of legal education was based is in fact a misnomer. The things which were studied were not cases but opinions. A study of the cases would mean at least a study of the records containing the facts and pleadings. But these records were not studied, although they are obviously useful and necessary for a real interpretation of the opinions since, in the language of a brilliant lawyer, "A judicial opinion is not only *ex post facto* with reference to the decision. It is a censored exposition, written by a judge, of what induced him to arrive at a decision which he had already reached." *

the contemporary problems of business and finance. He was instrumental in organizing a series of courses in finance and law given jointly by the Yale Law School and the Harvard Graduate School of Business Administration.

* Frank, "Why Not a Clinical Law School?" *University of Pennsylvania Law Review,* LXXXI (1933), 907, 911.

With this approach it likewise becomes apparent that the content of the records of the cases is likewise inadequate. Business practices, social philosophies, and similar imponderable factors, including "hunches," which produce many judicial decisions, become as obviously relevant to a true explanation of the specific result which a court reaches as do all of the pertinent documents which go to make up the case record. As stated by this same critical observer of the judicial process,

To study these eviscerated judicial expositions as the principal basis of forecast of future judicial action is to delude oneself. The lawyer will go wrong who believes that (in advising a client, drafting an instrument, trying a case, or arguing before a court) he can rely on the so-called reasons found in or spelled out of opinions to guide him in guessing what courts will hereafter decide. To do so is far more unwise than it would be for a botanist to assume that plants are merely what appears above the ground or for an anatomist to content himself with scrutinizing the outside of the body.*

Thus it is that any study of law which is restricted to the so-called case method; that is, to a study of judicial opinions, grossly oversimplifies and distorts the nature of law. After all, law is neither more nor less than a prediction of what a governmental agency or other agency of control will do under a given situation. A study of the legal literature exemplified by judicial opinions supplies part, but only part, of the material necessary to make such a prediction. The other psychological, political, economic, business, social factors necessary to complete that prediction are innumerable. The weakness of the old system was that all of these more general and imponderable factors were eliminated from consideration. It was for that reason that the nonconformists in legal education † began to raise disconcerting notes. They began not to attack the logical consistency of the syllogisms but to discard these syllogisms and talk about "the facts," "social policy," "effects on business," "desirable and

* *Idem*, p. 912.

† I refer to men like Cook, Moore, Llewellyn, Arnold, Clark, Frankfurter, Landis, Powell, Hamilton.

undesirable social consequences," "incidences" of particular rules, "good policy," "bad policy," etc. This was called either "ferment in legal education" or "loose thinking," dependent on the point of view. In any event, it blasted out the more conventional methods when it was employed, for it entailed a fundamental shift in point of view and a fundamental shift in techniques.

The result was that law teachers of this faith no longer restricted their exploration and study to the opinions but entered the preserves previously restricted to psychologists, sociologists, economists, bankers, politicians, etc. They began critically to study decisions in their entire setting. They not only opened up for study the case records, but they engaged in extensive exploration into the economic theories of particular judges, they entered into a consideration of the social and economic maladjustment which particular rules of law engender or permit, and into the question of the kind and quality of business practices and customs with which particular decisions were dealing. The result was that the whole horizon of the law was broadened and new vistas brought into view. The movement which was thus started has gained great momentum during the last decade. The difficulty with this new point of view was that it entailed not only a shift in point of view but also a shift in techniques. A shift in point of view was quite easily made; a shift in techniques was not. The result has been that perhaps some of us who made the transition have been at times wallowing either in the trough of idle chatter or of whimsical speculation. The charge is frequently made that under this new method hard analysis has tended to disappear, intellectual discipline has diminished, and the heavy and reliable doctrine of law, as expressed in opinions, has assumed a secondary place. If true, it means that the resultant product has lost some of the vigorous quality of the old and has fallen far short of the objectives of the new.

The new approach is largely in the blueprint stage because of the volatile character of the phenomena being studied. The quality of business practices is so dynamic that once a specific legal-business issue was adequately explored, the investigator would be apt to find that he had been studying history rather than current life. The process of catching up would thus be costly, breathless, and futile. A closely related fault is the fact that we are probably seeing only the bare beginnings of an endeavor to study the social and economic phenomena of our times.

To state the matter comparatively, the nonconformist in the law probably is not far behind—and at times he is ahead of—his brethren in the allied fields of psychology, sociology, economics, government, and business in his efforts to treat the phenomena, with which he deals, on a scientific basis. But the fact remains that, with minor exceptions, the whole area of human conduct with which the law deals is not yet capable of treatment on any scientific basis. The failure then of the nonconformists in legal education to produce a substitute system as vigorous, orderly, and complete as the one they seek to displace must be shared by all other students of human behavior. It is likewise probably true that no significant achievement in the direction of a really scientific method can be made for many generations to come, if ever.

But short of such achievement lie vast areas for exploratory work. Few of these have yet been traversed. Take, for example, the field of corporation finance. I suppose that most teachers in this field still treat only the conceptualistic and doctrinaire principles of corporation law. The interest and energy are given to the philosophical and metaphysical aspects of what corporations are or are not, what they are like or unlike, what they can or cannot do—all based on word pictures taken from judicial opinions. The impact of the corporate device on our social and economic life is almost wholly neglected. The corporation as an object of control and as a method of control is passed by. Even the nonconformists have only started on the task of broadening the horizon in the corporate field. True, they are sensitive to the importance of the problems. Yet when it comes down to the ultimate fact of studying the corporation in its modern environment, most of the major tasks lie ahead. Now it seems apparent that a study of the corporation in its modern environment is the essence of the law of corporation finance. The question of the responsibility of the investment banker calls for appreciation of the functions he actually or ostensibly performs, the techniques he employs, the niceties of his requirements, the malpractices in which he engages, his impact both on issuer and security holder. Such matters cannot be fully seen through the window of the law, even assuming abundant legal literature, which there is not. Exploration of such matters leads one directly to the market place and, more recently, to the files of the Securities and Exchange Commission. The question of dividends likewise calls for much more than is contained in the legal concepts of capital and surplus. It leads one directly into accounting and financial management. To forsake these areas and to hew strictly to the line of the legal concepts is to neglect the legal problem of control over dividends. Nor can the important issue as to the responsibility of the corporate trustee under modern trust indentures be met by adhering solely to the literature of the law of trusts and of contracts. The institution of the corporate trustee needs to be studied—its functions, the manner in which it performs or fails to perform them, its relationship to underwriter and issuer, its compensation, its conflicts of interest, the devices available to it for protection of investors, the responsibility which the law should place on it for what it does or does not do. Such examples in the field of corporation finance could be multiplied on end through watered stock promoters' liability, parent and subsidiary corporations, nonvoting stock, cumulative preferred stock, etc.

A consideration of such aspects of each of these problems is as much a legal as business one. The legal issue of liability or responsibility brings to the fore all of these so-called business considerations. It is with the business institution that the law deals. It is the business institution which needs to be understood in order that the legal control be so fashioned as to be adjusted to the requirements of the total situation.

The upshot of what I have been saying is not merely that adequate treatment of the law of corporation finance calls for use of so-called business materials. The point is that any considered treatment of this subject would entail a subtle fusion of the so-called legal and business aspects since in final analysis they are one. As a practical matter, viewed either from the legal or business point of view, it would be difficult, except in terms of emphasis, to differentiate between a law course and a business course on corporation finance.

What is true of corporation finance is likewise true of most other areas of the law. In the commercial law field the examples are more striking. Yet the same holds true in varying degrees throughout most other subjects. To rebuild our law courses along the lines mentioned would necessitate drawing heavily from all of the allied fields of the social sciences.

To reconstitute our law-school curricula along these lines obviously would not be to reduce the study of law to any scientific basis. It would still be on a literary or argumentative level. But it would have wider horizons than its present dialectics permit; it would have in it the true ferment of realism. The result would be that students would be more closely attuned to the practices and institutions with which the law deals. The insight and appreciation of the modern requirements of society which such education would produce should go far toward awakening in the Bar a greater social consciousness. Practitioners of the law acquire at least a technical appreciation of the workings of these business institutions. This is acquired from necessity so as to be able to handle the work of their clients. But it must be remembered that almost the sole tutoring which our lawyers obtain in such matters comes from their clients and their elders who are more concerned in getting what they want than in critically appraising and weighing the validity of the fundamental hypotheses that underlie their transactions and practices. It is because there is such a narrow trade view in the typical lawyer's approach to these problems that we are so sadly lacking in real legal statesmanship in these areas of law.

I mentioned above that in legal education we were over a generation slow. That we are will perhaps be now more apparent to you when I tell you that no real fusion of law and business—let alone other social sciences—of which I speak has been accomplished. The nonconformists, whom I mentioned, have been moving in that direction. But in no single field of law has there been any substantial integration of the kind described.

The path lies clearly in that direction. But progress in that direction calls for more than the law teacher has been taught or expected to contribute. It requires not research in the library but research in the market place and in other appropriate laboratories where human conduct may be observed. It requires treatment and study not so much of century-old legal precepts (though they may be relevant) as of the current cinema of life. That means that the law teacher's task is to a large part research —not research in the sense of compiling a corpus juris but research in the sense of keeping up with the fast-moving stream of human activity. To do this he requires new techniques, new approaches. In fact he often will need a new education. For that reason perhaps the nonconformists made no more progress than they did. For that reason it may be that a special educational task of training such teachers will have to be undertaken. The only thing certain is that the job remains to be done.

It must and will be done for the reason that the modern requirements of the law demand it. And that brings me to the second reason I had for calling legal education over a generation slow. The content and nature of our law curricula were pretty well set over a generation ago. As I stated, their content and objectives have remained fairly constant, although the quantum of courses has increased. The objective at the time these curricula were crystallized was pretty largely the education of country practitioners. I use the word "country" not so much with a geographical connotation as in the sense of general practice. What were conceived to be the requirements of general practice of that era fashioned the contents of the courses. The emphasis was on a thorough training in the common-law system. It is not difficult to see that the training, limited as it was in view of its restriction to the judicial opinion, was primarily for the courtrooms. The emphasis was on the meaning and application of the legal words of art, the nature of various legal proceedings, the basic factors in legal strategy, the philosophies of the system of common law and equity. The scene has changed materially since then in two important respects. In the first place there has developed a demand for lawyers who are doctor and nurse to the great financial and commercial institutions. For such service the cream of the profession has been drafted. These men are engaged as much in business as in law practice. Yet the training which they have had in preparation for this work is in large part inappropriate. They have in effect been trained for one profession while they practice in another. I do not contend that law schools should divert any of their energies to turning out bigger and better corporation lawyers. I do, however, maintain that if we are to make measurable progress in effecting more adequate social control over finance we must undertake seriously the training of enlightened corporation lawyers. We can do that if we address ourselves to the task. We cannot do it with the vehicle of legal education which we have known. If done, it must come through means of an educational system based on a study of the phenomena of finance, neither through the translucent window of judicial opinions nor from the limited vantage point of the technician, but from the broad social point of view.

In the second place we have fast adopted new and permanent governmental agencies of control. Depending on the point of view, these new agencies are called either administrative or bureaucratic. The vital fact is not that the number of these governmental agencies has increased. The material factor is that government has moved permanently into control over new social and business areas. This new problem of control does not require, nor can it countenance, the techniques of common-law litigation and adjudication. Frequently it entails disposition of litigated matter. More often it calls for formulation of policies, drafting of rules and regulations, preparation of forms, standardization of practices, etc. Lawyers have been and will continue to be conspicuous in such activities—those representing clients on the one hand, those representing government on the other. The lawyer is of necessity and perhaps by tradition the general handy man in such activities. This means that the mass of material with which he is constantly dealing consists of statistics, banking practices, finance, accounting principles and practices, problems of securities distribution, problems of securities exchanges, problems of marketing, of prices, of labor, of production, etc. With these raw materials he must work—he must interpret, analyze, and appraise. Out of these raw materials he must shape policies and make vital decisions. But more often than not the lawyer brings to bear on these problems nothing but native intelligence, for his common-law training has little or no application. There is, to be sure, no substitute for native intelligence, common sense, and character. Yet if any educational program is justified, education in preparation for these important and significant experiments in social control should come first, for on their success or failure turns the fate of our social and economic welfare. This, of course, entails more than training for law in the conventional sense—it entails training for law in the sense of training for government. And in view of the traditional proclivity of lawyers for such posts it means that fundamental changes in our legal education must be made.

These fundamental changes which must be made relate both to content and to techniques. The enlargement and expansion of the conventional course along the lines of integration of relevant business, social and economic material, which I have mentioned, indicate the character of one of the necessary changes. Another is in a sense ancillary thereto. That is the development in the students of techniques for handling and interpreting factual material, in obtaining broad social points of view on current issues, and of appreciating the tasks and limitations of government.

Such changes are fundamental. If they were adopted, legal education would move out into new zones. It would traverse some of the ground presently covered by business schools. The experience of business schools in this field would be helpful. Yet it is to be doubted if there could be salvaged from present business-school curricula much which could be readily adapted to this new objective, for we would be apt to find them costly collections of irrelevant facts. This is true because the niceties of the requirements for integration of law and other social phenomena are great and demand special effort and precise objectives. Also, I suspect that business schools have had at least as narrow a trade or professional point of view as have law schools.

The significance and importance of these changes would doubtless be more readily and quickly recognized by practitioners than by teachers. The reason for this is that they call for the use of techniques with which lawyers are familiar. Practitioners would be the first to admit that the content of a judicial opinion is an unreliable guide for determining or predicting the result of the next case. Practitioners would be among the first to recognize the utility of exploration into these other areas. Practitioners would be among the first to admit the relevancy of much of this so-called nonlegal material to the study of law. They would be among the first to do so because the techniques which they themselves consciously or unconsciously employ involve consideration of these other factors. It is thus that the teacher of law rather than the practitioner tends to the narrow view of legal education.

Such a movement must have the same quality of discipline

and vigor as the present methods of legal education. If it de-
generates into chatter of "what the business man thinks" or into
the musings of fireside philosophers, it may not have failed more
genuinely than the present system of legal education, but it will
have fallen far short of its ultimate objectives. To assure these
stern and vigorous qualities the development of such a program
must be painstakingly slow. It will take years to develop. Its full
development will entail either partial mergers of law and business schools or the growth of offshoots of our present law schools,
devoted to higher ideals of public service than either schools of
law or schools of business have yet attained.

CHAPTER XXV

THE DEMOCRATIC IDEAL

Mr. Douglas delivered this address in New York on February 9, 1939, at the annual dinner of the Fordham University Alumni Association. It was his last public address before his appointment to the Supreme Court.

MR. DOOLEY once said, "Historyans is like doctors. They are always lookin' f'r symptoms. Those iv them that writes about their own times examines th' tongue an' feels th' pulse an' makes a wrong dygnosis. Th' other kind iv histhry is a post mortem examination. It tells ye what a counthry died iv. But I'd like to know what it lived iv."

Mr. Dooley typifies the right of every American to express himself profoundly on broad questions of which he has no expert knowledge. When I leave my own field of law and government, I too avail myself of this privilege.

I think we all share Mr. Dooley's belief that the important thing for us to know about our country is "what it lived of." To know what makes our country live is to have the key to the immortality of its democratic ideal. That, perhaps, is what President Roosevelt had in mind when he said that this generation had a real "rendezvous with Destiny." It is our generation's destiny, in a time of great distress, to make democracy live, to make the democratic ideal survive the many assaults that beset it.

Unwittingly, I fear, we have in various ways slowly slipped away from that ideal. Over the years we have been preoccupied with materialistic and mechanistic matters. We have been incessantly employed in serving the physical wants and needs of man. The main current of our modern times has been a sweeping advance of technology and too often it has overshadowed all else. The problems of research, of production, of distribution, of finance have quite properly occupied a high place in our thought and activity. But the underlying values have been largely materialistic. Our material progress has often failed to reckon with the deep, spiritual factors of the democratic faith.

One aspect of modern life which has gone far to stifle men is the rapid growth of tremendous corporations. Enormous spiritual sacrifices are made in the transformation of shop-keepers into employees. The materialistic god of efficiency may dictate it in certain cases. But the extent to which it has been carried has been ruthless in its loss of human values. The disappearance of free enterprise has led to a submergence of the individual in the impersonal corporation in much the same manner as he has been submerged in the state in other lands. As a corollary the growth of the corporation has impersonalized and made materialistic many of our most important social and personal relationships. As a most gracious and polite lady in the drawing room may be transformed into a most impolite person behind a steering wheel of an automobile, so gentlemen may be propelled into ruthless raiding of other people's money once they take the corporate veil. The convenient and impersonalized use of the corporate device has unquestionably contributed to moral decadence. That has been especially true with the growth of bigness. Empires so vast as to defy the intimate understanding of any one man tend to become playthings for manipulation. The fact that railroads, or banks, or operating utilities lie somewhere deep underneath the corporate maze becomes incidental. Values are translated. Service to human beings is made subordinate to profits for manipulators. The stage setting is perfect for the disappearance of moral values. Individual responsibility before God has no counterpart in the corporate system.

In some countries this flood of materialism has risen so high as to drown out the spirit. Communism places complete reliance upon the satisfaction of physical needs, making of man a wholly economic creature. Fascism goes so far as to deify the corporate state, making man responsible to the state instead of to God. Both of these systems have suppressed the spiritual values which are the essence of democracy. Neither recognizes the principle that men are "endowed by their Creator with certain inalienable rights." Those alien systems have expurgated the words of the philosopher who said: "Pride not yourself in this, that you love your country, but rather in this, that you love mankind."

Fortunately in America the ideal of democracy is still alive and vigorous. This ideal includes both equality of economic opportunity and equality of political opportunity. It is broader and more embracing than either. It recognizes that man is not simply a biological organism, or merely the product of economic forces. It gives preëminent recognition to the principle that man is also a spiritual and ethical being. The ingredients of that faith are not solely materialistic; they are spiritual and ethical as well. They recognize the importance of the inward satisfaction of confidence in one's self, the deep desire for the respect of one's fellow man, the longing to be identified with some cause dedicated to the interests of humanity. Basically this is the democratic ideal. In practice even in this country it has at times seemed to lose some of its vitality. To revitalize it is the first order of our day.

I have often wondered what would happen if for a generation we had no new patents, no new discoveries, no new technological advances, no new mergers. If the wheels of invention were stopped and the processes of discovery were stilled, we would, I am sure, continue to live in comfort. Known skills and devices could go on servicing the physical needs of man interminably. They might not be as efficient as scientists could make them. But I have no doubt that the needs and desires of man could be met on the physical side.

I do not mean for a moment to suggest this as a proper course for us to take. Nor do I mean to minimize the importance of filling abundantly the basic physical needs of our whole people.

I recognize fully that man physically impoverished is a poor cornerstone for a free democracy. A strong, efficient, well-balanced national economy will ever be one of our indispensable assets. But without the meaning and guidance of a vigorous set of spiritual values, I doubt that the other will alone enable us to meet successfully our "rendezvous with Destiny."

One great source of strength to which all of us look in keeping alive the democratic ideal is the university. It may be that in the years immediately ahead our universities will again be called upon to play that great role in the protection of civilization which has been theirs for centuries. This responsibility has been recognized by more than one distinguished educator. President Conant of Harvard, in his recent annual report,[1] made the following statement:

Today we all realize that democracy is not a self-perpetuating virus adapted to any body politic—that was the assumption of a previous generation. Democracy we now know to be a special type of organism requiring specific nutriment materials—some economic, some social and cultural. Among the latter the emotional stability and intelligence of the electorate are obviously of importance; these are intimately connected with the type of education we give our children. Another requisite for a flourishing democracy would appear to be the existence of a ladder of opportunity; again the educational process is involved. From these and many similar considerations it is evident that if we wish the present type of society in this country to survive and to improve along thoroughly democratic lines, we must, as a people, pay due attention to our schools.

Yet even colleges and universities are not impervious to the dominant and engulfing materialistic influences of our time. Excessive trends toward purely technical training have been continuously observed by experts in education. At certain times and places it was a close question as to whether or not the main efforts and resources of some institutions of learning would not be devoted to simple trade-school curricula.

This I know has been evident in legal education where purely

1. For the year 1938.

professional training has been too often the dominant note. This has been true to such an extent in the past that legal education at times resembled a course of instruction in contract bridge. And I have often thought that the medical profession has been so busy dividing man into neat little compartments and placing him in so many separate test tubes that man as a total organism has often been little comprehended. Emphasis on the purely biological aspects of man has too often led to diagnosis of disease in terms of outward physical manifestations rather than of inward spiritual and emotional maladjustments.

The foregoing are merely small examples of a larger trend in the universities today. There is demand for a reawakening of the ancient concept of the university as the custodian of the things of the mind and the values of the spirit. The rise of materialism is today the greatest single challenge to the universities, not for the purpose of resisting technological advance but of attuning that advance to the spiritual need of man. All of us, and particularly the universities, can well heed the recent words of President Roosevelt:

Democracy, the practice of self-government, is a covenant among free men to respect the rights and liberties of their fellows.

International good faith, a sister of democracy, springs from the will of civilized nations of men to respect the rights and liberties of other nations of men.

In a modern civilization, all three—religion, democracy, and international good faith—complement each other.

Where freedom of religion has been attacked, the attack has come from sources opposed to democracy. Where democracy has been overthrown, the spirit of free worship has disappeared. And where religion and democracy have vanished, good faith and reason in international affairs have given way to strident ambition and brute force.

An ordering of society which relegates religion, democracy, and good faith among nations to the background can find no place within it for the ideals of the Prince of Peace. The United States rejects such an ordering, and retains its ancient faith.[2]

2. Message to Congress, January 4, 1939.

It is that spiritual ingredient which is necessary for great strength and vitality of nations as well as of individuals. That spiritual ingredient is itself the solvent of many social ills, and perhaps even economic ills. It is also the preventive of planetary disintegration. Of equal significance, it is the cohesive element which mystically binds men together in a common cause and makes strong and united, groups torn by dissension and turmoil.

Faith alone will not solve all problems. Basic economic and social issues will persist. But give us faith and we will have the driving force necessary to solve the other problems. With that faith our economic system can be revitalized. With that faith and with that revitalization, foreign ideology need breed no fear here. Such ideology, like a germ, can gain a foothold only in a diseased system. Spiritual well-being as well as physical health are both necessary preventives against such disease.

Such a renaissance constitutes the principal responsibility and opportunity of all of us—including universities and government—who are interested in the preservation of the American democratic ideal. Universities train the men that government needs. Men trained in the democratic faith are indispensable on the governmental front. Men with technical competence, men with humility, men with the quality of selflessness, men with a sense of responsibility—these are the needs and demands of democracy. Training of such men is a task of education and of stimulation. With such men, government in its strong position of leadership can make a continuous contribution toward a revitalization of the democratic ideal. With such a program our whole national life can be continuously enriched by the influx into government, business, and the professions of men basically conditioned in the democratic faith. But technical training will not alone suffice. We must reorient much of our materialistic philosophy in terms of humanitarian principles.

We have observed enough on our contemporary scene to know that a supreme spiritual effort must go hand in hand with an economic and social program. We have seen enough to convince us that dilution of ethical principles weakens rather than invigorates our present system. Therefore, we know that on the basis of sheer self-interest such a renaissance is a prerequisite to a strengthening and invigoration of both capitalism and democracy.

INDEX

Administration, problems of, 248 ff.
Administrative process, 243 ff.
Administrative Process, The (James M. Landis), 242
Aldrich, Winthrop W., 63
American Association of Collegiate Schools of Business, Address before, April, 1936, 278
American Bar Association, Address before, July, 1938, 143
American Gas & Electric Co., 153
American Gas & Power Co., 156
American Power & Light Co., 153, 154
American Water Works & Electric Co., 143, 153, 154
Ames, 278
Annalist, The, 134
Arkansas Missouri Power Corp., 156
Arnold, Thurman, 280
Association of Customers' Brokers, 107

Bankers' compensation, 34
Bankruptcy, result of abuses, 7
Bankruptcy Act, as amended, chap. x of, 59, 174 ff.
Bankruptcy Act, Section 77B of, 172, 174 ff., 207, 214, 219
Barkley Bill (S. 2344), 199
Barkley, Senator Alben W., 172
Bigness, consequences of, xii–xiii, 14, 15, 16
Bond Club of New York, Address before, March 24, 1937, 5, 32
Bond trading, 90
Boston, Mass., Address at, April, 1936, 278
Boston Edison Co., 153
Brandeis, Mr. Justice, vi, xii, xiii, 14, 32, 37

Brokers and dealers registered with S.E.C., 22, 25
Business-government relationship, xi, 247, 263

Capital market, 18, 20, 21, 22
Catholic University of America, 230
Central Arizona Light & Power Co., 154
Centralization of industrial control, 6
Central Public Utility Corp., 156
Certificates of deposit, 193
Chandler Bill (a bill to amend the National Bankruptcy Act), 173, 214, 217, 219
Chase National Bank, 63
Chesapeake & Ohio Railroad Co., 37
Chicago, Ill., 74, 128, 173
Chicago Stock Exchange, 74
Cincinnati Union Terminal Co., 37
Clark, Charles E., 280
Clark, Evans, 94
Cleveland, Address at, July, 1938, 18
Cleveland Union Terminal Co., 37
Commonwealth Club of Chicago, Address at, February, 2, 1938, 128
Commonwealth Edison Co., 153
Commonwealth Light & Power Co., 156
Commonwealth & Southern Corp., 153
Competitive bidding, 37, 38
Conant, J. B., 293
Congress: administrative agencies, 242, 243; delegation of power by, 244, 246, 260, 261; financial reforms, vi–vii; Holding Company Act, 129, 133, 139, 165; protective committee study, 172

Consolidated Edison Co., 153
Consolidated Gas, Electric Light, & Power Co. of Baltimore, 153, 161
Constitution, 253
Consumers Power Co., 37
Continuity of banking relationships, 37
Conway, Carle C., 79
Conway Committee, 75, 79, 81, 82
Cook, W. W., 280
"Corporate kidnapping," 29, 43
Corporate reorganization, 7, 30; function of S.E.C. in (see Securities and Exchange Commission); plans, 188 ff.; reforms in, 172 ff.
Corporation laws, 13
Customers' men, 107

"Death sentence," 130, 144
Deposit agreements, 208
Detroit Edison Co., 153
Directors, 42 ff.; inactive, 46, 47; in Great Britain, 51; paid, 52; public, 53
Discretionary accounts, 118
Dividends, 134 ff.; arrearages, 134 ff.
Dooley, Mr., v, 290
Duality of interest, 12
Duke Bar Association, Address before, April 22, 1934, 231
Dunn, F. J., 150

Eastern Law Students Conference, Address before, March 20, 1937, 230
Economic Club of Chicago, Address at, February 1, 1938, 5, 18, 74 ff.
Education, legal, 270 ff.
Electric Bond & Share Co., 127–128, 143, 154
Engineers Public Service Co., 153
Europe, 19

Federal Reserve System, 92, 95, 106; Regulation T of, 92, 94, 117; Regulation U of, 92, 94

Federal Trade Commission, 128, 148; investigation of utility companies by, vi, vii, 128
Florida Power & Light Co., 154
Fogarty, J. F., 143
Fordham University Alumni Ass'n, Address before, February 9, 1939, 290
Fort Worth, Texas, Address at, January 8, 1939, 46
Fourth Federal Reserve District, 25 ff.
Frank, Jerome N., vii, 279
Frankfurter, Mr. Justice, 280
Free credit balances, 87

Gay, Charles R., 79, 92
Groesbeck, C. E., 143

Hamilton, Walton, 280
Hancock, John M., 120
Hancock Committee, 120, 122, 123
Harriman, W. Averill, 28
Harvard Business Review, 150
Harvard Club of Boston, Address at, November, 1938, 163
Harvard Graduate School of Business Administration, 279
Harvard Law Review, 240
"High Finance," 7, 8, 9, 10, 13, 16
Holding Company Act. See Public Utility Holding Company Act of 1935
Holmes, Mr. Justice, 11
House of Representatives: Committee Report on Securities Exchange Act of 1934, 102; Report 8046 (on Chandler Bill), 173; statement before Interstate and Foreign Commerce Committee, June 8, 1938, 197
Hughes investigation, 76

Indenture trustees, 41, 42, 180 ff.
Independent trustee, 180 ff.
Inland Power & Light Corp., 156

Institute of Public Affairs, University of Virginia, Address before, July 11, 1936, 92

International Management Congress, Address before, September 27, 1938, 56

International Paper & Power Co., 141

Investment bankers, control by, 11; proper function of, 32 ff.

Investment banking, 32 ff.

Investment trusts, xii–xiii, 37, 39

Kansas Gas & Electric Co., 154

Kennedy, Joseph P., vii, 51

Kreuger and Toll, 172

Labor, 43, 44

Landis, James M., vii, 242, 280

Langdell, 278

Law teaching, 278 ff.

Lawyers, 168; role in reorganizations, 230 ff.

Lea Bill, 197, 199, 206, 207, 217

Lehman Brothers, 120

Liquidity, 98, 101, 102, 103–106

Llewellyn, Carl, 280

Lotos Club, Address at, November, 1938, 256

Louisville & Nashville Railroad Co., 37

Management, 44, 56

Margin regulations, 94

Middle West Corp., The, 156

Midland Utilities Co., 156

Minnesota Power & Light Co., 154

Monongahela West Penn Public Service Co., 154

Monopoly, 15, 36

Monopoly Message, Franklin D. Roosevelt, 159

Montana Power Co., 154

Moody's *Manual*, 154–155

Moore, Underhill, 280

Municipal Debt Readjustment, 221 ff.

Murphy, Grayson M. P., 168

National Association of Credit Men, Address before, June, 1937, 173

National Municipal Debt Readjustment Act, 222

National Power & Light Co., 153

National Power Policy Committee, 147; *Report on Public Utility Holding Companies* by, 148

Nebraska Power Co., 154

New Dealers, 81

New England Power Association, 150, 153

New York, N.Y., 6, 8, 19, 23, 74, 75, 131, 133; address at, February 9, 1939, 290

New York Curb Exchange, 104; floor trading, 104

New York Herald Tribune Forum, Address before, October, 1938, 243

New York Stock Exchange, vi, xii, 5, 23, 63, 65, 69, 70, 71, 72, 75, 79, 81, 87, 92, 94, 98, 104, 120, 168, 275; brokers' loans, 94; Committee on Customers' Men, 118; margin accounts, 94; paid president of, 81; president of, 76; reorganization of, 79; Stock List Committee, 120

New York Times, 28, 32, 37, 127

Niagara Hudson Power Corp., 153

North American Co., The, 143, 153

Northwestern Electric Co., 154

Odd-lot market, 105

Odd lots, 70, 71

Ohio, 25

Old Guard, 245, 275

Options, 35

Other People's Money (Louis D. Brandeis), vi, 32–33, 37–38

Pacific Gas & Electric Co., 153, 155, 161

Pacific Power & Light Co., 154
Paramount Publix Corp., 172
Pecora, Ferdinand, vi
Peoples Light & Power Co., 156
Pools, 84, 85, 99
Potomac Edison Co., 154
Powell, Thomas Reed, 280
Prentiss Hall, 271
President Roosevelt, 157, 247, 290; Message to Congress, January 4, 1939, 294; Reorganization Bill, 276
Press conference, March 15, 1939, 120
Protective Committees, 197 ff.; S.E.C. Report on, 172
Public Influence of the Bar, The (Mr. Justice Stone), 240
Public Service Corp. of New Jersey, 153, 161
Public Service Co. of Northern Illinois, 153
Public utilities, 127 ff.; diversification, 154 ff.; "diversity of investment," 157; dividends, 134; integration, 143 ff.; overcapitalization, 136 ff.; recapitalization, 136; voluntary reorganization, 139
Public Utility Holding Company Act of 1935, 29, 58, 127, 129, 136, 138, 139, 143, 146, 159, 163, 166, 167, 210, 212, 220, 245, 246; administration by the S.E.C., 263; Section 11 of, 144 ff.
Public utility industry, 134 ff.
Public Utility Integration (F. J. Dunn & Associates), 150

Regional capital markets, 20, 21, 22, 24, 31
Regional finance, 18 ff.
Regionalism, 18
Reorganization Bill (S. 2970, 75th Congress, 1st Sess.), 276
Reports. *See* Securities and Exchange Commission; U. S. Senate; House of Representatives
Reynolds Hall, 271
"Rights," 35
Roosevelt, Franklin D. *See* President Roosevelt
"Round table," 91, 262

St. Louis–San Francisco Railway, 172
St. Louis Union Terminal Co., 37
San Francisco, Address at, June, 1938, 18
Securities Act of 1933, 23, 24, 25, 26, 28, 57, 209, 210, 212, 220, 228, 248, 249, 251; amendments to, 120; registration costs, 57
Securities and Exchange Commission, administration of Holding Company Act, 163–170; as an administrative agency, 243; analysis of security underwritings, 24; brokers and dealers registered with, 22; career service in, 277; corporate standards, 56; corporation mangement, 57–59; delegation of power to, 244, 260, 261; flexibility of, 262; history of, vi–viii, 10; injunction suits against, 127; opinion *In the matter of the Application of International Paper and Power Co.*, 141; prevention of abuse by, 54; public utility reorganizations, 140; regional philosophy of, 29; in reorganization proceedings, 191 ff., 214 ff.; reply to Hancock Committee, 120–124; Report of Public Utilities Division, 134; *Report on Study and Investigation of Protective and Reorganization Committees,* 172 ff., 197 ff., 221 ff.; responsibilities of, 257; staffed by youth, 275; stock exchanges, 63–73; stock-exchange reorganization, 75–92; study of protective committees, 172; thin markets, 106

Securities Exchange Act of 1934, 29, 58, 63, 64, 72, 78, 92, 93, 95, 172, 210, 212, 220, 244, 245, 246, 248, 249; amendments to, 120

Segregation of broker and dealer, 96; S.E.C. report on, 96, 101; rules on, 97

Short selling, 69

Small industry, 20, 28

Southern Bell Telephone Co., 37

Southern California Edison Co., 153

Standard Gas & Electric Co., 156

Specialists, 68, 100

Speculation, 103–105

Stock exchanges, as private clubs, 82; floor trading, 97; management, 75 ff., 82; members' trading on, 68, 69; memberships of, 67; professional trading on, 67; regional, 74; reorganization of, 63 ff., 74; rules, 63, 65, 66; trust institutions for, 88, 89

Stock Exchange Institute, Address at, November, 1936, 107

Stock trading, 23

Stone, Mr. Justice, 239

"Termites," financial, 8 ff.

Texas Electric Service Co., 154

Texas Power & Light Co., 154

"Thin" markets, 95, 102

Time, biography of William O. Douglas, viii–x; quoted, 32

Trust Indenture Act of 1939, 172

United Gas Improvement Co., 153

United Light & Power Co., 153

U. S. Conference of Mayors, Address before, November, 1936, 221

U. S. Department of Commerce, 172

U. S. District Court, Southern District of N.Y., 127

U. S. Senate: Banking and Currency Committee's investigation of stock-exchange practices, vi; Committee on Interstate and Foreign Commerce, 159; Report No. 621, 74th Congress, 1st Sess., 159

U. S. Supreme Court, 128, 163, 222

United Telephone & Electric Co., 156

Underwriters' fees, 35, 36

Underwriting participations, 23, 24, 25

Underwritten issues, 23, 24, 25, 26

University of Chicago, Address at, October 27, 1936, 1, 5

Utilities Power & Light Corp., 156

Walla Walla, Wash., Address at, June, 1938, 271 ff.

Wall Street, 6, 13, 26, 63, 129

Wall Street Journal, The, 134

Washington, D.C., 84, 120, 130, 259

Washington Water Power Co., 154

West Penn Power Co., 154

Whitman, Marcus, 277

Whitman College, 271 ff.; Address at, June, 1938, 271 ff.

Why Not a Clinical Law School (J. N. Frank), 279

Write-ups, 164

Yale Club of Washington, D.C., Address at, April, 1936, 248

Yale Law School, 278, 279

Yale University, 172